ORIGINAL

CHRISTIANITY

Also by Peter Novak

The Lost Secret of Death

The Division of Consciousness

PETER NOVAK

ORIGINAL

CHRISTIANITY

A NEW KEY TO UNDERSTANDING
THE GOSPEL OF THOMAS
AND OTHER LOST SCRIPTURES

HAMPTON ROADS
PUBLISHING COMPANY, INC.

Hampton Roads Publishing Company, Inc.
1125 Stoney Ridge Road
Charlottesville, VA 22902

434-296-2772
fax: 434-296-5096
e-mail: hrpc@hrpub.com
www.hrpub.com

If you are unable to order this book from your local
bookseller, you may order directly from the publisher.
Call 1-800-766-8009, toll-free.

Library of Congress Cataloging-in-Publication Data

Novak, Peter, 1958-
  Original Christianity : a key to understanding the Gospel of Thomas and other
lost scriptures / Peter Novak.
      p. cm.
  Summary: "A new key to understanding the Gospel of Thomas and other Lost Scriptures.
Proposes a theory called Binary Soul Doctrine which allows for both reincarnation and an
eternal afterlife. Offers fresh insights on the beliefs and politics of the early church
founders, and helps explain the current flight from traditional religions"--Provided by
publisher.
  Includes bibliographical references.
  ISBN 1-57174-445-2 (6x9 tp : alk. paper)
  1. Gospel of Thomas (Coptic Gospel)--Criticism, interpretation, etc. 2.
Apocryphal books (New Testament) I. Title.
  BS2860.T52N68 2005
  229'.8--dc22
                                        2005015665

                    ISBN 1-57174-445-2
                    10 9 8 7 6 5 4 3 2 1
              Printed on acid-free paper in Canada

Contents

Introduction

Return of the King of Terror

Life is rough. Almost as soon as we are born, we start to realize that we are going to die some day. And to make things worse, everyone else we care about is going to die as well. Our parents, our siblings, our spouses, our children, our friends, and even our enemies are all in the same sinking boat. The only question is whether we will see them off first, or if they will witness our passing instead. For many of us, our mortality doesn't truly register until someone close to us dies, but sooner or later, each of us comes to accept this painful truth in our own way.

The older we get, the more the dark inevitability of death weighs on our minds. This soul-wrenching realization is perhaps the ultimate common denominator of the human experience. It is something we share with people in all corners of the globe; as different as human cultures can be, everyone struggles with this same disturbing thought. This burden is also something we have in common with people who lived a hundred years ago, a thousand years ago, and even a hundred thousand years ago. Can a mere *thought* be eternal? Perhaps so; the same mortal worries and uncertainties in our heads today were also in theirs.

All human activity is, in effect, a cry of defiance against this fate, a refusal to admit that death is truly our end. Continuously lurking in the back of our minds, the unpleasant awareness of our impending destruction is, perhaps more than anything else, what separates us from the animal kingdom. This curse of consciousness is a burden we carry within us every moment of our lives, and it has shaped, and perhaps even unilaterally directed, the evolution of human culture. Everything we do in life, every time any of us lifts a single finger, it is with the implicit assumption that doing so makes some sort of difference. In order to function at all, in order to carry out even the most basic and elementary tasks of life, it is necessary for human beings to first sidestep our debilitating awareness of death. We need to *disbelieve*.

We have found many ways to do this. All cultures (all modern cultures as well as all known ancient cultures) embraced some sort of religious belief in life after death. This is as inevitable a human trait as the need to eat, sleep, or reproduce; no one could build or maintain a civilization with a populace that was paralyzed by grief, hopelessness, and despair.

Our Western culture today is built upon the afterlife beliefs of Christianity, but those foundations are starting to crumble. As more and more people begin to question their inherited religions, that long-repressed grief, hopelessness, and despair are starting to reemerge as an active factor in the human psyche, and therefore also in human culture. Our generation has a momentous problem to address: We need to continue to disbelieve in death in order to survive as a civilization, but, for the majority of people in the West, that means believing in Christianity, and Christianity is in trouble.

Christianity began with the teachings of one man, but today it has fractured into literally thousands of different sects, denominations, teachings, and belief systems, each of which feels that it alone is correct and all the other versions have got it wrong. Although the church was once the bedrock of European culture, today the majority of Europeans don't even consider Christianity a significant element of their lives. And why should they? Every year, more and more Christian "leaders" are revealed as immoral frauds, thieves, and perverts. In addition to this moral crisis, Christianity also finds itself at odds with modern science on many issues and, as the decades pass, more and more people are siding with science in such disputes. The current teachings of the church are also at odds with the theory of reincarnation, which is threatening to become an even bigger problem for the church, due to a steady stream of scientific evidence supporting reincarnation that has been collected in recent years. And although for the last 2,000 years the church has steadfastly defended its version of the origins of the faith, a large cache of lost early Christian scriptures was found in 1945 that seriously challenges church doctrine about those earliest years.

All these issues have conspired to seriously erode the general population's confidence in and commitment to Christianity, and the social effects of that erosion are apparent for anyone to see. The loss of confidence in Christianity may involve more serious consequences in the United States than in Europe because, in the latter, religions that believed in life after death existed long before the advent of Christianity. But American culture was founded on the Christian faith and has no other belief system to fall back on if Christianity ever falls away. Left without any cultural basis for a belief in life after death, the American public would be completely vulnerable to all those threatening torrents of grief, hopelessness, and despair that Christianity is still able, just barely, to hold back. Like the story of the little Dutch boy afraid to remove his finger from the dike, we may fully discover what psychological and cultural terrors Christianity has been holding at bay only after it is finally gone.

From a sociological standpoint, of course, it does not matter if America believes in Christianity, Hinduism, Islam, or even the Pharaonic religion of ancient Egypt, as long as the population is able to maintain some sort of belief in life after death. Any such belief is a stabilizing cultural influence. Shifting from one such belief to another is very *de*stabilizing to a culture, however, and such social transitions often only occur via extreme social unrest. In matters of religion, public opinion is like a colossal ocean vessel: Its unwieldy bulk has tremendous inertia and it takes a long time to start, stop, or change directions. America has no substantial infrastructure ready for any alternate belief system; if we had to abandon Christianity and make the transition to an alternate belief, it would probably prove to be a very tumultuous period in American history. The shift of the Roman Empire from paganism to Christianity is probably a valid example of what we might have to expect from such a transition today. It would engender great cultural destabilization.

Even from a purely sociological perspective, then, it would be preferable for us to preserve Christianity, if possible, rather than allowing it to self-destruct and then looking blithely about for something else to take its place. Unfortunately, this is no small task. Each of the many social factors conspiring to derail the church is formidable on its own; together they cast a seemingly insurmountable shadow over the future of the faith. First, we would have to determine why Christianity has been fracturing into different sects and teachings ever since its inception, and then find some way to reverse that process. We would also have to reconcile Christian doctrine with the teachings of modern science, possibly even including the new research on reincarnation. And we would have to find a way to increase the moral integrity of the church so the many financial, sexual, and pedophiliac scandals of today's religious headlines become a dim memory of the past. Perhaps most important, we would have to find a way to integrate the revolutionary new testimony about early Christianity found in the lost scriptures of Nag Hammadi, including the now-famous Gospel of Thomas. No small task indeed. Nonetheless, the stability, and possibly even the survival, of our civilization depends on our success.

Fortunately, a seemingly tailor-made solution to all these dilemmas is already at hand. The binary soul doctrine, an ancient belief system once held in common by Egypt, Greece, India, and China (and, judging by the Nag Hammadi scriptures, also early Christianity), would seem to satisfy all the aforementioned requirements. In this work, I argue that the ancient world's widespread belief in soul duality is the missing key to the entire Christian religion, a lost fulcrum of the faith that not only resolves all the sociological problems the church is currently confronting, but also explains many enduring mysteries of church history and theology.

This book is the third in my series of explorations into the binary soul doctrine. The first, *The Division of Consciousness: The Secret Afterlife of the Human Psyche,* offers a multicultural introduction to the concept of soul duality. The second, *The Lost Secret of Death: Our Divided Souls and the Afterlife,* explores humankind's many different traditional and sociological reports of death and the afterlife, and demonstrates their common denominator in the binary soul doctrine. This third book revisits the early history of Christianity, probing evidence of a substantial revision of Christ's original teachings centuries after His death and revealing the presence of the binary soul doctrine in early Christian doctrine, still preserved in its original, pre-edited condition in the lost scriptures of Nag Hammadi. The doctrine of soul duality found in these lost gospels transforms the very substance of Christianity, reconciling the West's doctrine of resurrection with the East's doctrine of reincarnation, reasserting the importance of personal integrity as a nonnegotiable prerequisite for salvation, and anchoring the entire Christian promise within an established scientific framework. In short, it restores an ancient religion that has been lost to human culture since the fourth century.

Relics of an Ancient War: The Lost Scriptures of Early Christianity

When war is declared, truth is the first casualty.

—Arthur Ponsonby[1]

At the start of the twenty-first century we find ourselves in the middle of a religious war. Islamic terrorists have attacked America, Israel, Spain, France, and Russia in recent years, and the president of the mightiest nation on Earth has openly doubted if the West can ever win this war against these religious extremists.[2] Most perpetrators of suicide operations around the world for the past ten years have professed to be devout Muslims, but their claim to representing true Islam has been widely disputed. Their fellow Muslims around the world have not universally united in support of this jihad against the West—but they have not done so in condemnation of it either. This should not surprise us, because Islam was born with a warlike nature, and aggression will probably always be in its blood. Although Mohammed preached peace, history leaves no doubt that he supported the use of violence for the advancement of Islam, and his followers have never forgotten that injunction. This distinguishes Islam from other religious approaches, such as Buddhism, that are not so warlike.

Official Christianity, the foundation of Western civilization, was *also* born of war, and will probably always have war in its blood as well. By this, I do not mean the original religion Christ taught, but rather the imposter that came later and modified His teachings. This imposter shows no evidence of being the true offspring of the Prince of Peace, but seems instead to be, much like Islam, born of a warlike parentage. The official church has been in a fairly constant state of war since its inception, fighting the Jews, the Gnostics, the Muslims, dissenting sects, and even a good portion of the scientific community. True Christianity, however, unlike that imposter that came later, could not have been originally a warlike religion. Its Founder never carried a sword, refused to defend Himself when attacked, and taught His followers to "love their enemies," "give to those who ask," "worship not money," "turn the other cheek," and "resist not evil." Not only did the Founder of Christianity go quietly like a lamb to His own slaughter, he also actually told His disciples that if they wanted to be saved, they would have to follow His example and do the same.[3] There seems little doubt that that person is *not* represented by our Western civilization today. He is not represented by our politicians, or our priests, or by Wall Street, academia, or Hollywood. He is virtually unknown. And so are His true teachings.

That could be a problem just now. While the Islamic militants attacking the West believe they are being loyal to Mohammed's teachings in fighting this war, anyone acquainted with Christ's Gospel knows He did not advocate warfare. For the West to respond in kind to these terrorist attacks violates the teachings of our religion's Founder, putting us in the untenable position of trying to win a religious war by betraying our religion, even as our enemy remains loyal to his. Such a strategy provides them a formidable psychological advantage.

These terrorists already enjoy at least one advantage over the West. Islam is visibly growing stronger and more robust around the world, while Christianity seems to be dying the fabled "death of a thousand cuts." In Europe, once the stronghold of a vast Christian Empire, an increasing percentage of the population considers religion irrelevant. In America, Christianity's supposed new center of gravity on the planet, a corrupt ministry's sexual and financial scandals have managed to make the vulgarities of popular television seem tame by comparison. And in science, more and more evidence is piling up in support of reincarnation, an idea which, if true, spells doom for conventional Christian theology.

Still, despite all the systemic weaknesses of modern Christianity, the only way the West is going to win this war is to stay united and focused, and in this particular conflict that means we have to remain true to our cultural and religious ideals, whatever they may be, at least as much as our enemies do to theirs. Make no mistake about it, this is a conflict over cultural ideals and perspectives, and if we are less devoted to our cultural vision than these Islamic militants are to theirs, we will be at a serious disadvantage. Once, *all* wars were "religious" wars, and some would say that reality has never really changed. People used to believe that an army's strength stemmed from the god it fought for; people today might instead say that an army's true power is found in the ideal it uses to rally people to its cause. In either case, if we find ourselves entering a conflict that is at odds with our cultural ideals and religious vision, our hearts will not be in the struggle. And a halfhearted army rarely wins wars, especially against an enemy as single-minded as the suicidal militants facing the West today.

If this conflict did not come to us dressed as a religious war, these sorts of ideological issues might not bring the same weight to bear on our psyches that they do today. But this is, at least in the minds of the Islamic jihadists attacking us, an authentic religious war. And if truth be told, our response has largely been cut from that same cloth. Immediately after 9/11, images of the American president preaching at church podiums were broadcast all over the world. Bush characterized our enemy as pure "evil" and labeled his war against them a "crusade," using terminology guaranteed to reawaken memories of other religious wars. But even with all this posturing, it was still surprising when Bush promoted a general who *openly* argued for religious war. In the summer of 2003, Lt. Gen. William "Jerry" Boykin was made deputy undersecretary of defense after spending the previous two years giving public speeches condemning Islam as a tool of the devil, preaching that the Christian God is "bigger" than Allah, and that America's war on terrorism is a Christian fight against Satan.[4] This rhetoric so outraged the Church of England that Archbishop of Canterbury Dr. Rowan Williams scolded both Bush and Britain's Tony Blair for using religious language and Christian imagery to justify their war against Iraq.[5]

Is this truly a religious war, or is it just being made to appear as one? Certainly a great many on both sides of the conflict view it as such. Unfortunately, defining this conflict in religious terms may have a psychological downside that Bush and Blair failed to anticipate. It has become clear from the last century's archaeological finds that what the world follows today is not Original Christianity, but a heavily edited, modified, and incomplete substitute.

From a purely political perspective, the timing for such revelations couldn't be worse. At a time in history when most educated people assumed the days of religious wars were long behind us, events beyond our control seem intent on thrusting our world into yet another one. But at the same time, archaeology informs us that everything we thought we knew about Original Christianity may be wrong, disarming us of our faith at the very moment we need it most.

Accusations about Christianity having been corrupted long ago are nothing new. From its very inception, sects began splitting off from the main trunk of the faith, accusing the church of betraying and corrupting Christ's original teachings. This accusation has been repeated by every denomination of Christianity.

While these sects don't agree on what the true teachings of Original Christianity actually were, they *do* agree that those original teachings were betrayed and corrupted. Solid proof to back up those claims came in 1945, when a large cache of previously unknown early Christian scriptures was unearthed in Nag Hammadi, Egypt, a small southern village on the west bank of the Nile. These 52 early Christian writings had once so threatened the official church that it sought out and destroyed all existing copies and murdered any poor soul who happened to be caught in possession of one of these illegal scriptures.[6] The only reason any copies of these works remained to be found at Nag Hammadi is because the official church never knew they were buried there.

The Lost Gospels

Never before had such a collection been recovered; this find brought the first serious defeat to the church's 2,000-year censorship campaign, which had alienated the world from the earliest flowerings of Christian thought. Thanks to that censorship, some of the teachings and recurring themes in these early scriptures now seem totally alien to Christianity. In the Gospel of Thomas, for example, we are repeatedly instructed to "make the two one"; in the Gospel of Philip, we are told that Jesus Himself "divided" in two when He died; in the Secret Book of James, we read that salvation revolves around the relationship between one's own soul and spirit; in the Gospel of Mary, we are warned against having a divided heart; and in the Gospel of Truth, we learn that Jesus' mission was to repair a great division. This theme of division and duality obviously permeated early Christian thought, but was later erased from the canvas of history.

A great many of these lost scriptures have been dated to the first or second century, making them some of the earliest Christian literature. Despite that, these teachings were erased from the church's legacy; we never inherited them because the church didn't want us to. For 1,500 years, from Constantine's conversion in the fourth century until the end of the Spanish Inquisition in 1834, the church burned these books and killed their owners. It was the longest censorship campaign in human history.

There is no way to calculate how much we lost. Although a few listings of titles of missing early Christian scriptures still exist, we know these listings aren't inclusive. They are just the only listings that managed to survive the editing process of the church. Still, they are enough. They make it clear that many more early Christian scriptures once existed. In the first centuries of the church, the faithful once read the following, alongside the familiar titles in today's Bible:

The Acts of Andrew
The Gospel of Andrew
The Gospel of the Twelve Apostles
The Gospel of Barnabas
The Gospel of Bartholomew
The Gospel of Basilides
The Gospel of Cerinthus
The Revelation of Cerinthus
Epistle from Christ to Peter and Paul
The Gospel of the Egyptians
The Gospel of the Ebionites
The Gospel of the Encratites
The Gospel of Eve
The Gospel of the Hebrews
The Book of the Helkesaites
The Gospel of Hesychius
The Book of James
The Acts of John
The Gospel of Jude
The Acts of the Apostles by Lentitus
The Books of Lenticius
The Acts of the Apostles by Leucius
The Acts of the Apostles by Leontius
The Acts of the Apostles by Leuthon
The Gospel of Lucianus
The Gospel of Marcion
The Gospel of Matthias
The Traditions of Matthias
The Gospel of Merinthus
The Gospel of the Nazarenes
The Acts of Paul and Thecla
The Acts of Paul
The Preaching of Paul
The Revelation of Paul
The Gospel of Perfection
The Acts of Peter
The Doctrine of Peter
The Gospel of Peter
The Judgment of Peter
The Preaching of Peter
The Revelation of Peter
The Acts of Philip
The Gospel of Philip
The Gospel of Scythianus
The Acts of the Apostles by Seleuccus
The Revelation of Stephen

The Gospel of Thaddaeus   The Gospel of Titan

The Epistle of Themison   The Gospel of Truth

The Acts of Thomas   The Gospel of Valentinus

The Gospel of Thomas

Today's official New Testament only offers its readers the four gospels of Matthew, Mark, Luke, and John, along with a handful of letters from Paul, Peter, James, and Jude. Early congregations also read dozens of gospels and holy scriptures that no longer exist. All we have left today are a few of the titles, which stand as witness to the power and thoroughness of the church's censorship campaign.[7] Although only eight authors are represented in the official New Testament, in the earliest years of Christianity the faithful read the work of at least 38 additional authors that we know of. The earliest disciples spent their lives teaching a literate culture about Christ, and, as Luke himself testifies, a great many written works emerged from their passionate commitment to that mission:

> Many have taken pen in hand to draw up an account of the things that have taken place among us, just as they were handed down to us from the first eyewitnesses and ministers of the word. Since I have perfectly followed all these things from the very beginning, it therefore seemed good for me to also write you an orderly account. (Luke 1:1–3)

Before Luke got around to writing his version of events, many others had already done so. The official church, however, condemned *all* of those early reports, all except the 27 books that made it into the New Testament. In making those decisions, the church demonstrated favoritism toward one author in particular: Paul, who wrote 14 of the 27 books in the New Testament—and never even met Jesus in the flesh. Today the official church embraces Paul's letters as the standard by which all other Christian scripture is to be judged, primarily because his work, before the discovery of the Gospel of Thomas, seemed to be the oldest surviving Christian literature. Paul's writings were given preference over a great many other scriptures, including many allegedly written by some of the actual Twelve Apostles, such as Peter, James, Andrew, Thomas, and Philip. The church's only possible defense of this would be if all those writings were falsely attributed and were not actually written by the true Twelve; for if they were authentic, then the testimony of those who spent a year or more being instructed by Christ during His ministry would surely be preferred over someone who had only had visions of Him after His Resurrection.

The church does deny that these scriptures were written by members of the original Twelve. There are two things wrong with this position, however. First, if these scriptures were not originally written by the apostles, then where are the scriptures they wrote? Luke says that a sizable percentage of the apostles wrote their recollections or teachings. If these recently discovered scriptures are not the ones they wrote, then where are the ones they *did* write? Second, a very good case can be made that both the Gospel of Thomas (found at Nag Hammadi, Egypt, in 1945)[8] and the Gospel of Peter (found in Akhmim, Egypt, in 1886)[9] actually date from the mid-first century, which is exactly when the Twelve would have been most likely to produce written works.

We know our lists of lost works are incomplete, because the Nag Hammadi find contained no fewer than 41 early Christian scriptures that we'd never heard of. Their titles had previously appeared in no list, no correspondence, no surviving document of any kind. These scriptures were considered so dangerous to the church that not one mention of them was allowed to survive. In the last century, for example, we discovered that there had once been a Gospel of Mary. We never knew that because the church didn't want us to. If the church had wanted that text to survive, no power on earth could have erased it from our heritage.

These texts and all trace of them were to be rooted out, the church decided. History was wiped clean of any memory or mention of the ideas in these works, until their texts were unearthed in Egypt.

How many more were there? Were there another 41 scriptures written in the earliest years of the church that we still don't know anything about? Were there a hundred? Two hundred? There doesn't seem to be any way to know. If the church could successfully erase all memory of these 41 scriptures, it could do anything; 1,500 years is a long time to get a story straight.

Truth through Censorship

The official church openly admits this censorship. It claims that all these lost texts were erroneous representations of Christianity and so deserved to be destroyed; and in support of that position, it points to some extant writings of early church figures that say as much. This argument is disingenuous, however, for the church is arguing its case with evidence it has admitted tampering with. For all we know, the vast majority of Christians in the first two centuries preferred these forbidden scriptures over those the official church canonized. But now that all evidence that might have reflected this has been erased, we will never know. As soon as the official church began tampering with the evidence, it lost all credibility.

Over the years, many have accused the church of betraying its original integrity in order to gain political strength and stability, and such a motivation may be understandable. Christians suffered horrific persecution in its first 300 years. Many of the original apostles endured beatings, stonings, and imprisonments. Anyone who accepted a public position as a Christian leader was asking for a short and troubled life. For example, in 235 A.D., the Roman bishop Pontian was arrested almost as soon as he was ordained. Rome sent him to the lead mines of Sardinia, where prisoners were forced to toil 20 grueling hours per day on nothing but one meal of bread and water. Most died within months. Like Pontian, many high-ranking Christians were sent to the Sardinian mines in those years, or persecuted in other equally miserable ways. Less than a century later, however, after the Roman emperor Constantine converted to Christianity, everything changed.[10] In 314 A.D., the new Roman bishop found himself showered with prestige, wealth, pomp, and the favor of the emperor. Instead of facing persecution, he was now living in the lap of luxury, with a beautiful palace, a glorious cathedral, and all the trappings of power.

It was only natural for Christians to welcome a more politically approved status for the church. But ever since that status was granted, historians have been asking if accepting it was a mistake. Before Constantine, the church had been a pure fellowship of selfless heroes, people so committed to serving Jesus that they endured any hardship. There was no question of their personal dedication to the church's ideals and teachings, since they were putting their lives on the line just to be a member. But after Constantine's conversion, the newly "politically correct" church became an attractive career option for the average person. Simply claiming to be a Christian could bring power, prestige, and promotion, where it had previously brought persecution. This placed the church at risk of being infiltrated by unscrupulous people seeking nothing more than worldly power and political advancement. Such people, if they succeeded in securing a foothold in the ecclesiastical hierarchy, could ascend to positions where their ambition could compromise the church.

The Emperor's New Sword

As Constantine came to power in the fourth century, the Roman Empire was struggling with a dilemma. After centuries of persecutions, it had become obvious that the flood of Christians refusing to pay religious homage to the emperor was not going to end, even under penalty of death. Constantine knew a radically new approach was needed. The masses had become unacceptably unruly, and the empire needed to find something to render them servile and cooperative again.

Until Christianity entered the picture, state and religion had operated in tandem in Rome. The emperor had been viewed as a god and had exercised a god's unlimited control over his subjects. Christianity was the first real interruption of that privilege. This strange new religion gave its followers the courage to defy the state, as they so famously did during the Christian persecutions. This open defiance made a huge impression on Rome. It left the emperor looking weak, which threatened the stability of the whole empire.

But the emperor eventually realized that this new faith might be made to work for him, just as all the former religions had done. Constantine tried to increase his control over the population by reunifying state and religion. With Christianity working for the state, the emperor reasoned, he could reestablish his traditional control over the populace, giving commands the masses would again be afraid to disobey. Indeed, Christianity seemed to hold the potential to make the emperor's power over the masses greater than it had ever been before. With a renewed alignment of church and state, the people would no longer merely fear the ability of the state to take their lives, but would then also fear its ability to condemn their souls to eternal damnation in the afterlife. A government that could get the population to believe it had such power would possess the most successful populace control system imaginable.

But some adjustments would be needed first. The state's claim to religious power would rest on one assumption: that earthly authorities could damn one's soul to eternal punishment. That, of course, would require the people to believe that a single, eternal afterlife immediately followed one's present earthly life. There was no room in this picture for any idea that a person might have more than one chance to get things right. Belief in reincarnation, if it was there, would have to go.

Reincarnation in the Early Church

Belief in reincarnation *was* there. There's really no questioning the presence of the concept of reincarnation in early Christian theology. In fact, the doctrine of rebirth was so mainstream in the earliest years of the church that one of its most prominent teachers, Valentinus, almost became pope. Born in Alexandria around 100 A.D., Valentinus claimed to have been personally initiated by Theudas, a disciple and initiate of the apostle Paul, who had passed down secret teachings and rituals from Christ Himself. Like Paul, Valentinus also claimed to have had a vision of the risen Christ. After this mystical experience, he began teaching in Alexandria but migrated to Rome around 135 A.D., where he quickly became an influential and widely respected member of the official church. His pro-reincarnational teachings were so well received there that he became a candidate for the papacy. After losing what is said to have been a very close election, he continued to teach in Rome for many years, and his theology attracted a large following, especially in Egypt and Syria.

The official church openly admits that some portion of pre-Nicene Christianity believed in reincarnation, and the recovered gospels from Nag Hammadi, preserved for 1,500 years in their original unedited condition, say the same thing. In fact, it would have been surprising if the concept of reincarnation had *not* been a part of the original teachings of the church, since the world in which Christianity arose was utterly saturated with the idea.[11] In Egypt, that massive cultural force on Israel's western border, the doctrine was so ancient that a number of Pharaohs even had the idea incorporated into their very names.[12] And the concept of rebirth was at the foundation of India's entire culture. But by far the most direct influx came through Hellenistic thought; ever since Alexander the Great conquered the Mediterranean world in the fourth century B.C., the pro-reincarnational teachings of Plato and Socrates flowed like water through the Holy Land. By enforcing the spread of Greek language, Alexander and his successors brought everyone into communication in an unprecedented way.

Many ancient reports that came out of Egypt insist that the belief was common among the earliest Christians, being imparted in secret to the faith's most advanced initiates.[13] According to tradition, Christianity was originally brought to Egypt by Saint Mark in the second half of the first century. Although we possess no records describing the theology of Mark aside from the canonical gospel, he may have authored a Secret Gospel of Mark that contained more advanced teaching for those being initiated into the Christian mysteries.[14] Excerpts from that "secret gospel," rediscovered in the twentieth century, seem to portray Jesus initiating a student into secret mysteries of the church. From the very beginning of the Egyptian church, then, a "secret doctrine" seems to have been taught to those who were deemed worthy.

The Alexandrian Catechism

The intellectual center of the Roman Empire at the time was in Alexandria, Egypt, and the Catechetical School, an official institution of the church, was founded there sometime in the second century. Before the establishment of that school, the Christian sects of Carpocrates, Basilides, Isidore, Valentinus, and Heracleon all flourished in Alexandria. These groups all taught a form of Christianity that included the doctrine of reincarnation, which put them in familiar company in that corner of the world. The famous Jewish philosopher Philo, also an Alexandrian, taught a version of Judaism that included belief in reincarnation and, back then, Christianity was widely thought of as another Jewish sect. Alexandria's Judeo-Christian reincarnationist schools have been dated as far back as 117 A.D.

The original founding date of the Catechetical School is unknown; any documents that might have provided that information have been deleted from the historical record. In any case, we know the school dates at least as far back as 175 A.D., when it was headed by a man named Pantaenus. Although this school became very famous and influential, history has left no record of the teachings of Pantaenus. All we know is that he passed the leadership of the school to Saint Clement[15] in 190 A.D., who ran the institution until he, in turn, passed the reins to Origen in 203 A.D.

Born about 150 A.D., Clement of Alexandria was deeply respected in the early Christian community; in addition to being the head of the most prestigious theological college of his day, he was also a presbyter in the church of Alexandria. He was exceptionally well read, holding a comprehensive knowledge of Judeo-Christian literature, including both "orthodox" and "heretical" works. Clement used and honored many scriptures that the official church later condemned, including the Gospel of the Egyptians, the Gospel of the Hebrews, the Traditions of Matthias, the Teaching of Peter, the Epistle of Barnabas, the Apocalypse of Peter, and the Preaching of Peter, all of which he seems to have considered authentic. He claimed to have received a secret esoteric Christian tradition from Pantaenus, which had been passed down directly from the apostles Peter, James, John, and Paul. These mysteries had to remain hidden, Clement insisted, and could never be written or taught publicly:

> . . . the wise do not utter with their mouth what they reason to council. "But what ye hear in the ear," says the Lord, "proclaim upon the houses," bidding them receive the secret traditions of the true knowledge, and expound them aloft and conspicuously; and as we have heard in the ear, so to deliver them to whom it is requisite; but not enjoining us to communicate to all without distinction, what is said to them in parables. (Clement of Alexandria, "The Mysteries of the Faith Not to Be Divulged to All")

Did those secret teachings include a belief in reincarnation? The ninth century Greek theologian Photius thought so, accusing him of teaching reincarnation in his work *Hypotyposeis* (*Outlines*).[16]

Although he possessed an extraordinary education and was hailed as a theological pioneer, Clement was dwarfed in all of these by his student Origen, who is widely recognized as the most prominent, distinguished, and influential of all the early church fathers. The most prolific theologian of early Christianity, he is said to have written over 6,000 works, although the vast majority of those failed to survive the church's later censorship. Still, in Origen's extant works, we seem to catch a far more substantial glimpse of the esoteric teachings passed down to him from Pantaenus and Clement. And one of Origen's contemporaries, Saint Jerome, publicly accused him of teaching reincarnation in his writings. Origen makes a curious distinction, however. Whereas he enthusiastically condemns belief in the reincarnation of the *soul,* he seems to openly support belief in the reincarnation of the *spirit.*[17] Origen taught that the living are born into this world after having already experienced previous lives:

The soul has neither beginning nor end . . . [They] come into this world strengthened by the victories or weakened by the defeats of their previous lives.[18]

Constantine's Choice

In addition to Valentinus, Clement, and Origen, we know that many other prominent figures in the early church taught a form of Christianity that included belief in reincarnation. But we know too that the concept of reincarnation did not mesh with the empire's political needs. And, of course, we know that the church subsequently edited and modified the literature of the time to suit its purposes. Knowing all that, only one question remains: Did Constantine intentionally compromise Christ's original teachings to further his political ambitions?

Our knowledge of the history of these first centuries is far from complete, and scholars still dispute various details of the early church councils. Nonetheless, it is quite clear that, like all emperors, Constantine didn't think anything was forbidden him. Although he paid lip service to Christianity, Constantine demonstrated virtually no loyalty to Christ's teachings. In the course of his life, he murdered his own wife, his eldest son, and many of his closest friends and reveled in the mutilation and torture of political enemies and prisoners of war. Despotic and ambitious, Constantine seemed ruthlessly determined to achieve complete dominance over the empire. And although he claimed to be a Christian, he at the same time also worshiped the traditional Roman sun god. Such a life would seem to be a far cry from the ideals and teachings of Christ, but it does seem to have a lot in common with the subsequent history of the official church, a parallel that has led many over the centuries to suspect that the true founder of the official church was not Christ at all, but Constantine.

Shortly after acquiring control of the united empire and ending the Christian persecutions, Constantine found himself facing yet another domestic crisis over religion. In the East, rioting was breaking out in one city after another; bishop was contending against bishop and people were fighting in the streets. Although Constantine did not fully comprehend what all the fuss was about, he resolved to put an end to it. He needed a united church for his united empire, so for the first time in the history of the church, the state intervened in a dispute about belief. It wouldn't be the last time.

By Constantine's orders, 1,800 bishops from all corners of the empire were invited to attend a great church council at Nicaea, but only about 300 answered the imperial summons, perhaps because they realized that Constantine intended to chair the meeting himself. The thought of a Roman emperor presiding over church affairs must have been very intimidating and troubling to the Christians of that era; many of the attendees still bore scars of torture from previous emperors.

At the heart of the matter to be addressed was a simple question: Had Jesus always been God, or had He once just been a man who at some point became God's Son? Was there, in other words, a time when the Father alone existed, but not the Son? This was no mere academic question. If Jesus was originally a man who later became God's Son, that implied that other men could potentially also become Sons of God. And if others could become Sons of God, then no one would need the church for their salvation, but could instead achieve that goal on their own, the same way Christ did. This question was ripping the church apart, just when Constantine needed it to hold the empire together.

It was decided in that meeting that Jesus had always been God, and that other men could not follow in His footsteps to achieve the same result. The council declared that the souls of men were not like Jesus' soul and did not, in and of themselves, possess inherent potential for divinity. While Christ's soul had always existed, the council decided, man's soul was a created thing and did not come into existence until the person was physically born. There was thus a huge gulf between God and man, and the church was the only bridge between them. In short, man had to rely on the church to acquire eternal life. In denying the soul's divine origin, the council implicitly ruled out all possibility of preexistence and reincarnation, while emphasizing the power and authority of the church over the individual.[19] In the end, one definition of Christianity was chosen in that meeting, and all others were rejected. Shortly after, the Christian persecutions began anew, this time orchestrated by the church itself.

Return of the Christian Persecutions

From the earliest days of the Roman Empire, anyone refusing to pledge allegiance to the emperor was put to death, and this did not change just because Constantine converted. After the Council of Nicaea,

all who practiced those rejected versions of Christianity were labeled enemies of the state, and officials began hunting them down. These new persecutions involved unprecedented literary censorship, starting with
Emperor Constantine's order that all writings of the Christian theologian
Arius had to be delivered up to the authorities to be burned, and that anyone found concealing them would be put to death. But that was just the
beginning.

When Emperor Theodosius made Christianity the official state religion a few years later, the Roman government published an edict requiring all subjects of the empire to profess the faith of the bishop of Rome.
Those who refused were again labeled enemies of the state. Much as
before, everyone was forced to pledge allegiance to the official state religion or suffer harsh punishment. Instead of being prey, Christians were
now the hunters. Church leaders became "heretic" hunters, mercilessly
killing any who dared disagree with them. All writings inconsistent with
the official teachings of the church were outlawed and those who read
them risked being killed.

Historians think that this was just about when texts began to be gathered up and buried at Nag Hammadi. For the next thousand years, the
church continued to hunt and kill "heretics."

Curiously, Jesus seems to have predicted all this: "The time is coming
when whoever kills you will think he is doing God a service" (John 16:2).

Thousands of books were destroyed, and hundreds of thousands of
"heretics" with them. Less than 100 years after Constantine's conversion,
the church burnt down the famous Library of Alexandria in Egypt. It continued to launch similar campaigns for the next 1,000 years. It massacred
tens of thousands of Christian "heretics" in France in the Albigensian crusade of 1209–1255, and possibly hundreds of thousands more during the
Inquisition.[20] Like George Orwell's fictional "Big Brother," the official
church sought complete control over public and private opinion. When
the printing press was invented in the fifteenth century, the church
demanded the right to approve all manuscripts before publication. The
church even refused to let people read its *own* book. As unlikely as it seems
today, it was actually illegal to possess the Bible, and simply reading it was
considered proof that someone was a heretic. Men and women were actually burned at the stake for reading the Roman Catholic Bible.

Obviously, something had gone horribly wrong. Christianity had taken
a wrong turn. Love had warped into hatred and fear. Before Constantine,

the church had been different, a pure fellowship of selfless heroes filled with the love, courage, and fruitfulness that only come from authentic health and wholeness. Even though the original church contained the disparate elements that would later become known as the Orthodox and Gnostic churches, they were originally very successful together. Before Constantine, Christians had been known throughout the empire for their remarkably advanced social innovations. Christian communities had been very organized, cohesive, and creative, introducing artisan associations, charitable groups, and retirement and funeral insurance agencies that supported all members regardless of social class. The Roman government tried to emulate their new social systems, but Rome bungled the job so badly that it only emphasized how well the Christians had done.

Orphans of War

After the Council of Nicaea, everything changed. Now there seemed to be two separate churches, the Orthodox and the Gnostic, at war with each other. Each believed that it alone represented the true Church, the original teachings of Christ, but—as we will see from the recovered scriptures from Nag Hammadi—they were both wrong. Neither half was the whole. A dynamic and creative complexity had been shattered, leaving two equally crippled halves. The official church, the Orthodox church, became a dictator, murderer, and thief, waging endless wars of conquest at home and abroad, while the Gnostic Church became a disorganized and ineffective dreamer that receded into the shadows of history, occasionally reappearing with new names like Manichaeism, Bogomilism, and Catharism. Each time it resurfaced, it taught an otherworldly version of Christianity that incorporated belief in reincarnation, and each time it was hunted down anew by the official church. Both halves are the orphaned offspring of Christianity's first war, and neither has known any peace since.

These two halves were very different, but their difference is familiar. One exhibited the characteristics of one half of the human psyche, while the other behaved like the other half of the mind. The Orthodox Church focused on objective left-brain issues like discrimination, order, and authority, while the Gnostic Church paid more attention to subjective right-brain issues like intuition, imagination, and personal experience. Like the conscious mind, the official church was more dominant and out in the open, while the Gnostic Church was more like the unconscious, carrying out its activity in the background. We will run across this pattern again and again in our search for Original Christianity.

The divorce between the Orthodox and Gnostic factions of Christianity did not actually begin in Nicaea. They seem to have started to differentiate from one another almost as soon as Christ was lowered from the cross; the Council of Nicaea just brought this process to a head. And ever since that first climactic division in Nicaea, Christianity has continued on the same self-destructive course, fracturing ever further with each new century. Where there had originally been just one church, there are now, according to the *World Christian Encyclopedia,* more than 34,000 different Christian denominations.[21] Each has its own unique teachings and practices, but none, the lost gospels suggest, reflect the original teachings of Christ.

And so, at the dawn of the first great conflict of the third millennium, the West finds itself unarmed, in a religious war without its religion.

2

The Potter's Soil: The Ground the Church Was Planted In

If anyone asserts the fabulous preexistence of souls, and shall assert the monstrous restoration which follows from it, let him be anathema.
—First Anathema against Origen,
Second Council of Constantinople, 553 A.D.

Despite the machinations of the official church, it remains clear that at least some early Christian groups originally believed in reincarnation. The question is, how did they reconcile this with resurrection, Christianity's single most fundamental and central belief? The whole promise of Christianity relied on the Resurrection. Jesus rose from the dead, and thanks to Him, it was declared, everyone else could. But if early Christians *already* believed that people regularly came back from the dead, returning to reincarnate again lifetime after lifetime, what need could they have seen for a general resurrection of the dead at Judgment Day—or, for that matter, for any savior's self-sacrifice to guarantee that resurrection? This has remained a long-standing mystery. For the past 1,500 years, it has not been understood how both beliefs could be held simultaneously. Thanks to church censorship, no documents existed that would explain it. With the rediscovery of the lost scriptures of Nag Hammadi, however, it has finally become possible to tackle this mystery. With these ancient works in hand, we are no longer totally dependent on the adulterated data stream the official church has been feeding the human race for the past 1,500 years.

But we still have work to do. These recovered scriptures do not paint as clear and direct a road to our goal as we might have preferred. Virtually all the texts found at Nag Hammadi are filled with mysterious and obscure passages; although scholars have been studying these works for decades, huge portions have defied comprehension. It is no secret why this is so; these works openly identify themselves as Jesus' *secret* teachings, not meant to be read, and certainly not meant to be understood, by all. The Bible itself says that Jesus had two separate and distinct sets of teachings—one for the masses, and quite another for His closest disciples:

> The disciples came to him and asked, "Why do you speak to the people in parables?" He replied, "The knowledge of the secrets of the kingdom of heaven has been given to you, but not to them." (Matt. 13:10–11)

These "heretics" considered themselves devout Christians, yet they believed in both reincarnation and resurrection. This mystery has never been explained. Some have suggested that Original Christianity *only* believed in reincarnation, and not resurrection, but we have enough evidence to rule out such suggestions. In the Gospel of Thomas, for instance, Jesus repeatedly praises the religious knowledge of Judaism,[1] and those Judaic scriptures clearly prophesy a coming Universal Resurrection at Judgment Day.[2] There is no doubt, then: Mysterious elements in the early church believed in both resurrection *and* reincarnation. But how?

There *is* an answer. A very popular and widespread theology once existed within the Roman empire that would explain this mystery (along with many other mysteries within Christianity), and this theology is readily apparent in the rediscovered scriptures found at Nag Hammadi. This ancient belief system is virtually unknown to the modern world, however. As one might suspect, it failed to survive the 1,500-year editing and censorship campaign of the official church.

The Binary Soul Doctrine

Thousands of years ago, numerous cultures all over the globe believed essentially the same thing about death and the afterlife. They thought that human beings possess not one, but two souls, which usually would divide at death, each going off to a very different sort of afterlife. These ancient cultures often described those two souls in very similar ways, frequently referring to them in the same way modern psychology now describes the two halves of the human psyche. One soul was thought to contain one's free will and intellect, while the other contained one's emotions and memory. The intellectual soul was said to possess the person's life force and could not leave the person's physical body without resulting in death. The emotional soul, however, was deemed capable of wandering free from the body and was said to commonly do so during sleep, disease, or mystical experiences.

Although these two souls were tied closely together inside a person's heart during life, they were generally believed to divide from one another at death, literally ripping the person's nonphysical essence apart into two disconnected fragments. After this division, which was often called "the second death,"[3] the intellectual half of the person was often believed to reincarnate, while the emotional half was generally thought to become trapped in a dark and dreary dreamlike netherworld.[4]

The Second Death: A Journey Written in Stone

Ancient Egypt is one of the best-documented examples of a culture that believed in this "binary soul doctrine" (BSD). It devoted huge amounts of its resources to the problem of death and the afterlife, and its most famous monument reflects this obsession. The interior of the Great Pyramid of Cheops, with its multiple chambers and forking passages, seems specifically designed around the binary soul afterlife theology. Just as Egyptians believed the living possess three elements—a body, a soul (Egypt's *ka*), and a spirit (Egypt's *ba*)—this pyramid has three unique chambers that seem to mirror the expected afterlives for each of these elements. Similarly, the passageways between these chambers closely reflect Egypt's vision of the processes and changes thought to occur along the journey from life to death.

Fifty feet above the base, the pyramid's entrance opens into a steeply descending, claustrophobically narrow corridor that descends almost to ground level, then forks into two branches. One branch plummets farther, to an underground chamber known as "the pit," while the other branch ascends again. This ascending passage eventually forks into two branches

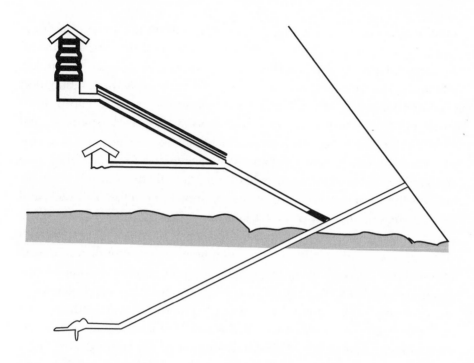

as well, one leading to the "Queen's Chamber" and another to the "King's Chamber." The first fork in the pyramid's corridor seems to represent the "first death," the initial change people experience upon their demise, when their mind and body disengage and go their separate ways. Similarly, the second fork seems to reflect the "second death," when the spirit and soul disengage as well, fracturing the mind.

At the first fork, one branch continues downward under the monument until it reaches a rough-hewn cave containing nothing but a shallow, empty pit. Crudely carved out of the actual bedrock, this grave-like cell is small, dark, and airless, perfectly symbolizing the end of the physical body at death. Meanwhile, the ascending branch rises just as sharply upward again, appropriately symbolizing the hopeful promise of the mind's survival as it separates from its failing corpse. The very beginning of this upward passage is blocked, however, by a thick granite plug, an appropriate reminder that nothing physical can escape the inevitable descent into death. Of the three components Egyptian theology credited a living person as possessing, only the two nonphysical elements, the *ba* and *ka*, could hope to pass into this ascending corridor.

On the other side of that granite plug, the person's *ba* and *ka* could continue together, proceeding up the passage until they reach the place where it also forks off into two directions, one path leveling out to the Queen's Chamber and another ascending higher still to the King's Chamber. The Queen's Chamber seems to represent the final destination and afterdeath fate of the *ka*. The room is void of contents except for a niche in the east wall thought to once hold a life-size "*ka* statue" of the king, within which his living *ka* would be able to endure eternity. This chamber is aboveground, perhaps symbolizing that the soul living here does at least successfully survive death. Multiple features of this chamber suggest the unpleasant nature of that existence, however. The walls and ceiling are smooth and polished limestone, but the floor has been left rough and uneven, suggesting that the soul will not find the afterdeath experience easy and joyful, but instead quite rough and unpleasant. Also, although the Queen's Chamber, like the King's Chamber, contains something like air shafts (tiny vents extending out toward the exterior walls of the pyramid), they come up short, stopping many feet before they would have reached open air. This seems to symbolize that the soul living here, even though technically still alive, remains imprisoned after death.

The air shafts of the larger and more luxurious King's Chamber, however, *do* reach all the way outside, making it the only room in the pyramid equipped with any way out. This reminds us that the ancient Egyptians believed the *ba* to be the only part of a person guaranteed to enjoy true freedom after death, going on to visit new realities and begin new experiences. Built entirely of beautiful rose granite, the finely polished stones of the King's Chamber are the heaviest in the entire pyramid, reflecting the magnificent afterlife of the *ba*.

But the *ba* did not have to enter the King's Chamber alone, for the second fork in the pyramid's passageways is quite different from its predecessor. Whereas the first fork had the upper path blocked off, the second fork leaves both its branches open. While all BSD cultures acknowledged the inevitability of the first death, some felt the second death was avoidable if the proper steps were taken. Egypt believed it was possible to prevent the *ka* and *ba* from dividing, in which case both could travel together to the paradisiacal afterlife symbolized by the King's Chamber. Indeed, not only does the second fork leave both branches open, but instead of blocking the upper branch, the structure actually seems to encourage one to choose the upper path. Known as the Grand Gallery, the ascending passageway from the second fork to the King's Chamber has an extravagantly tall ceiling, which is a huge relief after squeezing through all the tiny corridors that led to this point.[5]

Some BSD cultures taught that the after-death division of the soul and spirit was inevitable, but a few believed that it was possible to avoid it. Those nations believing that the second death could be avoided, such as Egypt and China, focused most of their religious efforts on helping people escape it. Those convinced the division was inevitable, on the other hand, tended to emphasize the importance of one soul and devalue the other, which made their imminent division seem less threatening.[6] But until Christianity came along, the second death was thought to be irreversible and permanent. If the second death caught you, all hope was lost. The person you had been in that lifetime, that "self," would be ripped completely apart and would never truly exist again. Even though it was widely believed that half of one's being might yet go on to reincarnate after the second death, this seemed small consolation for the perpetual loss of memory and identity lifetime after lifetime, and the endless suffering of the other half of one's being in its mindless netherworld prison.

This binary soul doctrine was the cultural mindset when Christianity was born. And, despite what the official church later maintained, Christ does not seem to have refuted this story. Instead, He added a new chapter to it. For the most part, Original Christianity assumed the same assumptions and spoke the same language as all the BSD cultures around it, only adding one new element to the story line—it was now possible to overcome the second death: "He who overcomes will not be hurt at all by the second death" (Rev. 2:11).

If Jesus had come bearing an entirely new and unfamiliar message, telling the citizenry of the Roman Empire to discard everything they had previously believed to come and follow Him instead, few would have listened. But that's not what happened. Instead, His movement picked up followers at an amazing rate throughout the empire because He and they were already on the same page in their underlying cultural beliefs. Christ provided a solution to a problem everyone already knew they had, a solution no one previously had thought possible. This was the great message that won so many converts to Christianity, the unprecedented breakthrough the world had been waiting for: Even if someone died and suffered the second death, it was now possible for them to live again. "Jesus said, 'I am the resurrection. He who believes in me will live, even though he dies'" (John 11:25).

No one had ever said this before. Although a few cultures claimed to know the secret of avoiding the second death *before* it struck, no one had had the audacity to claim that he could reverse its effects after the fact.

As we will see, a number of the lost Christian scriptures found at Nag Hammadi are unmistakably based on this ancient dual-soul religious system. Until now, the theology of these scriptures remained undeciphered; the Gospel of Thomas, for example, begins with a challenge, declaring that the whole book points to a single mystery, and if one can identify that mystery, one will never die. Until the rediscovery of the BSD, no analyst or theologian had been able to identify that common denominator in Thomas' passages. In addition to deciphering the Gnostic Gospels, the forgotten theology of the BSD explains a plethora of other mysteries about early Christianity; it immediately explains, for example, how the early church could simultaneously believe in both resurrection and reincarnation: While one soul might incarnate again and again, the other was thought to remain trapped in a static heavenly or hellish dreamworld reality after death, and so still needed to be rescued via resurrection. In book after book, and passage after passage, these Nag Hammadi scriptures demonstrate that the BSD was the original foundation of Christ's teachings.

One World Religion

> The identical thing that we now call Christian religion existed among the ancients, and has not been lacking from the beginning of the human race until the coming of Christ in the flesh, from which moment on the true religion, which already existed, began to be called Christian. (Saint Augustine)[7]

The binary soul doctrine was once very nearly a universal faith. It existed on the planet for thousands of years, in cultures all over the globe. Even so, it was no match for the 1,500-year editing and censorship campaign of the official church, which almost completely erased from the face of the earth a belief that had once been a common denominator across nations, continents, and even oceans. Today, only a few isolated cultures on the extreme fringes of the modern world, such as the Maku tribe of the Amazon, the Luba of Zaire, and the Mandaeans of southern Iraq, still subscribe to the BSD. Prior to Constantine's takeover of Christianity, however, innumerable cultures believed in binary souls that split at death. This afterlife tradition not only saturated the high cultures of ancient Egypt, Greece, India, Persia, and China, it left its footprints in the indigenous cultural traditions of Australia, the Americas, and numerous isolated islands around the globe as well.

The BSD was once the native faith of dozens of tribes in the Americas, such as the Inuit, the Dakota, the Toltecs, the Incas, the Mbua, the Guarani-Apapocuva, and the Waica. In Africa, it was held by the Ewe of Togo, the Mossi of Burkina Faso, and the Bambara of Mali. In Eurasia, it was professed by the Khanty and the Mansi of the Ob River region, the Samoyed of Europe and Siberia, the Tunguz of the Yenisei River, and the Yukagir of Siberia. And among island peoples, it was embraced in Australia, Hawaii, Haiti, and the Solomon Islands.

Greece called these two souls the *psyche* and the *thymos*, Egypt called them the *ba* and *ka*, Israel called them the *ruah* and *nefesh*, Persia called them the *urvan* and *daena*, Islam called them the *ruh* and *nafs*, India called them the *atman* and *jiva*, China called them the *hun* and *po*. Haiti called them the *gros bon ange* and *ti bon ange*, Hawaii called them the *uhane* and *unihipili*, and the Dakota Indians called them the *nagi* and *niya*. The list goes on and on.[8] In each case, these native cultures described their two souls the same way modern science now describes the conscious and unconscious halves of the human psyche.

Original Christianity subscribed to this doctrine; when Jesus was preaching along the dusty roads of Judea, it was understood both by Him and His audience that each living person possessed a body, a soul, *and* a spirit.[9] The soul and spirit were *not* the same thing. Although their distinction was radically de-emphasized later by the official church, originally these two spiritual elements were viewed as completely separate and distinct components of a living person. This teaching was a fundamental tenet of Original Christianity. Both 1 Thessalonians 5:23 and Hebrews 4:12 declare that people possess two very different spiritual components: both a soul and a spirit. And when he wrote to the Corinthian church, Saint Paul carefully distinguished between three different types of people, the *sarkikoi*, the *psychikoi*, and the *pneumatikoi*. Although these terms are usually rather deceptively translated into English as "carnal," "natural," and "spiritual," they actually refer to the three components of each human being: the body *(sarx)*, the soul *(psyche)*, and the spirit *(pneuma)*. While the Corinthians liked to think of themselves as *pneumatikoi* (spirit-oriented), Paul maintained, they were really *psychikoi* (soul-oriented) or even *sarkikoi* (physical-body-oriented). And like all the other binary soul doctrine cultures, Original Christianity recognized that, under certain unfortunate circumstances, one's soul and spirit could divide from each other: "The word of God is living and active and more powerful than a two-edged sword, and cuts so deeply it divides the soul from the spirit" (Heb. 4:12).

This is the only place in the canonical Bible where the once universally recognized division of soul and spirit can still be found, the only passage where the BSD's soul division is specifically mentioned.[10] And that may be why the official church was originally unsure whether it wanted Paul's Epistle to the Hebrews to become an official component of the canon.

Our Two Halves

In every BSD culture, these two elements were described in terms strikingly similar to modern science's right-brain/left-brain descriptions of the two halves of the human psyche. In culture after culture, we find one soul being described as more objective, independent, masculine, logical, rational, verbal, dominant, and active. This soul was thought to possess the person's individuality and autonomous free will. The other soul was considered more subjective, dependent, impressionable, changeable, intuitive, feminine, fertile, emotional, nonverbal, recessive, reactive, responsive, and receptive. This soul was generally credited as possessing the person's memory, and therefore the person's personality and sense of self-identity as well. The rational soul was generally considered immortal and unaffected by death, while the emotional soul was thought to be more vulnerable and at risk.

It is either an amazing coincidence, or a substantiation of the ancient world's binary soul doctrine, that modern science has *also* arrived at the conclusion that the psyche is divided into two distinct components. At the turn of the twentieth century, Sigmund Freud and Carl Jung revolutionized the world with their discovery that the human mind is differentiated into separate conscious and unconscious halves. And in the last 25 years, neuropsychological studies have reconfirmed the ancient belief that humans have two minds functioning in their brains at the same time. The left hemisphere of the brain, numerous studies have determined, is home to a more dispassionate and rational consciousness, while the right half contains a more intuitive, emotional, and introspective mentality. And just as the ancients warned so long ago, these two mental elements can and often do function independently of one another.[11]

This identification of the soul and spirit as known elements within the human psyche carries profound implications. The handful of ancient cultures that believed soul division could be avoided felt this could only be accomplished by unifying a person's two halves together so tightly in life that they wouldn't divide at death. Before Christ, this seems to have been the only "salvation" the world knew, the only hope anyone had of passing unharmed through the doors of death. It was thought that this achievement, often referred to as "perfection," "wholeness," "singleness," or "non-duality," would allow an individual to safely depart this world with personal identity and being completely intact; from that moment on, that person would know true immortality, and nothing could ever threaten him or her again.

This identification of the soul and spirit as familiar (if not fully understood) psychological components shows the salvation taught by the ancients to be a psychological achievement, just as the ancient Gnostics described it. This "salvation via wholeness and perfection" seems to stand in stark contrast to the "salvation by faith" taught by the official church, but in the earliest days of Christianity, *both* seem to have been viewed by the faithful as viable options.

The Emerging Signature of Soul Division

This identification of soul and spirit as the conscious and unconscious immediately explains the loss of memory between lives. In the early church, when the question of reincarnation was still an active and hotly disputed issue, one primary argument raised against its existence was the lack of memory of previous lives. If one's psyche divided at death, however, one would inevitably lose one's memory. Although the left-brain conscious part of the psyche might eventually reincarnate, it would do so without the right-brain unconscious half that possesses the memory. This was an incalculably huge loss. Without memory, reincarnation was pointless, and eternal life worthless.

In much the same way, this hypothesis that the two halves of the mind split apart at death seems to explain a number of other mysteries concerning the afterlife. For instance, if after death the subjective unconscious found itself still alive but deprived of both its physical body and its own objective conscious mind, it would quickly find itself immersed in its own memories, emotions, and fantasies, and would automatically weave its own personal heaven or hell dreamworld out of that subjective mental content.[12] This ancient concept of the mind dividing at death also seems to explain a great deal of what has been reported in recent years about near-death experiences, out-of-body experiences, past-life regression, ghosts, apparitions, deathbed visions, poltergeists, after-death communications, and other afterlife phenomena.[13]

Soul versus Spirit

The BSD is readily apparent in the Bible's description of the soul and spirit. In the Old Testament, souls are regularly referred to as "feeling" this or that, while spirits are always "doing" or "thinking" rather than "feeling." Terminology appropriate to the right-brain unconscious is consistently used when referring to the *nefesh*, or soul. More than 110 times in the Old Testament, the soul is presented as possessing attributes that we know today belong exclusively to the subjectively oriented, emotionally based unconscious—such as loving, hating, abhorring, loathing, lusting, grieving, longing, and mourning; feeling bitterness, joy, humility, thirst, desire, anguish, weariness, enjoyment, satisfaction, comfort, contempt, and delight. The contrast could not be more clear; *nowhere* in the Old Testament is it suggested that the *ruah*, or spirit, experiences such feelings.

Consistently, the left-brain soul was portrayed in BSD cultures as immortal. The right-brain soul, however, was far more vulnerable and could suffer greatly after death. This pattern also appears in the Bible. Whereas the spirit is said always to "return to God" after death, one's soul is in grave danger of being destroyed after departing the physical body. Thirty-two times in the Old Testament, the soul is described as being able to die, 20 times as being in danger of being "cut off," seven times as being in "the pit," three times as being in "hell," three times as being rent "in pieces," four times as being destroyed, twice as being "taken away," and once each as being thrust into "total darkness," "total silence," being "dried up," being "in prison," and being "gathered with sinners." Not once is the spirit referred to in any of these contexts. Whereas one's soul is in danger of suffering in all these ways after death, one's spirit is spoken of in only one way in reference to death: "The spirit returns to God who gave it" (Eccles. 12:7).

This spirit is not an abstract or inconsequential part of a person's being, but instead, much like the left-brain conscious mind, was thought to provide a person's intellectual powers and conscious awareness: "For who among men knows the thoughts of a man except the man's spirit within him?" (1 Cor. 2:11).

The church seems to have subscribed to some form of the BSD at least into the fourth century. While addressing the Apollinarius controversy during the Second Ecumenical Council of 381 A.D., the church accepted and approved the teaching that human beings are comprised of three distinct parts: body, soul, and spirit.[14] When the Fourth Ecumenical Council rolled around 500 years later, however, the church made an explicit about-face on this point, bluntly declaring:

> Though the Old and New Testament teach that a man or woman has one rational and intellectual soul, and all the fathers and doctors of the church, who are spokesmen of God, express the same opinion, some have descended to such a depth of irreligion, through paying attention to the speculations of evil people, that they shamelessly teach as a dogma that a human being has two souls, and keep trying to prove their heresy by irrational means using a wisdom that has been made foolishness. Therefore this holy and universal synod is hastening to uproot this wicked theory now growing like some loathsome form of weed.[15]

After Constantine commandeered the church in the fourth century, a few holdout sects steadfastly refused to abandon what they believed to be the original teachings of Christ, and the BSD is clearly evident in some of their teachings. Manichaeism, a once vigorous offshoot of early Christianity that believed both in reincarnation and binary souls, spread out over most of the known world in the early centuries of the church, surviving to the fourteenth century. During the tenth to fifteenth centuries, Catharism arose, which was yet another mixture of Christianity, reincarnation, and the BSD. And the Mandaean religion, a small but still-living relative of early Christianity, believes even today that living people possess both soul and spirit, and that these two elements of the self split apart after death.

Two Promises, Two Paths, Two Churches

Jesus said, "I am the resurrection and the life. He who believes in me will live, even though he dies; and whoever lives and believes in me will never die." (John 11:25–26)

Many ancient BSD cultures, such as Egypt and China, focused their religious efforts on trying to teach people how to live in such a way that their two souls would not split apart at death. In Egypt, it was thought that if a person achieved a perfect union between his *ba* and *ka,* they would bond together to form a singularity called the *akh.* In China, the same achievement was thought to produce the "immortal fetus." In both cases, it was thought that if individuals achieved this breakthrough, they would never again be in danger of having their two souls divide. Such people would then inherit "true" eternal life, never again losing their memories or sense of self-identity at the end of each life. As ancient Israel termed it, they would then possess an "eternal name."

Before Christianity, virtually all religions seemed to subscribe to some version of the BSD. Almost none of them had any expectation of a future resurrection, however. In their view, the only way a person could achieve "eternal life" was to prevent his two souls from dividing at death in the first place. If someone failed to do this and the two souls divided, that was the end of the story; the self from that lifetime would never exist again. But Christ, it seems, changed everything, making it possible for all the lost souls of the dead to be returned to life one day.

It was a huge change.

Christ introduced a whole new option—faith—for the person wishing to acquire eternal life. He did not end the old option, but just added another option alongside it. The old religions, which had always been based on acquiring eternal life through one's own personal wholeness and perfection, still existed as a valid option. Indeed, the Judeo-Christian tradition celebrates two legendary figures credited with doing just that: Enoch and Elijah. These two men did not inherit their eternal life by dying and then hoping (faith) to be resurrected again at some later date; on the contrary, they are credited as having never died at all. They remained whole. The second death never claimed them.[16]

They did not acquire their eternal life through Christ's first promise ("I am resurrection itself. He who believes in me will live, *even though* he dies"), but through His second one ("I am life itself. He who lives in me will *never* die"). From the testimony of the Gnostic Gospels, it seems that Original Christianity considered the Old Testament path of perfection to have been every bit as important and effective as the path of faith.[17] Whereas the canonical New Testament focused on the new path of faith, placing all hope in the resurrection of the Last Day, many Gnostic scriptures were devoted instead to the older path of wholeness and perfection, seeking to avoid the second death altogether. In the earliest church, there does not seem to have been any argument about this older path still being a valid option. Jesus claims in the "heretical" Gospel of Thomas, just as He does in the canonical Gospel of John,[18] that it is not necessary for the true Christian to wait until Resurrection Day to inherit eternal life. Instead, Christianity originally considered it possible for a person to inherit eternal life *before* he died, making it unnecessary for him ever to die at all: "He who discovers the meaning of these sayings will never taste death" (The Gospel of Thomas 1). "If he refrains from sin, he shall live forever" (from Judaism's Passover Haggadah).

Like so many other BSD cultures, Judaism had long acknowledged that a path to eternal life, difficult though it was, already existed before Jesus arrived on the scene. Enoch and Elijah were merely considered rare examples of a universal truth: A person perfect enough would never die.

Our Inner Dance

Identifying the soul and spirit of the ancient binary soul doctrine as the conscious and unconscious of modern science leads to some startling insights. Modern psychology has not merely rediscovered humanity's two legendary souls, but has also greatly added to the scant information about them that managed to trickle down to us through history. And what modern science has added to our knowledge about the nature of the conscious and unconscious seems to explain a great deal about the afterlife traditions of the ancients, as well as the reports of today's afterlife researchers.[19]

If the conscious and unconscious divide at death, however, one must ask if the relationship between these two in life has anything to do with that eventual outcome. When Freud discovered the existence of a secondary sublevel of the human psyche in the beginning of the 1900s, he was dismayed, and throughout the rest of his life he remained convinced that this binary structure was evidence of pathology, and that the human mind was fundamentally dysfunctional. Folk wisdom would agree, holding that everyone is mentally ill to some degree, and that we only use ten percent of our full mental capacity. Of course, this discovery was not really a new observation:

> The hearts of men, moreover, are full of evil and there is madness in their hearts while they live, and afterward they join the dead. (Eccles. 9:3)

The two halves of the mind see the world very differently. In many respects, they are opposites: The conscious is active, while the unconscious is reactive and responsive; the conscious seems to exercise autonomous free will, functioning under its own initiative and volition, while the unconscious functions automatically and instinctively; the conscious is objective, while the unconscious is subjective; the conscious is intellectual, while the unconscious is emotional. The left-brain conscious mind is verbally oriented, while the right-brain unconscious is nonverbal, thinking and communicating via images, symbols, pictures, gestures, and metaphors. The left-brain conscious mind sees the differences and distinctions between things, while the right-brain unconscious is geared to do just the opposite—see the connections, relationships, and similarities between things. The conscious sees the trees, the unconscious sees the forest; the conscious reads the text, the unconscious perceives the context; the conscious notices the details, the unconscious grasps the meaning.

Although everyone possesses both sides, most of us tend to identify more with one side or the other. The rational, objective, left-brain conscious mind seems to be worshiped more by scientists, businessmen, and neoconservatives, while the emotional, intuitive, nonconformist right-brain unconscious is the darling of artistic idealists and liberals. Although they are so different, these two halves of the mind are perfectly made for one another, and when they are healthy, they waltz together inside us as if they were a single unit. The conscious mind always leads in this dance, taking the initiative in making new choices and decisions. But whenever the conscious mind initiates a move, the unconscious automatically responds with a corresponding move. Whenever the conscious mind chooses or acts, the unconscious mind reacts immediately and directly to that choice or act, generating its own responses, in the form of feelings, emotions, impressions, connections, associated ideas, and insights, which are then released back into the conscious mind.

Like a mirror, the unconscious forces a part of us to be always looking back on ourselves and our own past thoughts. This seems to be a built-in self-monitoring mechanism, one apparently designed by our Creator to ensure that we be true to ourselves, and honor the ideals, goals, and values we embrace deep inside. Whenever the conscious mind makes any new choice or decision, the unconscious automatically responds by scanning for relationships, patterns, and connections with what has come before. Comparing that latest choice or decision with the full gestalt of all our previous memories, the unconscious instinctively evaluates the current decision in light of all our previous thoughts, attitudes, impressions, perceptions, decisions, and conclusions on the matter. Thus the dance automatically generates the human conscience, our inner sense of right and wrong, and since it is naturally created by the automatic processes of the human psyche, this moral awareness ultimately seems independent of any cultural influences.

The unconscious automatically records all our decisions and conclusions, treating them as commands to be followed, carrying them out as a computer carries out its programming or a hypnotized person carries out the commands he or she is given. Thus, if a person at one point decided that "this is bad," then at a later time does that "bad" thing, the unconscious compares the present act and the previous judgment, and generates appropriate and corresponding psychological material—that is, bad or guilty feelings. Like a mirror, the unconscious always responds in kind, good for good and bad for bad. It is always reflecting back to us our own decisions, showing us: "This is what you are," "This is what you did," "This is how you felt about this then, but then this is how you acted here, and the two don't match up." It is always comparing ourselves *to* ourselves, and when it finds an inconsistency, our sense of integrity, wholeness, and self-esteem suffers.

The Price of Self-Betrayal

Unfortunately, the relationship between these two halves of our being can get out of balance and become unhealthy. We often bring this on ourselves, side-stepping our conscience, the mind's built-in self-correcting mechanism, by refusing to acknowledge the whispering voice of the unconscious, denying the validity of the thoughts coming from that side of the mind. Being the stronger of the two halves, the conscious mind can repress the feelings, memories, and insights coming from the unconscious, disrupting the natural communication between itself and the unconscious. Blocking the messages trying to rise up from the unconscious is essentially a form of self-censorship, self-betrayal, and self-destruction, an insistence that "those feelings/memories/insights don't really belong to me."

Most forms of neurosis can be traced back to these dynamics. The unconscious is not only the source of our moral balance, but also the source of our emotions and feelings, so when we repress the unconscious in order to avoid its moral judgments, we often find that we become cut off from our feelings and emotions as well. This is why it is a classic cultural archetype that the most evil people in the world feel no emotions, for in the process of turning off the voice of their own morality, they had to block the voice of the whole unconscious and so became cut off from their own feelings. To lose one is to lose the other. When people violate their own sense of right and wrong and then repress the outraged reaction from their own unconscious souls, they are actually pushing their own souls away from themselves, unknowingly dividing themselves in two. By consistently violating their own inner moral sense and ignoring their unconscious soul's messages, they alienate themselves not only from those moral messages, but also from most of the other input that normally rises from the unconscious. Each time we reject this input, the gap between soul and spirit grows wider and wider.

Thus the mind is able to divide itself into two. The ancients knew this, and we know it today as well. The ancients didn't really know anything in this regard that we don't also know today, except for one little point that just might make all the difference: They believed that this mind, which is capable of existing in states of extreme self-division and self-alienation, is *immortal*. It can't die. It can't stop functioning. It can, however, continue to rip itself apart into smaller and smaller bits and pieces throughout all eternity.

Why do our minds disintegrate at death? The answer seems to be embarrassingly simple: because we divide ourselves in life. We betray our own wholeness and integrity by rejecting the voice of our own conscience and ignoring parts of our own inner being. We divide ourselves by acting differently on the outside from the way we feel on the inside, denying with our outer actions what our inner soul urges us to do. Every time we push aside input from our souls, rejecting it as too impractical or just too painful, we alienate our unconscious soul a little more from its conscious spirit.

Where Does This Leave Us?

The binary soul doctrine held that one half of our mental being would go on to reincarnate after death, while our other half would split off and be discarded, eventually becoming trapped in a fixed dreamlike experience. One half got reborn, the other wound up in heaven or hell. And this process, it was thought, would just keep repeating; the conscious spirit would reincarnate again and again, repeatedly developing and then discarding more and more unconscious souls, all the while completely oblivious that any of this was going on.

A few cultures, however, believed it was possible for people to live their lives in such a way that this division would *not* occur to them. Modern science suggests much the same thing, that even though many people end up divided, bitter, and self-alienated, things don't have to work out that way. If we are careful how we live our lives, and don't lie to ourselves or betray our own values and ideals, we won't end up as psychological basket cases. But just as the ancient BSD cultures believed that the vast majority of humans *would* end up divided, in much the same way, modern science also warns that most of us end up neurotic to some degree, quietly suffering from our own inner betrayals:

> The number one killer in the world today is neither cancer nor heart disease. It is repression. Unconsciousness is the real danger, and neurosis the hidden killer. Repression—a stealthy, hidden, intangible force—strikes many of us down. It does so in so many disguised forms—cancer, diabetes, colitis—that we never see it naked for what it is. That is its nature—diabolic, complex, recondite. It is all pervasive, yet everywhere denied because its mechanism is to hide the truth. Denial is the inevitable consequence of its structure.[20]

We all have our blind spots, our secret inner places where we have quietly agreed with ourselves to lie to ourselves about ourselves. And woe to those in our personal lives who do not intuitively discern and stay away from those sensitive issues, for we often defend them to the death, as if our personal safety and security utterly depend on those lies being maintained![21]

When Jesus arrived on the scene, this seems to have been the way things looked to much of the world. While a few cultures considered it theoretically possible to achieve the degree of wholeness and integrity necessary to avoid mentally disintegrating at death, on a practical level this was considered so difficult as to be almost impossible, and only a rare few, such as Buddha, Zoroaster, Enoch, and Osiris, were ever thought to have actually accomplished it. Most people were considered doomed to just keep on reincarnating and dividing, reincarnating and dividing, throughout eternity.

It was not a happy picture.

3

Literature's First Theme: Soul Division from Gilgamesh to Galilee

I will make my name a name that endures!

—King Gilgamesh of Uruk

Life had not always seemed so grim. In fact, the past seemed to hold an intriguing promise. Before the great flood, according to Sumeria's ancient king list, just eight kings in succession ruled the land for an inconceivably long stretch of 241,200 years (giving each an average life span of more than 30,000 years). After the deluge, 23 further kings ruled Sumeria for 24,510 more years. These incredibly long life spans remind us of the biblical report of Noah and his forefathers living hundreds and even thousands of years. Instead of being unique to the biblical tradition, the idea that people before the flood lived very long lives seems to have permeated the entire Middle East. Indeed, the ancient king lists of Egypt also held that, prior to the flood, their land was ruled for thousands upon thousands of years by "the dead," and before that by demigods, and before that, by gods themselves.

While life spans of thousands of years would clearly seem to be beyond scientific possibility for the frail human body, life spans of thousands of years for a human *individual* might not be impossible—if it were possible for a person to incarnate again and again into successive lives without suffering loss of memory. The BSD suggests that this *is* possible, and some of the most ancient Egyptian king-names suggest that Egyptians once believed this as well. Modern Buddhism claims something very similar—that the holiest among us are sometimes able to recall their past lives.

Unfortunately, if humanity's masses indeed did once know how to transfer their memories and sense of identity from one incarnation to the next, that precious knowledge was eventually lost, at which time death became a far more pressing problem. From the very moment they appear on history's radar screen, the cultures of China, Egypt, and Sumeria all seem to have been utterly obsessed with finding a way to beat death; indeed, the people of Egypt practically devoted their society's entire resources to this goal. The *Epic of Gilgamesh*, perhaps the oldest written story on Earth, seems to be a tale of that same effort. Coming to us from ancient Sumeria, it describes the adventures of the historical King of Uruk (who lived sometime between 2750 and 2500 B.C.E.), who sought the secret of death. The aforementioned cultures were all exhibiting this same mortality-obsessed behavior at essentially the very moment in human history when writing was invented. We don't know if people were acting like this for thousands of years before writing showed up, or if writing and this cultural obsession with death arrived simultaneously.[1]

The *Epic of Gilgamesh* was essentially the Bible of ancient Sumeria and Babylon, home of the famous pyramid-like ziggurats. Predating Homer's *Iliad* by at least 1,500 years, the ancient tale was reintroduced to the modern world when tablets written in Akkadian were found at the library of the Assyrian king Ashubanipal by archaeologists in the nineteenth century. And, like so many other pyramid-building cultures, Sumeria seems to have subscribed to the binary soul doctrine.[2] From beginning to end, the *Epic of Gilgamesh* is a perfect allegory for the BSD. It explores the meaning of death and the afterlife via a tale of a partnership between two men who are equal opposites of one another. At first, their partnership is very successful, happy, healthy, and fruitful, but eventually death takes the one and leaves the other.

Gilgamesh the Strong

The tale starts out by describing Gilgamesh, who turns out to be a classic archetypal symbol of the left-brain conscious spirit. Sole ruler of his realm, he was a mighty king who enjoyed unlimited power and control over his kingdom. Although he was supremely strong and fiercely intelligent, he seemed to have had no empathy for others. Young and arrogant, he oppressed his people harshly and immorally. All this, of course, is consistent with the characteristics of the left-brain conscious spirit, which is strong, dominant, and intelligent but possesses no subjective sensitivity or moral center. And since the conscious spirit reincarnates without any memory, it possesses no record of its distant past and so always feels itself to be young. Also, Gilgamesh is said to have been two-thirds god and one-third human, which reminds us that two of a person's three parts, the soul and spirit, are immortal, but the third part, the physical body, does die.

Enkidu the Pure

At first, Gilgamesh ruled alone, but the story soon pairs him with a partner. Because of Gilgamesh's great cruelty, his people called out to the gods for help and, in response, the gods created Enkidu. Designed to be an equal but opposite match for Gilgamesh, it was hoped that the two mighty beings would balance each other out, thereby providing the Kingdom of Uruk some peace. Enkidu was not only Gilgamesh's perfect equal in strength and size, but his visual double as well, virtually a second "self," right down to the hair. Again and again, the text repeats the same theme, emphasizing that Enkidu was Gilgamesh's exact equal and perfect partner: "Create him his equal! . . . Let him look into as mirrors—give a second self to him. . . . [Enkidu was] like unto Gilgamesh to the hair."[3]

Enkidu was not identical to Gilgamesh in every respect, however, but was more natural, enjoying an instinctual rapport with the world of nature. He had long shaggy hair and was ruled by his feelings, often being overcome by his own deep emotion. All this, of course, brings to mind the characteristics of the right-brain unconscious soul: Just as the right-brain unconscious is the equal but opposite partner of the left-brain conscious, so was Enkidu an equal opposite to Gilgamesh. Both Enkidu and the right-brain unconscious possess a strong sense of connection and relationship. Both are more natural, instinctual, and emotional than intellectual. And, possessing the memory, the unconscious provides a perfect record, like a mirror image, of the person's entire life. Just as the unconscious acts like a mirror for the conscious, so did Enkidu act like a mirror for Gilgamesh.

A Perfect Match

Before they met, Gilgamesh had two dreams. In the first, a meteorite so great that Gilgamesh could neither lift nor turn it fell to earth. He embraced it like a wife, but his mother forced him to compete with it. In the second dream, Gilgamesh dreamed of an axe so great he could neither lift nor turn it. Again he embraced it like a wife, but here too his mother intervened to force him to compete with the axe. The meteor and axe, the story explains, are symbols for Enkidu (and thus we find that symbolism is as old as literature itself; in this work, believed to be the oldest existing piece of literature in the world, we find the earliest use of symbolism). These dreams both fit the BSD; although the conscious and unconscious embrace one another within us as would a married couple, they also wrestle with each other as well. In the end, Enkidu and Gilgamesh were two of a kind and could not help but love one another: "You are so like him, you will love him as yourself."[4]

As soon as these two heroes met, Enkidu took on the role of Gilgamesh's moral advisor, the same job the unconscious soul performs for the conscious spirit. As king, the story explains, Gilgamesh cruelly insisted on raping all new brides on the day of their weddings, before they could be delivered to their husbands-to-be. When Enkidu heard of this inhumane practice, he objected to it with great moral outrage and proceeded to confront Gilgamesh about it. Enkidu blocked Gilgamesh's path into the bedchamber of his next victim, provoking Gilgamesh into a furious wrestling match. In the end, however, Enkidu finally relented, conceding Gilgamesh's superiority. The two then embraced, quickly becoming devoted friends and inseparable partners.

The same dynamic, of course, occurs between the soul and spirit; although the morally aware soul will struggle mightily to prevent the spirit from acting immorally, in the end the conscious spirit is stronger than the unconscious soul and always gets its own way. In the story, the two friends bonded closely; after each saw himself in the other, they made a solemn vow to stay together always.

Three Curses

Buoyed up by the arrival of his new friend, Gilgamesh felt inspired to tackle the greatest challenge of his era, deciding to go harvest the great Cedar Forest. The land of Sumeria lacked such timber and had to build all its buildings from sun-dried clay bricks. It had long coveted the natural wealth of the Cedar Forest. But those riches were guarded by a beast so fearsome that none before had dared this task. Enkidu repeatedly tried to talk Gilgamesh out of this foolish and arrogant mission, but to no avail. When others also protested, bringing up various objections about this adventure, Enkidu promised to go in front and always protect Gilgamesh's life. In much the same way, the unconscious soul always remains loyal to the conscious spirit, devotedly protecting its interests and defending its decisions. During this adventure, Gilgamesh was taunted for taking orders from a nobody like Enkidu. Similarly, the conscious spirit often discounts the value of the soul's guidance.

With Enkidu unable to convince Gilgamesh to abort this journey, the two ultimately found themselves fighting Humbaba, the monstrous guardian of the forest. Just before Gilgamesh killed the monster, Humbaba cursed Enkidu: "Of the two of you, may Enkidu not live the longer, may Enkidu not find any peace in this world!" Even though Gilgamesh was the true guilty party, Enkidu was made to pay instead. Thus, just as the soul passes away while the spirit continues on after death, the soul paying the price for the spirit's choices and decisions in life, so was Enkidu instead of Gilgamesh cursed to die, an innocent party forced to pay for his partner's crimes.

The goddess Ishtar became enraged after Humbaba's death, wanting revenge. If she was not allowed to kill Gilgamesh, she threatened, she would knock down the gates of the netherworld and let the dead return to eat the living. All the dead would arise, she threatened, and would outnumber the living. Unlike those of Judaism, Christianity, and Zoroastrianism, this ancient Sumerian prophecy of a coming Universal Resurrection of the dead specifically predicts that the resurrected dead will feed on the living. In much the same way, the BSD also suggests that when our past-life souls reawaken within us at Judgment Day, they will ravenously consume our minds like a pack of wild rats let loose at a feast.[5] When the gods held a conference to discuss these matters, however, they decided that Enkidu should die instead of Gilgamesh. Since Enkidu was condemned by the council instead of Gilgamesh, Ishtar's curse was presumably not averted, and so, the story would suggest, it still technically hangs over humanity's head.

The Quest for Immortality

After Enkidu succumbed to the curse and died, Gilgamesh became so grief-stricken that he resolved to find the secret of death, no matter what the cost. In the story, he quite literally traveled to the ends of the earth looking for Utnapishtim, the Sumerian "Noah," the only human being, according to the story, ever to have acquired eternal life. In many respects, this long journey seems to represent the afterlife journey of the conscious spirit after suffering the second death. On this long journey, Gilgamesh encountered many strange characters who always repeated the same message, saying that his quest was futile because all people must die.

But Gilgamesh refused to be dissuaded from this mission and, continuing on, eventually came to a place called the Road of the Sun, which was so shrouded in darkness that nothing could be seen in any direction. He traveled blindly on this dark path for many days, which reminds one of the first phase of near-death experiences (as well as the between-lives realm in past-life regression reports), when the conscious mind finds itself wandering aimlessly in a similar empty blackness after separating from its unconscious soul.[6] Once out of this darkness, Gilgamesh met a young maiden who inquired why he was so grief-stricken over the death of his friend. She advised him to forget his Enkidu, informing Gilgamesh that no one else remembered him anymore. This maiden seems to be speaking more about the BSD's tale of a soul discarded by its spirit than of true human relationships, where our bonds with and memories of our departed loved ones often remain strong for the rest of our lives. (This whole meeting-the-maiden scenario also seems related to a similar postmortem meeting between the *urvan* and *daena* souls in Persia's native religion, Zoroastrianism.)

The Sleep of Liars

At the end of his long journey, Gilgamesh finally met Utnapishtim in the Land of Far Away. He thus discovered, despite everyone's confident advice to the contrary, that it indeed is technically possible for human beings to conquer death, since at least one person had accomplished that goal. Curiously, Utnapishtim is said in the story to have a damaged eye, reminding religious students of Osiris, who gave one of his eyes to Horus.[7] When Gilgamesh asked Utnapishtim to tell him the secret of death, Utnapishtim agreed to do so, but only if Gilgamesh could stay awake for six days and seven nights. Accepting these conditions, Gilgamesh sat down, firmly intending to stay awake, but almost instantly fell fast asleep. While Gilgamesh was asleep, Utnapishtim peevishly complained to his wife that all men are liars. The text suggests that Utnapishtim might have actually given Gilgamesh the secret of immortality if he had simply been able to stay awake, but Gilgamesh failed the test, and in the end finished his journey empty-handed.

Utnapishtim's complaint about lying also suggests, however, that if Gilgamesh hadn't made a promise he couldn't keep about being able to stay awake, he might have been able to receive immortality. Both these story elements seem relevant to the BSD. Unconsciousness and lies are indeed the enemies of eternal life, the BSD maintains. In fact, they are the very same thing. If we lie to ourselves by keeping ourselves unconscious of portions of our own mental content (keeping portions of ourselves asleep), the BSD teaches, we will die; if we are truthful to ourselves by remaining fully conscious of the content of our own minds, we remain whole, and thus avoid dividing at death.

When Gilgamesh finally woke up and realized he'd botched his one chance for immortality, he despondently accepted his fate but then wondered about the value of his life. For whom, he wondered miserably, had he been laboring all his life? For whom had he journeyed? For whom, he despaired, had he suffered? He seemed to feel in the end that all his efforts and struggles in life ultimately gained him nothing. This is, the BSD student notes, the very same lament the conscious spirit might make about soul division: Since we lose our memories at the end of life, what good then did our toil accomplish in our lifetime?

Refusing to provide Gilgamesh with the secret of eternal life, Utnapishtim suggested instead that Gilgamesh just return home and be fresh and young again. While this is a most curious element of the story, it again seems consistent with the BSD. It suggests that the choice before Gilgamesh was to either remain in the Land of Far Away and enjoy immortality but also no longer ever again be "fresh and young," or return to his native land, where he could again be "fresh and young" but not enjoy immortality. This suggests to the student of the BSD that Utnapishtim thought it would be better for Gilgamesh to continue to incarnate again and again, getting a fresh new identity each time, than to continue his old identities.

The tale finally ends with Gilgamesh standing once more before the grand gates of Uruk, expansively extolling the greatness of his city and exploits. All this boasting, however, rings a little hollow after his forlorn evaluation of his mortality in the Land of Far Away. It is a profoundly bittersweet ending, apparently intended to leave the reader pondering his own impending mortality, but now, perhaps, viewing death not as an inevitability, but a problem that has simply not yet been solved. Even though the mighty King Gilgamesh failed to procure the secret of death, he came tantalizingly close, and that would seem to leave the matter, and the story, unresolved.

What is perhaps most interesting about this powerful piece of ancient literature (history? religion?) is that, even as far back as the dawn of writing itself, the powers-that-be at the time did not wish to come right out with a straightforward presentation of the binary soul doctrine and its vision of life and death, but instead felt it would be better to disguise the message as metaphor, placing it inside a cultural legend. We have seen this same dynamic in the scriptures of the Old Testament,[8] as well as in many other legends and myths from other cultures.[9] Was there really a Gilgamesh? Yes, the name seems to be genuine, appearing among Sumeria's king lists. Was there also an Enkidu? Perhaps not. In an age of no mass communication and complete state control over virtually everything, it would have been a simple matter to manufacture such a legend out of whole cloth and insert it into the cultural dialogue.

In any case, it seems that the custom of preserving some elements of religious knowledge as "secret" extends far back in time, at least as far as we are able to see, since this practice shows up at the very dawn of history, that is, the written word. And until the Roman Empire came along, this custom apparently worked quite well.

The Book of Baruch by Justin

Paradise came into being through the love of Elohim and Edem . . .

They made man a symbol of their union and love
and planted some of their powers in him.
Edem provided the soul and Elohim the spirit.
The man Adam was a seal of the wedding of Edem and Elohim.
And, as Moses wrote, Eve was image and symbol,
and the seal of Edem preserved forever.
Edem set the soul in Eve and Elohim the spirit . . .
Edem gave away all her power to Elohim, like a marriage dowry.

(from the Book of Baruch by Justin)

Similar allegories of soul division are found in creation myths around the globe. Every continent seems to have independently spawned its own collection of tales about primordial beings dividing into or otherwise generating two equal but opposite halves, the marriage or interaction of which then creates the universe in which we live. Such tales are found in the Babylonian creation myth of the Enuma Elish, the Hindu myth of Indra and Vritra, the Egyptian myth of Seth and Apophis, the Canaanite myth of Baal and Yamm, the Sumerian myth of Kur and Enlil, and the Hebrew myth of Adam and Eve. Similar myths can be found in creation myths from China, Africa, Australia, and North and South America.[10]

Christianity is not exempt from this pattern. Numerous examples occur in early Christian literature, such as the Book of Baruch by Justin, thought to date to the transitional period between Judaism and Christianity.[11] We only know of this lost scripture because a sizable fragment of it happened to be preserved as a paraphrase in Hippolytus of Rome's *Refutation of All Heresies*. We know virtually nothing of its author, Justin, except that Hippolytus tells us he was a Gnostic. This may be one of the very earliest Gnostic texts ever written, reflecting a transition between first-century Judaism and Christian Gnosticism. To the student of the BSD, it is a remarkable find, clearly reflecting the story line of the binary soul in a very early Christian document.

The basic structure of the Book of Baruch is very simple. Three divine beings are also divine principles, "the roots and pools from which all springs." They are the Good, who alone among the three possess omniscience, along with the divine couple Edem and Elohim, both of whom are limited and fallible. Edem is female, and both represents soul and provides soul to human beings. Elohim is male, and both represents spirit and provides spirit to human beings. These two deities fell in love and mated, and when that happened, Edem gave away her power to Elohim. From their union, the whole universe was created, including humankind. Human beings were specifically designed to be a seal and reflection of the loving union between Edem and Elohim. The human beings created by these two deities possess part of each deity; Edem gave them soul, and Elohim gave them spirit. And just as Edem gave away all her power to Elohim, so too, the text declares, will humanity do the same.

The story does not stop there, but goes on, as so many creation myths do, to present an explanation for the existence of evil as well. Elohim eventually abandoned Edem and returned alone to heaven, leaving Edem behind on earth. In her grief at being abandoned by her lover, Edem decided to torture the spirits of all humans, and through their pain, she calculated, Elohim would also suffer for his "cold violation of their covenant." And so, because of Elohim's unfaithfulness and Edem's grief, soul was set against spirit, and spirit against soul, throughout all humanity.

Of course, the student of the BSD will immediately see the parallels. Not only does this early Christian work distinguish between soul and spirit, but it also declares that humankind's great spiritual dilemma is that our souls and spirits are in conflict, dividing us within ourselves. It suggests, furthermore, that just as Edem and Elohim divided from one another, so too our souls and spirits are in danger of dividing from one another as well, with the spirit "returning" to God while the soul is abandoned, left behind to cope as best it can on its own. It also suggests that the current enmity between our souls and spirits has its origins in a Primordial Division that predates our physical births.[12]

Just as Edem and Elohim mated, so too the conscious spirit and unconscious soul are wedded within the human psyche, and just as Edem gave up all her power to Elohim, so too does the conscious spirit have dominance over the unconscious soul. The conscious spirit possesses free will, while the unconscious soul always remains dutifully reactive, responsive, and reflective, possessing no independent initiative of its own. And just as Elohim willfully abandoned Edem, so too does the conscious spirit regularly choose to reject the messages of the unconscious soul, and finally abandons it altogether at death. And just as Edem strove to cause Elohim to suffer after he abandoned her, so too does the unconscious soul generate psychological pain for the conscious spirit to feel whenever it rejects the soul's messages.

We can see, then, that this same hidden message of soul duality and soul division continued in our literature throughout the ages. From the *Epic of Gilgamesh*, written at the very dawn of literature itself, all the way up to the earliest years of the Christian revolution, the same message was being repeated again and again: Humankind comprises not one but two divine elements, which are at odds with one another in the human breast and are in danger of dividing from one another at death. Interestingly, in the years between Gilgamesh and Galilee, the perceived threat of soul division seems to have increased rather than decreased; in the *Epic of Gilgamesh*, this division was merely associated with death, but in the Book of Baruch it was deemed responsible for *all* of humankind's woes.

Self-Correction of a Natural System: The Two Faces of Resurrection

Light the light within you. Do not extinguish it!
Raise your dead who have died,
for they lived and have died for you.
Give them life. They shall live again!
Knock on yourself as upon a door,
and walk upon yourself as on a straight road.
　　　　　　　　—The Teachings of Silvanus (a lost second-century
　　　　　　　　　　Christian scripture recovered at Nag Hammadi)

Before Jesus arrived on the world scene, most people despaired of ever acquiring the perfection needed to survive death intact. Although many remained convinced, like Gilgamesh, that the personal achievement of immortality was technically possible, on a practical level this goal seemed beyond the reach of all but a select few. Still, believing this goal to be achievable, numerous cultures painstakingly outlined paths people could take to effect their own salvation. The Jews catalogued a bewildering array of laws intended to ensure personal purity and integrity, the Egyptians designed elaborate rituals and procedures to bond their *ba* and *ka* souls together, and the Hindus and Buddhists sought their wholeness and nonduality through prayer and meditation. These religious disciplines appear to have the same goal: conquering death through inner wholeness, integrity, and perfection.

Unfortunately, when all was said and done, very few succeeded in such efforts. For every Enoch or Elijah who beat the odds and survived death, millions failed. While it was occasionally effective on the level of the individual, this approach of achieving immortality through personal wholeness and perfection was a miserable failure on the level of the collective. It worked wonderfully when people actually tried it, but it was a path few ever started down, and fewer still completed. Even though a scattered few had been able to escape the revolving wheel of soul division, the vast majority of the Earth's tired, insecure, misinformed, and perpetually distracted population never even tried. Despite all the different religions intended to promote spiritual wholeness and integrity, humanity's masses still found themselves trapped in a downward spiral of unconscious self-deceit, self-betrayal, and self-destruction. The old religions, when all was said and done, were just not enough to turn the tide in humanity's ancient war against itself.

Which Resurrection?

Christ's promise of resurrection seems to have been exactly what the world was waiting for. For the first time in history, the average person could hope for a real future; with this new guarantee of personal salvation, the grave no longer had the last word on who one was and what one's life really meant. This was such a powerful cultural suggestion, and one the masses were so primed and ready for, that it eventually enveloped—indeed engendered—the whole of Western civilization.

From the perspective of the BSD, however, Christ's promise of resurrection takes on a whole new dimension and explains some very curious teachings that circulated in the earliest years of the church. Conventional Christian theology, of course, holds that at the prophesied Universal Resurrection of Judgment Day, every person who ever lived on Earth will not only be brought back from the dead, but will also be retrofitted with their very own physical body for the occasion. Christ reportedly rose from the dead in the same body He was buried in, and the official church has always assumed that everyone else's resurrection would work the same way. Reincarnation, however, throws a curve into this scenario: How would this process work for a person who lived in one century as George Smith and in another century as Frank Jones? Would George get a body but Frank wouldn't, or would the one entity who lived in different eras as both people then be physically divided into two separate people, each with his own unique body at the same moment in time?

The BSD suggests a third, seemingly more likely possibility—that the souls of both George and Frank would reawaken together within the same mind, both of them waking up inside the body and mind of their current incarnation. If George had reincarnated as Frank and then Frank reincarnated as Robert, and the Universal Resurrection occurred during Robert's lifetime, Robert's past-life souls as Frank and George would return to his conscious awareness, causing him to recall those past lives and selves as clearly as his present life. These past-life selves would indeed have arisen from the dead fully embodied, just as Judeo-Christian prophecy always promised (albeit in a somewhat less dramatic fashion than previously expected). This scenario, which explains many perplexing biblical passages about the Universal Resurrection, is explored in depth in my book *The Division of Consciousness*.

Resurrection Now or Later?

This scenario would also seem to explain a great deal about the mysterious Christianity of Nag Hammadi texts. In the earliest years of the faith, resurrection was a subject of no little dispute; while the official church insisted that our resurrections could only occur during that end-time event known as Judgment Day, the Gnostic Church enigmatically insisted that a person would be better off seeking his resurrection *before* death: "Those who say they will die first and then rise are in error. If they do not first receive the resurrection while they live, when they die they will receive nothing" (The Gospel of Philip 73:1–5).

This, of course, would not even be possible using conventional Christianity's definition of resurrection, but it makes perfect sense from a reincarnationist perspective. If "resurrection" returns one's past-life souls from the dead, it could theoretically occur at any time. If reincarnation is real, such a restoration might even be inevitable. The human mind is, after all, a natural system, and all natural systems are self-correcting, automatically tending toward a state of healthy balance. The disassociation of past-life souls and past-life memories would seem to be an unnatural and artificially imposed imbalance in this system, and thus a temporary condition that, given enough time, would probably correct itself. And if, as virtually all our ancient religions once held, the human mind indeed is immortal, then it would have as much time as it needed to correct this neurotic imbalance. In other words, the "resurrection," or restoration of the mind's original wholeness and integrity, probably *would* happen sooner or later.

While the official church rested all its hopes on the "later" scenario of Judgment Day, the Gnostic Church seems to have thought that sooner was better than later, and this too makes sense. If this "resurrection" were delayed until the last possible moment at Judgment Day, then all one's past-life souls would chaotically reemerge into one's consciousness simultaneously. The Gnostics seem to have thought that this transition did *not* have to be chaotic and destructive, but could instead be experienced well in advance of Judgment Day, presumably under far more safe and controlled conditions.

The Danger of Resurrection

If this restoration was inevitable anyway, would that mean that Jesus' promise to resurrect His followers was just an empty gesture? Not at all. Even if it was predestined that all this lost mental content would eventually be restored within each of us as our fractured minds were made whole again, that doesn't necessarily mean that the transition would be easy. The divided fragments of our immortal minds reuniting wouldn't necessarily *integrate*. Instead, they could all just melt together into a meaningless mess. Instead of ending up integrated and functional (like the highly organized ones and zeros of a complex computer program), all the memory data of a person's multiple past lives could wind up shuffled haphazardly together like a deck of cards, losing all meaning and functionality in the process.[1] This coming psychological reunion thus posed the ultimate danger for humanity, threatening to dissolve all memory and identity as we know it. "The end will come like a flood" (Dan. 9:26).

The prospect that all the psychological experiences humanity has recorded since the beginning of time—all our lost feelings, thoughts, hopes, dreams, loves, hates, grudges, fantasies, insights, experiences, traumas, fears, complexes, compulsions, desires, and identities—could one day all come flooding chaotically back into our conscious awareness at once is inexpressibly horrendous and begins to explain why the coming of this "Judgment Day" was portrayed so dreadfully in the Old Testament, and so frequently as an unstoppable invasion of foreign barbarians:

> "O house of Israel," declares the LORD, "I am bringing a distant
> nation against you—an ancient and enduring nation, a people whose

language you do not know, whose speech you do not understand. Their quivers are like an open grave; all of them are mighty warriors. They will . . . devour your sons and daughters." (Jer. 5:15–17)

Caught in the middle of such a chaotic inner invasion of images, memories, and past-life selves, the average frail human psyche wouldn't stand a chance. While our immortal spirits would survive this passage, our fragile souls could be lost, and with them, all our memories of everything we'd ever been, done, or achieved. Whereas our living consciousness itself would pass unscathed through this fiery test, our memories and senses of identity were at risk:

> If any man's work survives, he will receive a reward. If any man's work is burned up, he will suffer loss: but he himself will be saved; yet so as by fire. (1 Cor. 3:14–15)

In such a scenario, the most Jesus could have done would have been to make it possible for His followers' souls to *survive* this traumatic reunion, helping us safely integrate all our past-life memories, feelings, and selves into some kind of cohesive and meaningful order. It would still be a painful transition, but no longer a fatal one:

> "The days are coming," declares the LORD, "when I will bring my people Israel and Judah back from captivity . . . Cries of fear are heard—terror, not peace. Ask and see: Can a man bear children? Then why do I see every strong man with his hands on his stomach like a woman in labor, every face turned deathly pale? How awful that day will be! None will be like it. It will be a time of trouble for Jacob, but he will be saved out of it. In that day," declares the LORD Almighty, "I will break the yoke off their necks and will tear off their bonds . . . So do not fear, O Jacob my servant; do not be dismayed, O Israel," declares the LORD. "I will surely save you out of a distant place, your descendants from the land of their exile. . . . I will not completely destroy you. I will discipline you but only with justice; I will not let you go entirely unpunished." (Jer. 30:1–11)

The author of the Gospel of Thomas, however, believed that Christ promised far more than that.

5

The Gospel of Thomas: A
Primer on Living in Christ

In its opening words the Gospel of Thomas offers a stunning hermeneutic challenge: "whoever finds the interpretation of these sayings will not experience death." Unfortunately, modern readers come to this incipit devoid of a technique of interpretive reading—an hermeneutics—that grants entry into the mysterious meaning vouchsafed by such words. Current academic studies respond to the challenge of the text with modest modern techniques of historical and sociological analysis, conceptual dissections of parallelisms, and suppositions about obscuring temporal stratifications within the compilation of the sayings. Unable to find any hermeneutic method for unlocking a coherent meaning in the Gospel of Thomas, some critics simply deny the organic function of this incipit relative to the remaining logion. In sum, they conclude the sayings of the living Jesus collected in the Thomas gospel are a hodgepodge with no integral, coherent intention. The question I pose is this: Was there an original tradition of interpretation—a hermeneutic technique—implicit in early transmissions of the Thomas tradition that gave an organic coherence to readings of the text, and if so, is that hermeneutic method still accessible? Can modern readers meet the challenge of the Thomas incipit?

—Lance S. Owens[1]

The discovery of the Gospel of Thomas may prove to be the biggest turning point in Christian history since Constantine's conversion. If proved authentic, this scripture would single-handedly change the world's entire understanding of Christ's message to humanity. Of all the early Christian works recovered at Nag Hammadi, this lost collection of sayings attributed to Jesus is the oldest and most important. In the first centuries of the church, Thomas' work was considered a genuine eyewitness account of Jesus' teachings and was revered by the faithful right alongside those of Matthew, Mark, Luke, and John. We know it circulated widely in the early church because references to the Gospel of Thomas appear in numerous early Christian writings.[2] Later historians, however, were under the impression that all copies had been destroyed; for over a thousand years, the Gospel of Thomas remained one of Christianity's greatest mysteries, thought to have been permanently deleted from history by the official church's censorship campaign. All that changed when a copy of this legendary work resurfaced from its long exile in 1945. Ever since, Christiandom has been collectively holding its breath over what revolutionary secrets the Gospel of Thomas might contain.

Although the Coptic manuscript found at Nag Hammadi dates from the fourth century, no one knows precisely when the Gospel of Thomas was originally written. Heated academic debate has persisted over this issue ever since the work was discovered; some scholars point to a mid-second century origin, but others argue compellingly for the mid-first century. In any event, we know the Gospel of Thomas had to have been written no later than 140 A.D. because a second copy, written in Greek, was found 50 years earlier on the site of an ancient Egyptian library. Although this Greek version of the text only contains 20 of the 114 sayings found in the Coptic version (plus one other saying not found in the Egyptian version), the two are otherwise essentially the same, and the Greek version has been dated to about 140 A.D. While the Coptic version is about two centuries younger, it is clearly a translation of the Greek version, which tells us that most if not all of the Coptic text was written before 140 A.D., and also that the work circulated among Christianity's faithful for at least 200 years, and possibly as many as 300. There are various opinions about its specific date of origin, but the majority of scholars place the Gospel of Thomas somewhere between 50 and 140 A.D., which would make it fully contemporary with the New Testament.

Most scholars agree that the biblical gospels were not actually written by people who had met Christ during His lifetime, but this disappointing caveat may not be true of the Gospel of Thomas. If Thomas' gospel is an authentic eyewitness account, it would be the world's single most important source for historical knowledge about Jesus of Nazareth, which, given the unorthodox contents of its text, would radically revise modern assumptions about Original Christianity.

A pure sayings gospel, the Gospel of Thomas contains a collection of 114 sayings (logia) attributed to Jesus without any accompanying narrative. Many of its logia are slightly different—seemingly earlier—versions of familiar biblical passages, while other sayings, some of which seem quite obscure, have no known parallels in New Testament literature.[3] The Gospel of Thomas seems to contain forgotten traditions from the earliest years of the church, restoring lost teachings. If so, it may provide the modern world with its first real window into a Christianity—and a Christ—that history turned its back on millennia ago.

Twin Traditions

> There were originally two primitive kerygmas, two early proclamations of salvation, two separate spheres of Christian theology.[4]

Long before the discovery of the Gospel of Thomas, religious scholars had already figured out that something like it must have existed in the earliest years of the church. A study of the Gospels of Matthew and Luke suggested they had a common source in some unknown collection of Jesus' sayings. Noting the recurrence of numerous similar passages in those two gospels, scholars came up with a hypothetical document they named Q, a lost sayings gospel that lacked narrative structure and references to Jesus' death and Resurrection.[5] The subsequent unearthing of the Gospel of Thomas shook the scholarly community to its core, for this was exactly what they found in it.

Since that discovery, further research convinced many in the academic community that Q/Gospel of Thomas represents a previously unknown second tradition in early Christianity, one largely independent of the Pauline tradition that focused so heavily on Jesus' death and Resurrection. One of the most striking aspects of both Q and the Gospel of Thomas is their apparent silence on Jesus' redemptive sacrifice—the very core of Paul's message.[6] The Didache, an early Christian "believer's manual" that once widely circulated in the nascent church, is also strangely silent on Jesus' death.[7] These recently recovered Christian documents appear to disprove the orthodox assumption that Original Christianity unanimously viewed Jesus' death and Resurrection as the cornerstone of the faith, as they all seem to find Jesus' primary meaning and value in His words rather than His death.[8]

Was there a divided tradition in early Christianity? Many eminent religious scholars believe so. John Kloppenborg, Helmut Koester, and John Dominic Crossan all hold that there were two distinct arcs of Christian theology in the early church, one based on Jesus' life, the other on His death. Two separate proclamations of salvation, they insist, developed side by side in the primitive church. One of these traditions, represented by Q and the Gospel of Thomas, focused on the importance of Jesus' life and teachings, while the other, represented by Paul's Epistles, focused on Christ's death and Resurrection. Today, numerous Christian historians argue that instead of one of these traditions coming before the other, both date to the very foundations of the faith.

Both traditions promised salvation through a Kingdom of Heaven, but only one of them was apocalyptic. Whereas the resurrection tradition believed the arrival of that kingdom was scheduled to occur at some point in the future, the sayings tradition viewed it as already realized, present, and immediately available for the taking:

> From the days of John the Baptist until now, the kingdom of heaven has been pressing forward, and assertive men can grasp hold of it. (Matt. 11:12)

On a number of levels, these two primitive traditions seem related to the two salvations predicted by the binary soul doctrine. One path, the sayings tradition, taught the immediate acquisition of salvation and immortality in this current life through holiness and integrity, while the other path taught the eventual achievement of salvation and immortality through resurrection *after* death. The first path was more demanding, requiring one to be completely perfect and sinless, while the second path accommodated greater levels of human imperfection, providing some forgiveness of sins in exchange for a more delayed salvation. The New Testament seems to meld these two into an inconsistent theological hybrid, simultaneously demanding that Jesus' followers be completely perfect and sinless,[9] but at the same time accommodating imperfection by providing "forgiveness" for their sins.[10]

In time, it seems, the path of immediate salvation through personal perfection became the focus of the Gnostic Church, while the path of eventual salvation through faith in forgiveness and resurrection became the focus of the official church. But when Jesus proclaimed Himself to be both the "life" of those who would *not* die, and at the same time the "resurrection" of those who *would* die, it seems that Christianity originally recognized *two* paths to salvation, both a "path of life" and a "path of death." Is it any surprise, then, to find that the text of the Didache begins with just such a message? "There are two ways, one of life and one of death, but a great difference between the two ways" (Opening to the Didache).

Whereas the "way of life" described by Q and the Gospel of Thomas required a person to live a life of perfect holiness to qualify for its immediate reward, it seems that the "way of death" embraced by Paul and the Orthodox Church allowed for sin and merely required a person to have faith in order to qualify for its more eventual salvation. The Didache not only seems to refer to both these traditions in its opening "Two Paths" section, but also suggests elsewhere as well that the faith originally recognized two separate sets of teachings that existed side by side in the church:

> Every tested and true prophet who performs rites of the cosmic mystery of the church but does not teach others to do what he himself does, he shall not be judged before you, for he has his judgment before God, for, in such a way, the ancient prophets also acted. (Didache 11:11)

Saint Paul taught much the same thing himself, distinguishing between two distinct sets of Christian teachings, one which he refers to as "milk," the other as "meat" or "strong meat." He wrote that "babes" in the faith can only be given the milk of elementary instruction, being unready for the meat of deeper spiritual doctrines, while the "mature" are provided "God's secret wisdom."[11] The Didache reflects this same distinction. It instructs settled Christian communities how to deal with the itinerant Christian prophets and apostles that were wandering through their towns and villages in the first decades of the church. The Didache tells us that many of those wanderers were recognized as fully legitimate representatives of Christ's original teachings, even though they had a reputation for practicing mysterious rituals they did not share with these Christian communities. According to the Didache, there were two separate sets of teachings and practices in the early church, one that *was* shared with these communities, and another that was not. What were these enigmatic "rites of the cosmic mystery of the church"? The author of the Didache does not say and indeed gives every suggestion that even he does not know, and yet he unreservedly accepts these secret practices as authentic expressions of Christ's original teachings.

Since the discovery of the Gospel of Thomas, much has been made of the fact that the document fails to mention Christ's death and Resurrection. Many scholars have taken this omission to mean that its author did not support the Pauline death/Resurrection tradition. The actual text, however, does not support that conclusion, for it clearly presents itself as a *supplemental* gospel, not an alternative gospel. Its text starts out with the words "These are the secret sayings which the living Jesus spoke," thus implying both that another more public and open set of Christ's teachings also existed, and also that the likely readers of the Gospel of Thomas would already be familiar with those more widely published teachings. While it does represent the sayings tradition rather than the resurrection tradition, it clearly presents itself as only half of the story, indicating that another tradition existed alongside it. Thus, rather than denying the validity of the resurrection tradition, the Gospel of Thomas implicitly confirms and supports it. Much like the Didache, then, it also seems to date from a very early period when the faith recognized the existence of two separate but complementary and equally salvific traditions.

Unfortunately, even though the discovery of the Gospel of Thomas confirmed the existence of that primitive sayings tradition, it failed to fully clarify just what that tradition originally had to say. The problem is, it contains many mysterious and obscure passages that have, until now, defied all attempts at interpretation. Although this lost work has been intensely studied since its reappearance 60 years ago, most scholars feel the hermeneutical key to unlocking the meaning of its passages has yet to be found. This is, apparently, as Thomas intended it. The very first words in the book warn the reader that it contains a mystery, a riddle not easily unraveled, but one with a huge payoff for those who successfully solve its challenge:

> *These are the secret sayings which the living Jesus spoke and which Didymos Judas Thomas wrote down. And he said, "Whoever discovers the meaning of these sayings will not taste death." (The Gospel of Thomas 1)*

The Gospel of Thomas reports that Jesus taught "secret sayings," of which the Bible also hints.[12] This archaeological confirmation of the existence of those legendary secret sayings suggests that there were indeed not one, but two separate sets of Christ's teachings, a position long denied by the official church, but nonetheless held by many Christian sects over the centuries. This, of course, explains why certain elements found in the biblical gospels do not appear in the Gospel of Thomas.

This gospel is attributed to "Didymos Judas Thomas." The word *didymos* is Greek for twin, and the word *thomas* is Aramaic for twin. His name was actually Judas, but his nickname "the twin" is perplexingly given in two separate languages,[13] which leaves the book apparently authored by a figure named "Twin Judas Twin," or, perhaps, "Double Judas Double." In the Bible, Didymos Thomas was one of Jesus' Twelve Apostles, better known as "Doubting Thomas" (John 20:24–25). A huge body of tradition in the Syrian church insisted that Thomas was Jesus' twin brother.[14] The full name Didymos Judas Thomas is found in only two works: the recently recovered Gospel of Thomas and the Syrian Acts of Thomas.[15] In John 11:16, however, the apostle Thomas is specifically identified as "Didymos Thomas" ("twin twin") and then, apparently because the point was deemed so important it needed repeating, it is reiterated in John 20:24. And the text points out the same thing yet again in John 21:2. For some reason, the early church seems to have felt that this point needed to be greatly emphasized. Even more curiously, if the Gospel of Thomas predates the Gospel of John (as seems to be the case), then John felt, for some reason, that it was necessary to *edit out* Judas' name from the moniker "Didymos Judas Thomas,"[16] which left him using the even more awkward and unlikely appellation "Didymos Thomas," or "twin twin."

Thomas being Jesus' twin brother has been traditionally viewed as doubtful, primarily because it was never mentioned in the canonical accounts. Nonetheless, the Bible does admit that Jesus had a brother named Judas, which seems a curious coincidence.[17] Even more curious, the Gospel of John, a book devoted exclusively to the story of Jesus Christ, takes pains to point out three times that Thomas was "the twin," but doesn't bother mentioning *whose* twin he was.[18] The Syrian church connected these dots, insisting that twin was Jesus' own brother Judas.

While some might theorize that this double entry of the term "twin" in the Gospel of Thomas was merely the author's translation error, this seems unlikely. Saying 12 suggests that the Gospel of Thomas was written before the fall of the original church in Jerusalem in 70 A.D., when James the Just was still the head of the Christian community. At that early date, most Christians would have still been Jews by birth, and those who would have been able to read Thomas' gospel probably would have been familiar with both Greek and Aramaic, and so would have instantly recognized that these two words mean the same thing. It seems, then, that the author of this gospel may have *intentionally* referred to himself as a "doubled double," or a "twinned twin." This sort of repetition is an ancient, time-honored literary technique used to draw attention to a point of special significance. In the Old Testament, one finds numerous examples of this.[19] The double use of this term in both the Gospel of John and the Gospel of Thomas emphasizes the term "twin" and, by extension, emphasizes the whole idea of duality. Appearing as it does at the very beginning of the Gospel of Thomas, this doubled use of a word that itself means "double" is the first clue to the author's hermeneutics. Indeed, since this work is entitled the Gospel of Thomas instead of the Gospel of Judas, perhaps the correct (i.e., originally intended) translation of the title should be the Gospel of the Twin, or the Gospel of the Two, or even the Gospel of Duality. Or, as we will see, perhaps it was meant to suggest the Gospel of the Binary Soul Doctrine.

The Sayings

> *And he said, "Whoever discovers the meaning of these sayings will not taste death." (The Gospel of Thomas 1)*

The first Saying in the Gospel of Thomas suggests that the whole book has but a single theme to explore, and all the rest of the passages relate to and elaborate on that same theme. Until now, no commentator has been able to demonstrate such a hermeneutical link between all the different passages, but as we will see, they do have a common denominator: the binary soul doctrine.

If the text is to be taken at face value, this first passage must be seen as defining the entire purpose and message of Thomas' gospel. It is therefore not intended as a discourse on social design, nor as a discussion on the principles of social interaction, politics, morality, familial obligations, or gender roles. Those who come away from this work with such ideas miss the point entirely. The Gospel of Thomas declares itself to be one thing only: a primer on how to avoid death.

Thomas wastes no time in getting to the heart of Christianity—the promise of eternal life. But rather than discounting the threat of death, his Gospel says that some people *will* experience death, whereas others will not. This first saying should remind its Christian readership of similar promises given in the Gospel of John:

> "Lord," Martha said to Jesus, "if you had been here, my brother would not have died. But I know that even now God will give you whatever you ask." Jesus said to her, "Your brother will rise again." Martha answered, "I know he will rise again in the resurrection at the last day." Jesus said to her, "I am the resurrection and the life. He who believes in me will live, even though he dies; and whoever lives and believes in me will never die." (John 11:21–26)

In the Gospels of both Thomas and John, Jesus makes a stunning and seemingly impossible promise: that it is possible for a person to never die. This promise is contrasted, in the Gospel of John, with another option in which a person does die, but then is raised up via resurrection, as was the case with both Lazarus and Jesus. But the opening passage of Thomas' gospel refers to avoiding death altogether, a fate more along the lines of Enoch's and Elijah's. This book is discussing matters fundamentally alien to conventional Christian exegesis, which focuses exclusively on the hope of a future resurrection, never even entertaining the possibility—briefly hinted at in the Gospel of John and stated more boldly in that of Thomas—that a person might be able to avoid death altogether.

The first saying in the Gospel of Thomas issues a command: Find. Search. Look. It leaves the reader asking himself, "How? How do I search?" The second saying addresses that question.

> *Jesus said, "Let him who seeks continue seeking until he finds. When he finds, he will become troubled. When he becomes troubled, he will be astonished, and will reign over all. And after he has reigned he will rest." (The Gospel of Thomas 2)*

Although this passage is considered obscure by most commentators, its meaning is self-evident to the student of the binary soul doctrine. Humanity's primary spiritual problem is the division between the spirit and the soul, the alienation between the conscious and the unconscious. Anyone wishing to heal this division will seek to remove the barrier dividing them. That barrier is composed, Freud maintained, of nothing but pure resistance, but in *The Lost Secret of Death* I described this barrier as built out of grief:

> Some people sincerely insist that they have no such inner wall. But *everyone* has grief. Our tendency to hold and cling to things, as well as our tendency to judge and condemn ourselves and others, is the day-to-day voice of this hidden grief, screaming about these unfulfilled needs.
>
> When we don't allow ourselves to fully experience grief and sadness, they cannot fall away naturally. Instead they continue to influence our behaviors and attitudes. Prevented from dissipating naturally, these unacknowledged feelings accumulate silently and invisibly within us, becoming ever more solid and formidable. So long as that wall remains in place, we are cut off, to at least some degree, from our normal moment-to-moment feelings and emotions. We don't feel fully "here." This cuts us off from our own past, as well; all the traumas, feelings, and emotional reactions that we never allowed ourselves to fully release and experience remain, still in their original condition.
>
> By the time we are adults, most of us have gone through years of bitterness and frustration, never letting ourselves fully experience, express, and thereby release this grief. This psychological sediment severely restricts the healthy exchange of communication between the head and heart, between the conscious and unconscious.[20]

Sooner or later, the persevering spiritual seeker will discover this mountain of repressed pain and fear and, as the Gospel of Thomas warns us, that find is very surprising and troubling, because we usually do such a successful job of repressing those feelings and memories. The greatest danger is that we as spiritual seekers will be so troubled by this first glimpse of the magnitude of our own inner darkness that we will turn away from it in disgust and horror. But those of us who are fortified with courage and faith can persevere, fully experiencing—and thus neutralizing—this inner psychological content. When we do, we will emerge from this inner journey in a state of complete astonishment—astonished first that we were able to make it through that soul pain—astonished later that we allowed the fear of that pain to control our lives so completely—and astonished later still by the riches that lay hidden within our souls behind that wall.

Once we have dismantled our own inner wall, we will "reign over all." With our conscious spirit and unconscious soul functioning at long last in harmonious union, we will feel unified and whole. We will be in control of all our actions and reactions, aware of—and at peace with—our mental content. We will no longer spend precious psychological resources trying to repress our souls' natural feelings, insights, and memories. No longer fighting against ourselves, no longer lying to ourselves, no longer betraying ourselves, we will enjoy true repose, a natural, restful inner peace beyond all imagination.

Christianity begins with this transformation. The story of the faith opens not with Jesus, but with John the Baptist's call for all to submit to such a "baptism of repentance" (Mark 1:4). Although the ritual known as "baptism" today no longer seems to have anything to do with such an intimate inner purge, the BSD suggests that John's baptism was the original initiation into the Christian mystery movement for a very good reason: it produced a genuine, palpable transformation within the mind and heart of the initiate.[21] This baptism of grief and tears also goes by another name—the dark night of the soul—a lengthy stretch of intensely private suffering that all spiritual pilgrims are said to pass through. This dark journey forces us to relinquish our psychological hang-ups and emotional attachments by taking us beyond our denial into territory we habitually avoid.

Because it is genuinely effective, the rejuvenating effects of such soul-searching techniques have been known and embraced in many different cultural settings. Hundreds of years ago, the Toltecs are said to have called the process "recapitulation"; in more modern times, the Alcoholics Anonymous organization incorporated it into their famous Twelve Step program as "making a searching and fearless moral inventory of ourselves." Unfortunately, it is typically at this point on the spiritual path, when we feel most alone, depressed, disoriented, afraid, uncertain, inadequate, and defeated, that many of us give up. Numerous contemporary religious teachings fail to mention this angst-ridden trial, not realizing that superficial and naively optimistic spirituality cannot heal what ails the human soul. Only honest confrontations with our own darkest selves can lead to authentic spiritual awareness and restore us to wholeness.

Jesus said, "If those who lead you say to you, 'See, the kingdom is in the sky,' then the birds of the sky will precede you. If they say to you, 'It is in the sea,' then the fish will precede you. Rather, the kingdom is inside of you, and it is outside of you. When you come to know yourselves, then you will become known, and you will realize that it is you who are the sons of the living father. But if you will not know yourselves, you dwell in poverty and it is you who are that poverty." (The Gospel of Thomas 3)

Saying 3 explains that the same inner wall that alienates us from our souls alienates us from the rest of God's Creation as well. Once that wall is down, we are more in tune with both our inner selves and the outer world. Repeating the message of Luke 17:21, Thomas' gospel insists that "the kingdom of God is within you"—it is a psychological matter, something that can be possessed immediately, rather than something that must await the arrival of Judgment Day. But at the same time, the Gospel of Thomas points out, the kingdom is something that touches, affects, and directs the outer world as well, that seemingly quite separate universe on the *other* side of our skin. Once we find the kingdom within, Jesus suggests, we mysteriously find that our outer world is in complete sync with that inner world, and the two are indeed one. This is one of the major themes in the Gospel of Thomas, being revisited in Sayings 13, 14, 19, 41, 106, and 113.

The passage reminds us of the Buddhist saying that "the eye you see God with is the same eye with which He sees you," insisting that we will not become "known" by God until we first "know" ourselves. This concept of "knowing oneself" fits quite well with the binary soul doctrine's psychological integration of the conscious and unconscious.

Upon entering this inner kingdom, the Gospel of Thomas suggests, the apparent rules of the physical world reveal themselves to be subservient to our will.[22] But those of us who remain divided within ourselves, traveling through our lives in a state of perpetual self-alienation, remain ignorant of these ready riches; not knowing ourselves, we do not know what we have and go through life deprived of the wealth and power within our grasp.

Jesus said, "The man old in days will not hesitate to ask a small child seven days old about the place of life, and he will live. For many who are first will become last, and they will become one alone." (The Gospel of Thomas 4)

Jesus poses a riddle in this passage, the first of many eschatological references in the Gospel of Thomas: How can an old man converse with a seven-day-old infant? This passage must refer to the Resurrection, the only such opportunity history could provide. The conventional Christian view of the Resurrection would not allow such a conversation, but the psychological version of that event expected by the BSD *would*. The binary soul doctrine suggests that while we have been incarnating again and again, these past-life selves have not actually ceased to exist but are still functioning "programs," or "complexes," buried deep within our psyches. These fractured-off shards of our minds will be reintegrated into our waking psyches sooner or later, since all natural systems tend toward a state of balance, health, and equilibrium. This resurrection of our own dead—this reintegration of our fractured minds—can happen whenever we wish, so long as we do the necessary preparation and groundwork first. But even if we never do that work, these fragments of our minds, these past-life selves, will return to us sooner or later because the division keeping them separated from us is an artificial and therefore temporary construct. And when that reintegration happens, all of our different past-life selves will be able to interact consciously with and learn from one another.

The result of this integration will be that all our past-life selves will become fully integrated, becoming "one alone," a single self. Those separate selves will have, however, greater and lesser places within that singularity, having been united into a highly *integrated* rather than *homogenized* state. They will not lose their separate qualities, but instead will all be integrated into a highly complex and cohesive organization. Within that greater psychological organization, some past-life selves that wielded great power during their earthly lives might find themselves relegated to positions of relative humbleness, while those that previously lived far more simple lives might find their relative power and influence greatly expanded. Some who were first will be last, and some who were last will be first, and yet, at the same time, they will all be effectively united together into a single self-aware being. And that new being, whole at last, will be far greater than the sum of its parts.

> *Jesus said, "Recognize what is in front of your face, and that which is hidden from you will become plain to you. For there is nothing hidden which will not become manifest, and nothing buried that will not be raised." (The Gospel of Thomas 5)*

In his second eschatological passage, Thomas gives us the greatest news anyone could ever hope to hear: The path to the kingdom is not to be found way off in some isolated monastery in Tibet, but right here, right now, at home, at work, in all the most intimate and familiar details of our everyday lives. In Saying 5, the Gospel of Thomas returns to its readers' first question: "How do we search for the kingdom?" Jesus answers that we need but recognize those issues troubling us right now. If we follow them to their roots, they will lead us directly to our own inner divisions, and thus to our integration, and thus to the kingdom.

"Why does _____ always upset us so?" "Why don't we ever seem to find time for _____, even though we insist it is important to us?" "Why don't we ever seem to get _____ right?" "Why do we always let _____ get under our skin?" "Why do we always ignore _____?" "Why do we always do _____ when we know we should be doing _____?" "Why do we always avoid _____?" "Why are we always so grouchy toward _____?"

The Gospel of Thomas promises that, if we open our eyes enough to recognize the personal issues and psychological blind spots we end up tripping over every day, and if we consider those questions deeply enough to follow them all the way back to their roots, ever greater spiritual mysteries will be revealed to us. These sort of questions, both the Gospel of Thomas and the BSD suggest, are nothing less than the path to the kingdom of God—the *only* path. These questions will lead us into greater self-honesty, wholeness, and psychological integration; in time, this path will even lead to the unveiling of our past lives, and beyond that, to full comprehension of our relationship with our Creator. The entire kingdom of God indeed *is* to be found within, the Gospel of Thomas explains, and the signs toward it are all around us, literally right in front of our faces. When we encounter challenges and difficulties in this world, Thomas' gospel suggests, we ought to view them as signs to open our eyes wider, not to shut them against the pain.

Jesus ends this saying with both a promise and a warning: "There is nothing hidden that won't become manifest." In other words, everything we have managed to bury deep down inside our souls will all have to come out again sooner or later. If we search out this psychic material now, the Gospel of Thomas promises, we will not be unsuccessful. It can and will emerge *now,* if we seek it out. But if we don't willingly search it out, it will still all come out eventually, so we'd better not count on avoiding it forever.

> *His disciples questioned him and said to him, "Do you want us to fast? How shall we pray? Shall we give alms? What diet shall we observe?"*
>
> *Jesus said, "Do not lie, and do not do what you hate, for all things are plain in the sight of heaven. For nothing hidden will not become manifest, and nothing covered will remain without being uncovered."* (The Gospel of Thomas 6)

In the third eschatological saying in the Gospel of Thomas, Jesus distances Himself from the familiar cultural practice of spelling out a specific list of dos and don'ts. Instead, He suggests that the best answers to such questions are found within. Be true to your soul before all else, Jesus says. Do not lie to yourself or to others. Things like fasting, praying, giving to charity, and observing a certain diet could end up being lies if the person doing them does not sincerely believe in their value. If so, then following such rules would be just another form of self-betrayal and self-alienation. If one half of us hates what our other half is doing, we are growing closer neither to ourselves nor our Creator. Instead, such actions add more psychic debris to the inner wall of grief, more soul pain that will have to be dealt with sooner or later. The more parts of ourselves we sacrifice, cutting away from ourselves, the more trouble we end up causing for ourselves. A similar sentiment can be found in another early Christian scripture: "I came to do away with sacrifices, and if you don't stop sacrificing, you won't stop experiencing wrath" (The Gospel of the Ebionites 5).

Although that repressed psychic material will not remain hidden forever, it will remain preserved within our souls until the day we finally experience it consciously. There is no reason to add to it, nor to do anything in the name of any religion that adds to our state of division and self-alienation. Everything we hide within our souls, Jesus reminds us for the second time in two sayings, will be exhumed again one day, so we must take great care not to add anything more to that repressed ocean of soul pain. It will all just end up being regurgitated back into our faces one day. This is a true gospel of integrity and self-honesty, reminding us that the only sin Jesus really got worked up about in the Bible was hypocrisy.

> *Jesus said, "Blessed is the lion which becomes man when consumed by man; and cursed is the man whom the lion consumes, and the lion becomes man."* (The Gospel of Thomas 7)

Continuing on the same theme of integration, Thomas' gospel compares the repressed, unintegrated soul pain to a raging beast. If we spiritual seekers are strong and brave enough to consciously confront and integrate this raw and untamed inner material, this courageous act will ultimately make us spiritually whole and psychologically healthy. But if we instead continue along the path of self-ignorance, denying the raw emotions, nascent insights, and unprocessed memories trying to surface from our unconscious souls, that repressed material builds up more and more pressure inside our psyches. Occasionally, this inner pressure erupts in fits of uncontrolled irrational behavior, transforming us into the epitome of a wild beast.

Thus, just as the Gospel of Thomas teaches, the man who "consumes" his inner beast in this way receives great rewards for his trouble, but he who ignores his inner beast does so at his own peril, eventually becoming overcome and consumed by it himself, suffering greatly for his self-ignorance.[23]

> *And he said, "The man is like a wise fisherman who cast his net into the sea and drew it up from the sea full of small fish. Among them the wise fisherman found a fine large fish. He threw all the small fish back into the sea and chose the large fish without difficulty. Whoever has ears to hear, let him hear." (The Gospel of Thomas 8)*

The first explicitly "Christian" message in the Gospel of Thomas, Saying 8 suggests that while multiple distinct elements are to be found and integrated within one's psyche, one particular element should be brought to the surface first: Jesus' own past-life soul. Seek out Christ first, and all else will be added.

How did Jesus' past-life soul wind up floating around inside other people's minds? The binary soul doctrine suggests that the same properties that made it possible for Jesus to rise from the dead also propelled His soul throughout time and space at His Resurrection, causing it to fuse with the souls of all other people everywhere.[24] If so, then in addition to our past-life souls remaining in the darkest depths of our psyches, the soul of Jesus Christ is *also* to be found there.

Many today are successfully experimenting with past-life regression, attempting to resurrect their past-life selves via hypnosis or other techniques. Thomas' gospel suggests that a much bigger fish is to be sought in those same waters. The Christianity of the Gospel of Thomas is, despite its seemingly Gnostic leanings, very much a savior-centered religion. It instructs its readers to work toward their own salvation, seeking the kingdom of God within themselves, but Jesus Christ is still central to that quest.

In many respects, this approach to recovering and reintegrating our past-life souls is similar to the Buddhist practice of Jivamala. Just as the Buddha was said to have recovered his past-life memories during his enlightenment, so the Buddhist faithful are instructed to follow in his footsteps. So long as all our past selves (jivas) remain unintegrated, Buddhism teaches, they consume and monopolize our psychological energy with their continuing presence and activity in the depths of our psyches. They also keep us unconsciously committed to their issues, hang-ups, and concerns. These past-life selves need to be freed from their unconscious imprisonment and integrated into our conscious minds, Buddhism declares, which can only be done through an inner guide. Buddhism calls this process of using an inner guide or guru "deity yoga." The Gospel of Thomas suggests that Original Christianity subscribed to the same practice, but identified Jesus as that inner guide. Spiritual seekers had to establish a relationship with that inner guide before they could hope to resurrect and integrate their past-life souls.

Note also that Saying 8 symbolizes Jesus with a fish. Since the Gospel of Thomas appears to have been one of the earliest gospels written, this may be the long-sought origin of the mysterious early practice of using a fish symbol—the *Ichthys*—to represent Christianity. As we will see in chapter 7, however, it was not the only reason.[25] The fact that the Gospel of Thomas was eventually outlawed left the movement with a lasting symbol, but no memory of why that symbol was originally adopted.

> *Jesus said, "Now the sower went out, took a handful of seeds, and scattered them. Some fell on the road; the birds came and gathered them up. Others fell on the rock, did not take root in the soil, and did not produce ears. And others fell on thorns; they choked the seeds and worms ate them. And others fell on the good soil and it gave up good fruit to heaven: it bore sixty per measure and a hundred and twenty per measure." (The Gospel of Thomas 9)*

This parable is similar to those found in the Gospels of Matthew, Luke, and Mark, but Thomas' version carries an interesting twist: It results in not one, but *two* fruitful crops—one of 60 per measure and another double that. This "double double" reminds us of the author's name, Didymos Judas Thomas; we will see this pattern again and again in our search for Original Christianity. In Matthew, only one crop was produced: "Still other seed fell on good soil, where it produced a crop." Conventional Christianity interprets this parable as discussing the teachings of the church, which had to fall on ready soil in order to produce fruit. But Thomas' twist on this well-known parable suggests that the teachings of Jesus Christ were recognized, even in Thomas' era, to be growing *two very different and separate crops* (i.e., churches), one of which would produce twice as much fruit as the other.[26]

What was that fruit? Although conventional exegesis interprets that seed as being the teachings of the church, that really doesn't fit the metaphor; seed, after all, grows into its own fruit, and the intended fruit of Christ's teachings is surely not just to produce more teachings. The BSD suggests that the seed represents Christ rather than His teachings, and if so, Christ would not have intended to merely produce more teachings, but more *Christs*. And while the teachings of the official church may have produced more professed Christians, the *other* crop, the Gnostic Church, has always claimed to produce more Christs, people who had achieved the integrity and wholeness necessary to avoid the second death.

> *Jesus said, "I have cast fire upon the world, and see, I am guarding it until it blazes." (The Gospel of Thomas 10)*

Although this fourth eschatological passage in the Gospel of Thomas parallels a biblical passage, we find that one version describes the present and the other the future. Luke's gospel has Jesus exclaim, "I came to cast fire upon the earth, and how I wish it were already kindled!"[27] but in Thomas' gospel the fire *is* already kindled. While Luke's version is clearly eschatological, discussing Judgment Day, some analysts feel that Thomas' version does not anticipate the future arrival of a Judgment Day. Jesus' anticipation in the latter that His fire will erupt into a blaze sometime in the future suggests otherwise, however.[28] And as we see, many other eschatological hints also appear in the Gospel of Thomas.

What is this fire? The binary soul doctrine maintains that our "sins," that is, our self-betrayals and self-divisions, have built up massive amounts of repressed psychological pain inside us, and even though we avoid all this soul pain by repressing it, Jesus personally experiences it all because His soul bonded to ours at His Resurrection. Although humanity has collectively chosen to repress this pain, Jesus put Himself in a position where He is swimming right in the thick of it. Why would He do such a thing? The BSD suggests that Jesus' ultimate mission was to force this repressed material out into the open, so its fiery pain could finally be confronted, experienced, and thus *overcome* by humanity. In other words, He did it so this repressed fire *would* burn, so all our repressed soul pain would finally be freed to blaze to its full force, because he knew this was the only way humanity could be healed. He knew He had to open our wounds and let the poison out before our healing could begin.

Both the Gospel of Thomas and the binary soul doctrine offer the same advice about what to do in the meantime, before that fire is unleashed: Struggle to be true to ourselves so we avoid increasing our stored-up soul pain, which will only increase the magnitude of the coming flood. As we will see again,[29] the Gospel of Thomas advises us to do what we can to release this pressure now while there's time to do so in a safe and controlled fashion. By fully embracing our souls' input into how we live our lives, we become more whole, undivided, and authentic human beings, and reduce the potential trauma of the coming Judgment Day scenario, when the "storehouses of the deep" will be released.

> *Jesus said: This heaven will pass away, and the one above it will pass away; and those who are dead are not alive, and those who are living will not die. In the days when you ate what is dead, you made of it what is living. When you enter the light, what will you do? On the day when you were one, you made the two. But when you come to be two, what will you do? (The Gospel of Thomas 11)*

Although this passage contains many elements, they all address but a single subject: death and the afterlife. This passage also introduces the predominant theme of the Gospel of Thomas: duality versus unity. The idea that division and duality are to be rejected in favor of integration and unity comes up dozens of times in Thomas' gospel and shows that Jesus' teachings were originally in sync with the ancient binary soul doctrine.

The first saying in this gospel indicated that the whole message of the Gospel of Thomas had to do with death and the afterlife. Saying 11 focuses pointedly on that subject. The first line refers to heaven (the place of the blessed dead), the second mentions the dead, the third mysteriously mentions "eating" the dead, and the fourth brings up "entering the light," which those familiar with accounts of near-death experiences will recognize as another reference to the death transition. The last two lines, which discuss "becoming two," might seem mysteriously unrelated to what came before—but not to students of the binary soul doctrine.

Indeed, BSD students find much familiar in this passage. Like the Gospel of Thomas, they also expect the present "heaven"—the abode of the blessed dead—eventually to cease to exist. At Judgment Day, they expect the world's dead to be discharged from that divine "holding tank" and return to conscious life during the Universal Resurrection. Thomas' gospel also predicts that the next "heaven" after that, the abode of the dead *after* the Judgment Day events, will *also* be a temporary location, and again, the BSD says much the same thing. Once Judgment Day has come and gone, according to the BSD, the nature of the death transition will have forever altered. The Old Testament promised that after Judgment Day, there will be no more death, that it will simply no longer exist as an element of the human experience. The binary soul doctrine suggests that this promise refers to the "second death" rather than the first. While people's bodies will still eventually grow old and stop functioning after Judgment Day, we will no longer lose our memories between one incarnation and the next, nor will we fracture off and abandon parts of our minds to a heaven or hell dreamworld between lives. Whereas the soul currently tends to split off from the spirit at death, becoming trapped in the soul's afterlife realm (heaven or hell) while the spirit goes off to reincarnate, this will no longer be the case after Judgment Day. After Judgment Day, the souls of the dead will no longer have to spend extended periods of time in any "realm of the dead" after death; instead, soul and spirit will reincarnate together. Thus, with soul and spirit remaining together after death, they will spend only a brief period of time between one life and the next.

The Gospel of Thomas then makes what seems an obvious statement—that the dead are not alive—and adds that the living will not die. The latter statement reminds the reader of the concept in Saying 1, that it is possible to avoid experiencing death altogether. But the apparent obviousness of "the dead are not alive" suggests that Jesus' definitions are not quite what one assumes. (These are, after all, supposed to be "secret sayings," the meanings of which are not clear and obvious.) The binary soul doctrine suggests that the "dead" spoken of here are all who are at least partially divided and self-alienated, and thus by definition are not *fully* alive or functional. The Gospel of Thomas seems to state that a person might *appear* to be alive but in fact is walking around as good as dead, and the BSD reports the same thing about those with disassociated souls and spirits. In the Bible, Jesus refers to people walking around as being essentially dead, with His retort "let the dead bury their dead."[30]

The Gospel of Thomas then introduces the subject of "eating," which is a useful metaphor for "integrating material into one's self." In Saying 11, Jesus suggests mysteriously that his audience already had some success with efforts to do this. And since the subject of Thomas' gospel in general—and of this saying in particular—seems to be death and the afterlife, it would seem that Jesus is talking about "eating the souls of the dead," a peculiar notion that nonetheless makes sense from the perspective of the BSD. The Gospel of Thomas seems to suggest that Jesus' listeners had already begun to seek out their past-life selves and reintegrate them into their present living consciousness, essentially returning them to life. Remarkably, this theme reverberates throughout much early Christian literature:

> Then, if one has knowledge [gnosis], he receives what are his own and draws them to himself . . . It is within Unity that each one will attain himself; within knowledge he will purify himself from multiplicity into Unity, consuming . . . death by life. . . . Raise up those who wish to rise, and awaken those who sleep. (The Gospel of Truth 21:10–14; 25:9–18; 33:5–10)

> Light the light within you. Do not extinguish it. . . . raise your dead who have died, for they have lived and died for you. Give them life. They shall live again. . . . Knock upon yourself as upon a door, and walk upon yourself as upon a straight road. (The Teachings of Silvanus 106:14–35)

> [Jesus said] You who have joined the perfect, the light [consciousness] with the Holy Spirit unite the angels with us also, the images [one's previous souls]. Do not despise the lamb [the soul which was slaughtered at death], for without it, it is not possible to go in to see the King [God]. No one will be able to go in to the King if he is naked [if he is not "clothed" with all his own past souls]. (The Gospel of Philip 58:10–30)

Similarly, millions of modern pioneers in past-life regression have reported success along these same lines.[31]

The text then introduces a question, notable as the first question Jesus asks in the Gospel of Thomas: "When you enter the light, what will you do?" This is the whole question of Thomas' gospel in a nutshell, the primary issue around which Original Christianity revolved: What will happen to you when you die? Then Jesus makes a statement that makes no sense at all to anyone but a student of the binary soul doctrine: "On the day you were one, you became two." In other words, on the day you were born, your psyche began to differentiate into two distinct mental elements. Whether one wishes to call them the conscious and the unconscious, or the left-brain mind and the right-brain mind, or the soul and the spirit, the Gospel of Thomas here shows itself again to be in step with the binary soul doctrine. Jesus ends this saying by warning people that when they die, they are in grave danger of dividing completely. He asks a second time, when they have died and find themselves "in the light" and dividing into two elements, "what will they do?" The Gospel of Thomas uses the same ending for two separate sentences here, attaching "what will you do?" to two seemingly very different beginnings: "when you enter the light" and "when you become two." This effectively associates these two phrases, seeming even to equate them, essentially saying, "When you enter the light, you will become two, and then what will you do?" The "light," of course, is indicative of God and His heaven, which may again remind the reader of Hebrews 4:12, where God's presence causes a person to divide into two separate elements, causing the soul and spirit to divide from one another.

In the Gospel of Thomas, Jesus is presented as the ultimate teacher. But in Saying 11, He offers no answers, only questions, suggesting that if His followers let things get so far out of control that they "become two" when they enter the light, they should resign themselves to the fact that they'll be more or less on their own after that. Later in the gospel text, however, Jesus returns to this subject again and again, repeating the solution: If you "make the two one" *before* you die, then you *won't* divide into two fragments when you enter the light.

> *The disciples said to Jesus, "We know that you will depart from us. Who is to be our leader?"*
> *Jesus said to them, "Wherever you are, you are to go to James the*

righteous, for whose sake heaven and earth came into being." (The Gospel of Thomas 12)

Recent scholarship has made it clear that James the Just, thought to have been Jesus' biological brother, was the first leader of the fledgling church after Jesus' departure, until his own death.[32] James is thought to have governed the church from roughly 33 A.D. to about 62 A.D. The precise date of James' death is not known, but it is certain that James died shortly before the church fled Israel when Rome sacked Jerusalem in 70 A.D. After the church fled Israel, its leadership moved to Rome, where it eventually melded with the monolithic political authority there. But during the earliest two or three decades of the church, James the Just was its leader, and the passage here makes no sense unless it was written during that period. Thus this passage suggests that the Gospel of Thomas may be the earliest of all extant gospels, written long before any of the four gospels of the canon. And as the earliest extant snapshot of Christ's teachings, of course, it is the most authentic witness of Original Christianity we have today.

> *Jesus said to his disciples, "Compare me to someone and tell me whom I am like."*
> *Simon Peter said to him, "You are like a righteous angel."*
> *Matthew said to him, "You are like a wise philosopher."*
> *Thomas said to him, "Master, my mouth is wholly incapable of saying whom you are like."*
> *Jesus said, "I am not your master. Because you have drunk, you have become intoxicated from the bubbling spring which I have measured out."*
> *And he took him and withdrew and told him three things.*
> *When Thomas returned to his companions, they asked him, "What did Jesus say to you?"*
> *Thomas said to them, "If I tell you one of the things which he told me, you will pick up stones and throw them at me; a fire will come out of the stones and burn you up." (The Gospel of Thomas 13)*

This saying tells us that Christ represented something so new, powerful, and unfamiliar to the disciples that they found themselves completely unprepared to wrap their minds around it or fit it into their previous culturally based notions of reality. At the same time, it suggests that the apostle Thomas may have possessed a unique status among the other disciples, perhaps one even equal to Jesus Himself.

The idea that Jesus' teachings were hard to understand is well documented in the canon; even the two pillars of Orthodox Christianity, Peter and Paul, are vulnerable to charges that they fully understood neither Jesus nor what He was trying to explain. (As we will see in chapter 6, this theme was expanded upon in the Gnostic scriptures that followed the Gospel of Thomas.)[33] In this passage, Jesus does not dispute being characterized as a "righteous angel" or "wise philosopher," nor does He attempt to clarify Thomas' inarticulate response. Instead, He seems to admit by His silence that He indeed is both like a righteous angel and a wise philosopher, and yet He is still more besides, also having the indescribable quality Thomas could not put into words.

Instead of responding to the articulate comments of Peter and Matthew, Jesus' reply seems to be addressed exclusively to Thomas, objecting to his use of the title "master." Jesus appears to single Thomas out from the other disciples in this passage, bluntly insisting that Jesus is not Thomas' master at all. This begs the reader to ask a question: Did Jesus view Thomas as His equal? As we will see in chapter 7, numerous elements in the early church not only believed that Thomas was Jesus' identical twin brother, but indeed a second Messiah in his own right. This passage suggests much the same thing, beginning by Jesus asking His disciples to identify someone else like Himself, and ending with Jesus declaring Thomas to be His equal, and sharing unique teachings and experiences with Thomas that He imparts to no one else. Indeed, the final three quarters of the saying focus on Thomas' unique relationship with Jesus. This is *very* suggestive.

This passage suggests that Jesus provided Thomas with a purer and more potent experience of life, consciousness, and reality. Like a man breathing pure oxygen, this richer experience left Thomas feeling lightheaded and intoxicated, and was so unlike anything he had known before that he was left completely speechless, lacking the vocabulary to describe it. Thomas' report that Jesus told him exclusive secrets again reinforces the "heretical" tradition that Jesus gave His disciples secret teachings that never got out into general circulation. This passage, however, indicates that Jesus shared even more exclusive teachings with Thomas, unique insights that were entrusted to no other apostle. The secret truths Jesus revealed to Thomas were so completely alien to and incompatible with the apostles' accustomed way of looking at reality, this passage declares, that they would have seemed like the most egregious blasphemy; but at the same time they were so true, and true on such a deep level of reality, that the physical universe itself would have jumped to their defense.

> *Jesus said to them, "If you fast, you will give rise to sin for yourselves; and if you pray, you will be condemned; and if you give alms, you will do harm to your spirits. When you go into any land and walk about in the districts, if they receive you, eat what they will set before you, and heal the sick among them. For what goes into your mouth will not defile you, but that which issues from your mouth—it is that which will defile you." (The Gospel of Thomas 14)*

The earlier passage "the kingdom is inside of you, and it is outside of you" is relevant to both this saying and the previous one; both describe the physical universe as an integral part of the Kingdom of Heaven, obeying its laws and supporting its goals. The previous passage showed the physical universe defending divine truths, whereas this one shows the physical universe providing dependable sustenance.

This passage contains what seem to be two very different and unconnected elements: (1) a surprisingly contrary attitude toward traditional religious behaviors,[34] and (2) a teaching that what one says and does is more important than what one consumes. In typical Thomas fashion, these two messages share the same theme, the idea that purity can only come from within.

Fasting, praying, and charity are worse than empty gestures if they do not proceed from one's deepest heart. If an act does not originate from a place of wholehearted purity, it will only further debase one's spiritual condition. The one who fasts, prays, and gives to charity only to fulfill some perceived religious duty will resent it at some level. Jesus warns that one who prays will be condemned; the binary soul doctrine would point out that it would be the person's *own soul* that would do that condemning. As Saying 6 reveals, the path to salvation is not to be found by doing what we hate.

With this passage, the Gospel of Thomas completely reinterprets traditional Jewish religious practices, which is something we also find in the first-century Epistle of Barnabas, in which it is claimed that those ancient obligations were always meant to be metaphors rather than objective rituals:

Look, this is the fast I have chosen, says the Lord: loosen every band of wickedness, untie the tightened cords of forcible contracts, send away the broken ones released. Tear every unjust bond into pieces. Break your bread with the hungry, and if you see someone naked, clothe him, and bring the homeless into your house. (The Epistle of Barnabas)

On the same subject, the Gospel of Thomas also indicates that the idea of "religious purity" was widely misunderstood in Jesus' day, having nothing to do with one's diet and everything to do with one's words, thoughts, and actions. It is worth noting that Jesus specifically counsels his followers to "eat what [others] set before you." This is interesting on a number of levels. For one, it seems to refute allegations that Original Christianity was strictly vegetarian.[35] But perhaps more interesting is the extension of that idea—that since the kingdom is "outside" a person as well as inside, sincere spiritual seekers can trust the universe to provide all their needs in the way of guidance, sustenance, and support. Jesus seems not merely to counsel his followers to eat what others put before them while they are on the path, but He seems to suggest that they accept whatever the universe itself puts before them as well. If the Kingdom of Heaven is both inside and outside, people ought to embrace what the kingdom places before them in *both* realms.

Jesus said, "When you see one who was not born of woman, prostrate yourselves on your faces and worship him. That one is your father." (The Gospel of Thomas 15)

Classic sexual symbolism holds that the male body represents a unity, singularity, or wholeness, whereas the female body represents a duality, a division, or a lacking. This theme of identifying the male with wholeness and the female with division is found throughout ancient literature, but probably nowhere more meaningful to the readers of this book than in the legend of Creation in Genesis. When Adam was first created, he was a solitary being, single and whole. Eve, of course, was brought into being by dividing Adam's body in two and, by her arrival, duality of the sexes came into existence where before there had only been unity. Before Eve, Adam had been complete; but after her creation, he was missing a part of himself. Thus with Adam's creation came wholeness, unity, and solitariness, but with Eve's creation came lacking, duality, and division.

The reader ought not read sexism into these observations, for these stories in Genesis and the Gospel of Thomas are not actually referring to human gender but to the two halves of the human psyche: the soul and the spirit.[36] In the Bible, Jesus referenced this same archetypal symbolism when He spoke of Himself as "the son of man" (the one who is whole and perfect), contrasting Himself against all others by calling them "all those born of women" (those who are divided). This passage employs the same symbolism when it refers to a person who is spiritually whole, or who proceeded from such wholeness, as being "not of woman."

> *Jesus said, "Men think, perhaps, that it is peace which I have come to cast upon the world. They do not know that it is divisions which I have come to cast upon the earth: fire, sword, and war. For there will be five in a house: three will be against two, and two against three, the father against the son, and the son against the father. And they will stand up, being one alone." (The Gospel of Thomas 16)*

This passage's mention of multiple generations "standing up" is a clear reference to the Universal Resurrection of Judgment Day, making this the fifth eschatological saying in the Gospel of Thomas. This passage, along with Saying 10 where Jesus "cast fire upon the world," and their parallel passages in the Bible (Matt. 10:34; Luke 12:49–53), seem to paint the "Prince of Peace" as a warmonger. Although this apparent incongruity has long posed a conundrum for biblical scholars, the binary soul doctrine makes sense of it. Jesus is not seeking to *create* a war, but to *end* one that is already in progress. Humankind, the BSD points out, is in a mindless, stalemated war against itself. Jesus' goal was to break the stalemate. All the repressed mental content of billions of past lives must be allowed to release its huge mental and emotional "charge" so it can finally be assimilated and integrated in our minds. In the process of this release, those who are alive will find their minds and bodies overrun from within by hordes of strange, foreign past-life selves, each of which feels it alone has the right to that body and mind.

Yes, the Gospel of Thomas, the BSD, and the Bible all insist that humanity's path back to health and wholeness must wind through a great war, but this is an entirely new kind of war, one that will play itself out within the psyches of the species instead of on a physical battlefield. As all the different past-life souls awaken to find themselves occupying a single body (i.e., house), they will, for a time, fight among themselves terribly. As the previous passages declare, the separate generations of the self will fight with one another, the incarnations that came before (fathers) struggling against the incarnations that came later (sons). But in the end, once their struggles are over, these many different selves, in being integrated, will restore the person's complete past history, creating a single, solitary, whole self out of them all.

> *Jesus said, "I shall give you what no eye has seen and what no ear has heard and what no hand has touched and what has never occurred to the human mind." (The Gospel of Thomas 17)*

Like Saying 13, this passage also emphasizes how completely unfamiliar spiritual reality is, and how profoundly alienated humankind is from its own true nature. The perfect health and wholeness that Jesus represents and offers to us are so far removed from our current experience of reality that not only do we not recall ever experiencing it before, but we are also not even capable of imagining it.

Interestingly, although there is no parallel to this passage in the biblical gospels, it is strikingly similar to a passage in one of Paul's letters:

> However, as it is written: "No eye has seen, no ear has heard, no mind has conceived what God has prepared for those who love him."(1 Cor. 2:9)

Paul introduces this quote with the words "as it is written," a clause that usually indicates an Old Testament source; however, there is no known source for this passage outside of the Gospel of Thomas. Was Paul quoting Thomas? If so, that would certainly indicate that Paul viewed the Gospel of Thomas as authentic, and more important, that it was *older* than Paul's Epistles!

> *The disciples said to Jesus, "Tell us how our end will be."*
> *Jesus said, "Have you discovered, then, the beginning, that you look for the end? For where the beginning is, there will the end be. Blessed is he who will take his place in the beginning; he will know the end and will not taste death." (The Gospel of Thomas 18)*

This passage and the next suggest the doctrine of preexistence, the idea that a person existed prior to his birth. Of course, the idea of preexistence is not completely foreign to Judeo-Christian thought; God claimed preexistence for Job in Job 38:21, and Jesus claimed preexistence for Himself in John 8:58. This passage in the Gospel of Thomas goes much further, however, claiming preexistence for *all*.[37] This was not an alien concept in early Christianity; even before the Gospel of Thomas was unearthed in Egypt, we knew that some of the earliest church fathers, such as Origen, believed in preexistence.

Jesus says here that those who recover their earliest memories will thereby acquire complete understanding of who they are and what their future will be. In the reacquisition of those lost memories, Jesus declares, they will find the self-knowledge necessary to survive the death transition without ill effect. This is in complete accord with the binary soul doctrine, which holds that all those lost memories are stored in the unconscious soul, and once the soul and spirit have been fully united and integrated, those memories will all be recovered. And of course, the purpose of the "end," or Judgment Day, is achieving that same soul-spirit union, when "all things will be restored."[38]

> *Jesus said, "Blessed is he who existed before he came into being. If you become my disciples and listen to my words, these stones will minister to you. For there are five trees for you in Paradise which remain undisturbed summer and winter and whose leaves do not fall. Whoever becomes acquainted with them will not taste death." (The Gospel of Thomas 19)*

Sayings 18 and 19 encourage us to become conscious of our immortality. Eternal life is not described as a gift that can be won or lost, but a possession we already have and only need to become aware of. The last line of Saying 18 and the first line of Saying 19 say essentially the same thing: "Blessed is he who discovers his original existence prior to his physical birth." The remainder of Saying 19 explores *how* such knowledge of our past will bless us in our future, suggesting that surviving future deaths will be easier if we realize we have already survived multiple deaths in previous lives.

This passage declares that one who becomes acquainted with certain mysterious trees of paradise will avoid the experience of death and will acquire the ability to work miracles. The binary soul doctrine offers no clear insights into just what these trees symbolize, nor why their number is reported to be five.[39] It is almost surely relevant, however, that the primitive church recognized five sacraments—baptism, chrismation, Eucharist, redemption, and bridal chamber—a subject we will return to in chapter 6. Since these trees are associated with the subject of immortality and surviving the death transition, the phrase "remain undisturbed summer and winter" suggests that they do not suffer any significant changes when shifting from summer (i.e., life, or embodiment) to winter (i.e., death, or disembodiment), nor do they drop off, discard, cut away, or otherwise lose any of their past-life souls ("whose leaves do not fall"). This fits. If we integrate our souls and spirits, the BSD promises, our sense of self will not change (be disturbed) with the transition between embodiment and disembodiment, and our various past-life souls (leaves) will thereafter remain attached to us from one incarnation (season) to the next.

As with many other passages in the Gospel of Thomas, the accomplishment of conquering death is also associated here with another great acquisition: the ability to perform miracles and control the physical universe. Not only would such fully integrated individuals suffer no change during the death transition, the text declares, they would also be so completely in tune with God and God's Creation that, just like Jesus Himself, even the elements (stones) would follow their command.

> *The disciples said to Jesus, "Tell us what the kingdom of heaven is like."*
> *He said to them, "It is like a mustard seed. It is the smallest of all seeds. But when it falls on tilled soil, it produces a great branch and becomes shelter for birds of the sky." (The Gospel of Thomas 20)*

The mustard plant has a small seed that, once planted and left on its own, spreads out far and wide, enveloping and overtaking the entire garden. This seed is a metaphor for one's original, undivided inner self, which in *The Lost Secret of Death* I referred to as the hidden "third soul." This seed is still present within one's psyche, but to one divided against oneself, it seems insignificant and easy to ignore, much like a mustard seed. However, one need only break up the hard ground of one's psyche (the wall between the spirit and soul) and fertilize it (with one's own psychological "waste" material—everything one's unconscious mind has generated that the conscious mind has not absorbed). Jesus did this, and expects us to do the same:

For he himself is our peace, who has made the two one and has destroyed the barrier, the dividing wall of hostility, by abolishing in his flesh the law with its commandments and regulations. His purpose was to create in himself one new man out of two, thus making peace. (Eph. 2:14–15)

Once our inner wall is down, our two will also become one, just as His did, and a new self will spread throughout our inner mental system, resurrecting and integrating all the lost fragments of our being. Just as a mustard seed spreads out to envelop a whole garden, all of our past-life souls will be absorbed into and sheltered by this developing canopy of wholeness.

> *Mary said to Jesus, "What are your disciples like?"*
>
> *He said, "They are like little children who have settled in a field that is not theirs. When the owners of the field come, they will say, 'Give us back our field.' They take off their clothes in front of them so as to give it back to them, and they return their field to them. For this reason I say, if the owners of a house know that a thief is coming, they will stay awake until the thief arrives and will not let the thief dig into the house of their domain and steal their vessels.*
>
> *"As for you, then, be on guard against the world. Gird yourself with great strength so the robbers can't find a way to get to you, since the advantage you look for they will find. Let there be among you a person who understands. When the crop ripened, he came quickly carrying a sickle and harvested it. He who has ears had better listen!"* (The Gospel of Thomas 21)

Thanks to the "harvest" metaphor, the fact that this passage also discusses future eschatological events should be obvious to any biblical student. The remainder of the passage, however, will be impenetrable to all but the student of the BSD. As I discussed in *The Division of Consciousness*, when resurrected past-life selves begin to enter our conscious minds during the Judgment Day scenario, they should not be resisted. Instead, we should allow them to assume control and push our soul down into the unconscious realms from which they just arose. These newly resurrected souls are our predecessors, and as the Gospel of Thomas points out, the "field" of the physical realm belonged to them before it belonged to us.

Thus we should willingly return that field to them by giving them control over the physical body we normally wear in life, essentially "taking off" the body and giving it back to them.[40]

To do so, however, is simply to make the best of a bad situation. The Gospel of Thomas doesn't see this invasion as a good thing at all, characterizing those returning "owners" as thieves about to break into the house (mind) and steal our possessions (body). These invaders, Thomas suggests, will be taking unexpected advantage of a situation that the home-owners had assumed would be working to their advantage instead. The Universal Resurrection, the very event all Christiandom looks forward to with hope, will be the very thing that allows these past-life souls to escape their unconscious imprisonment and return to overwhelm the living. Thomas portrays the invaders "digging" into our houses as if from below, just as the past-life souls of the dead would be rising up from below, emerging from the depths of the unconscious.

Fortunately, things don't have to go that far. If we know that these invaders are on the way, the Gospel of Thomas declares, we can prevent the invasion. How? The answer Thomas offers is the one he recommends for every problem—by allowing Jesus Himself, that is, "a person of understanding," to live within us. Jesus will come to intimately share in all the facets of our being, simultaneously allowing us to share Jesus' strengths and advantages.[41] The BSD suggests that the Judgment Day invasion can be avoided by resurrecting and integrating past-life souls *prior* to Judgment Day. Thomas suggests here, and in many other passages, that such integration cannot be fully achieved without Jesus' participation and assistance.

> *Jesus saw infants being suckled. He said to his disciples, "These infants being suckled are like those who enter the kingdom."*
> *They said to him, "Shall we then, as children, enter the kingdom?"*
> *Jesus said to them, "When you make the two one, and when you make the inside like the outside and the outside like the inside, and the above like the below, and when you make the male and the female one and the same, so that the male not be male nor the female female; and when you fashion some eyes in the place of an eye, and a hand in place of a hand, and a foot in place of a foot, and an image in place of an image; then will you enter the kingdom." (The Gospel of Thomas 22)*

Tying together two prominent commands in the Gospel of Thomas ("move from division to wholeness" and "become one with your universe"), this passage is but the first of many in the text that directly advises the reader to "make the two one," a peculiar phrase which also found its way into the Bible.[42] Jesus indicates that those who accomplish this task will find themselves in a physical and psychological universe that completely caters to all their needs and, just like a suckling baby, provides them with exactly what they require.[43]

Jesus describes "the two that must be united" in terms perfectly suited to modern psychology. He describes these "two" always as pairs of equal opposites; somehow they are simultaneously "the inside and outside," the "above and below," and the "male and female." These polarities reflect the two halves of the human psyche. The conscious is the uppermost, outermost half of the mind, and being objective, logical, and willful, it is often said to be the more "masculine" half. The unconscious is the lowermost and innermost part of the mind, and being subjective, emotional, and fertile, it is often called the more "feminine" half.

Jesus suggests in the Gospel of Thomas that when these two are properly united, a profound transformation will create an entirely new self-image, a new sense of the self, the body, and the universe that the self finds itself in. And, tellingly, while Jesus declares that our old perspective will be replaced and transformed with a new one—a new hand in the place of the old hand, a new foot in the place of an old foot—He makes an exception of the eye. Using the plural form in this one instance only, He says that multiple eyes will be given in the place of our previously single eye. The binary soul doctrine explains this: When we make the two one, completely uniting the conscious spirit with the unconscious soul, all of our past-life selves will then be reawakened and reborn within our consciousness, providing, as it were, multiple eyes looking out of the same head at the same time. Jesus thus suggests that we cannot hope to enter fully the kingdom until we have first resurrected and integrated all of our past-life selves.[44]

This passage's preference of unity over duality testifies to the authenticity of the Gospel of Thomas, since this was a well-worn theme in the earliest scriptures produced by the faithful. Both the Epistle of Barnabas and the Didache specifically condemn "double-minded," "double-tongued," and "double-hearted" people. The Testaments of the Twelve Patriarchs emphasize this theme almost as much as the Gospel of Thomas does, repeatedly condemning those who "wear two faces," those who are "double-faced," and those who have "double-sight," "double-hearing," or "two tongues," even as it blesses those "that are single of face." And, of course, this same theme appears in the canon; Psalm 119, James 1:8, and James 4:8 all condemn "double-minded" men. Obviously, this theme was originally thought of as a fundamental element of Christ's teachings.

> *Jesus said, "I shall choose you, one out of a thousand, and two out of ten thousand, and they shall stand up, they being one alone." (The Gospel of Thomas 23)*

Repeating the message of Sayings 4 and 16, this passage states that a day will come when multiple individuals will "stand up" together, becoming united into a single self. This seventh eschatological saying in the Gospel of Thomas also refers to the Universal Resurrection of Judgment Day, when all the generations of man will "stand up" again.[45] Thomas' gospel, however, puts a spin on the traditional vision of the Universal Resurrection, repeatedly emphasizing that when this reawakening occurs, many will be joined together into one. Most theological approaches could not explain this textual enigma, but the binary soul doctrine saw it as describing the eventual integration of all our past-life souls into a single, fully self-aware being with an unbroken consciousness of all our different lifetimes. This passage suggests that the average person will see thousands and even tens of thousands of past-life selves reawaken inside his or her mind during the Universal Resurrection. And, according to this passage, Jesus Himself will decide the order of that new self-organization, choosing which among all those past-life selves will have the greatest voice in that new integration.

> *His disciples said, "Show us the place where you are, for we must seek it."*
> *He said to them, "He who has ears should hear! There is light within a person of light, and it shines on the whole world. If it does not shine, it is dark." (The Gospel of Thomas 24)*

When asked for directions to His kingdom, Jesus counsels His disciples to look within themselves, for the light they seek is inside. If they do not see what they look for, then their own inner light is still darkened, and they are still divided. Darkness is not characterized here as the absence of light, but instead as light that does not shine, and since Saying 61 attributes darkness to a person who is "divided," we can conclude that light that does not shine is the same thing as light that is divided.

Reminding us again that the kingdom is both inside and outside a person, it is claimed here that an integrated person would consistently be a light to the world, and if someone did not consistently illuminate and improve all facets of the world around him or her, this would be a clear sign that the person is not yet fully integrated and enlightened.

Jesus said, "Love your brother like your own soul, protect him like the pupil of your eye." (The Gospel of Thomas 25)

Both this saying and the following one take on a whole new significance when considered from the perspective of reincarnation. Our closest brothers, of course, would be our other incarnations, and here Jesus pleads with his disciples not to consider those other selves any less significant or valuable than their current selves. It is our responsibility to provide protection for these past selves, Jesus teaches here, which is a very meaningful obligation in light of the approaching danger of the Universal Resurrection. The only way to protect these past-life souls from being damaged or destroyed by that event is to reintegrate them into our minds ahead of time, so the inevitable integration can be accomplished safely. If not, then when the integration is forced upon us at the Universal Resurrection, those past-life souls will be in danger of complete annihilation.

If Jesus' soul was bonded with the souls of all people everywhere, as the BSD suggests, however, then this saying points to another truth as well. If Jesus' living soul is inside each of ours, and all other people's souls are at the same time within His soul, then all people's souls are technically within all other people's souls. This speaks of a profound unity on a very deep level of the human psyche, very much like the "collective unconscious" described by psychologist Carl Jung. If such a unity does secretly exist, then even though we may all *seem* to be separated from one another in this physical universe, within the deepest cores of our being we are actually closer to each other than the closest biological twins. And with such an intimate connection to one another, whatever we do to the least of our brothers, we very genuinely do to ourselves as well, just as the Bible declares. Thus to love and protect our fellow man as the Gospel of Thomas recommends would not merely be an act of selfless altruism, but would be acting in our very own self-interest.

> *Jesus said, "You see the mote in your brother's eye, but you don't see the board in your own eye. When you take the board out of your own eye, then you will see well enough to remove the mote from your brother's eye." (The Gospel of Thomas 26)*

Conventional biblical exegesis assumes that this familiar biblical passage refers to interactions between separate people, but that would require a person to be able to *unilaterally* identify and repair the psychological blind spots of another, which is really not possible. While this inconsistency suggests that the conventional interpretation of this passage is incorrect, no better interpretation had been proposed until the BSD came along. If reincarnation is a piece of the Christian puzzle, however, such a thing *would* be possible: A past-life self *could* communicate with a present-life self within the same mind, and the one could help heal the other.

This, of course, is the very essence of the multi-incarnational integration proposed by the binary soul doctrine, but, as the passage suggests, it is not possible until the person's present-life psyche has itself already been restored to wholeness. This passage requires us to achieve full psychological health in our current life *before* attempting to integrate any of our past lives. If we try to integrate a past-life self while still indulgently holding onto our own psychological hang-ups, our efforts to heal others will be unsuccessful.[46] Our blind spots will prevent us from healing their blind spots. While we may be able to contact those past-life selves for brief moments, we will not be able to achieve full integration.

We all have these "motes" in our eyes, and they distort how we perceive the rest of the world, including our own past-life selves. We often fail to consciously recognize those aspects of our own personalities that are most abhorrent to us. Instead of admitting to ourselves that we possess these unattractive traits, we ignore and deny their presence within us. On an unconscious level, however, we always know the real truth about ourselves. Our unconscious still knows we possess this abhorrent quality and continues to attack it, still trying to purge this undesired trait from our being. This unconscious self-repulsion causes us to feel a tremendous urge to reject and condemn this trait, but since we are not admitting to ourselves that we possess it in the first place, we are unable to do so. Nonetheless, the unconscious does not stop pestering us until we consciously admit and repent our error.

That leaves us in a bind. Until we consciously acknowledge that secret inner fault, we cannot repair it, nor can we escape our continuing inner urge to repair it. Needing to condemn this trait, but unable to condemn it in ourselves, we look for other places where it might be found so we can condemn it there instead. This well-known psychological mechanism is called "projection." We project onto others those traits of our own that we hate but cannot admit we possess. We feel such a strong need to reject and condemn these faults that we unconsciously seek them out in others and convince ourselves that we do find them in others. We feel very comfortable condemning them in that context. But we cannot hope to integrate our past-life selves while we are still projecting our own faults onto them. We cannot unite with them while we are condemning them and pushing them away at the same time.

No matter how many others we are driven to condemn, that inner urge is never truly satisfied until we turn our searchlight back upon ourselves, finally rooting out and expelling our own inner fault. Only then will we find the peace we sought; once we have rooted out our own inner fault, we find, seemingly miraculously, that we no longer seem to see this hated fault everywhere else we look. That mote we thought we saw in our brother's eye, as it turns out, was really a board lodged invisibly in our own.

> *Jesus said, "If you do not fast from the world, you will not find the kingdom. If you do not observe the whole week as a Sabbath, you will not see the Father." (The Gospel of Thomas 27)*

Long ago, the whole law was summed up as "Love the Lord your God with all your heart and with all your soul and with all your strength." The quest for integrity, in other words, is not a part-time job. One must dedicate the totality of one's being to this search for wholeness, and take no time off from this venture, nor allow oneself to be distracted from this search by worldly matters. This passage is very much in keeping with the biblical passage "Seek first the kingdom of God, and all else will be added to you."[47] Only when one is completely whole will one enter the kingdom and see the Father, and no part of one's life can be left out of the equation.

> *Jesus said, "I took my place in the midst of the world, and I appeared to them in flesh. I found all of them intoxicated; I found none of them thirsty. And my soul gave me pain over the sons of men,*

because they are blind in their minds and do not have sight; for empty they came into the world, and empty too they seek to leave the world. But for the moment they are intoxicated. When they shake off their wine, then they will repent." (The Gospel of Thomas 28)

Not only is the entire human race intoxicated and blind, according to Jesus (unable to think and perceive clearly), but we feel no thirst for anything better. The communication failure between the conscious and unconscious has corrupted and compromised our natural abilities. Caught in the revolving door of self-betrayal, we lose our memories between one life and the next, always entering the next life with newly emptied hands, minds, and memories, having lost everything from our previous lives. And so long as we remain reluctant to confront our own inner soul pain in the present life, our souls and spirits will remain as divided as ever, condemning us to lose today's memories just as surely as yesterday's, leaving this life as empty as when we entered it.[48]

Jesus makes his eighth eschatological reference in the Gospel of Thomas when He predicts that a day will come when our minds *will* clear and our thinking and perception *will* improve. On that day, when we finally see the chain of action and reaction linking lifetime to lifetime and realize that we ourselves have been the sole cause of all our miseries, we will indeed repent.

Jesus said, "If the flesh came into being because of spirit, that is a marvel, but if spirit came into being because of the body, that is a marvel of marvels. Yet I marvel at how this great wealth has come to dwell in this poverty." (The Gospel of Thomas 29)

While taking a swipe at materialists who maintain that the physical world is the origin of consciousness (and thus that consciousness ends when the physical body dies), Jesus again returns to the theme that human spiritual reality is far greater than most people realize. While this passage commits neither to the position that spirit created flesh nor that flesh made spirit, it does show that Jesus valued the spirit far more than the flesh.

Most people, on the other hand, tend to be far more familiar with their flesh than their spirit. As we previously saw in Sayings 13 and 17, the Gospel of Thomas insists that humanity is profoundly alienated from its own true nature. In this passage, Christ refers to the physical body as a "great poverty," a sentiment in keeping with the well-known ascetic sentiments of the early church. For example, the leader of the Jerusalem church during its first three decades, Jesus' brother James the Just, was famous for his ascetic philosophy. This passage suggests that, in order to fully appreciate the "great wealth" of the spirit, one must first recognize the "poverty" of the flesh; but if one instead treats the flesh as a "great wealth," then one will never come to know the true riches of the spirit.

> *Jesus said, "Where there are three, they are without God. Where there is but a single one, I am with him. Lift up the stone, and you will find me there. Split the piece of wood, and I am there." (The Gospel of Thomas 30)*

When the body, soul, and spirit are at odds with each other, we cannot help but be alienated from our authentic selves. But the Gospel of Thomas suggests that to be divided within ourselves, and thus alienated from our own wholeness, is to be alienated from our Creator as well. We find much the same message in the Bible, where Jesus taught that "Any kingdom divided against itself will be ruined, and a house divided against itself will fall."[49] Both the Gospel of Thomas and the BSD proclaim the same message: God's essence exists in all parts of His Creation.

> *Jesus said, "No prophet is welcome in his home town; doctors don't cure those who know them." (The Gospel of Thomas 31)*

On one level, this seems to be a prediction that Jesus would not be accepted by His own people, and that a schism would occur between Judaism and Christianity. But this passage also explains the mystery of why, if Jesus' soul has been implanted inside the souls of all other human beings in order to heal their divisions and restore them to health, His presence within our souls is hidden until we make the effort to bring it out into the open. Some might ask why, if He is there, He doesn't directly reveal His presence and allow us to enjoy a fully conscious ongoing conversation/communion with Him within our minds. This passage suggests that this would actually make it more difficult for Him to achieve His objective. Allowing us to perceive that we are not alone in our minds before we are ready for such a realization would produce a strong impulse in us to struggle against that "foreign agent." If Christ's soul is left free to operate behind the scenes, He can avoid that unproductive struggle and therefore achieve His goal more efficiently.

Jesus said, "A city built on a high hill and fortified cannot fall, nor can it be hidden." (The Gospel of Thomas 32)

As a united collection of selves, a city is a ready metaphor for having successfully assembled all our different past-life selves into a single unit. A high hill, of course, is a metaphor for higher levels of consciousness, and the fortifying support Jesus promised to His followers is also well known. Thus this passage can be seen to declare that those of us who raise our past-life selves to the height of full consciousness and, with Jesus' help, unify them together into a single integrated mind, will never "fall," never die again. Nor will we be "hidden." This contrasts with the message of the previous passage, which discussed how Jesus' active presence is hidden inside the souls of those who do not actively seek to know him. We who accomplish full integration will not only know both ourselves and Jesus, but will also be recognized by the world as well.

Sayings 30–34 all explore this theme of hiddenness. Saying 30 explains that God's presence exists within us even when we are divided and cannot readily perceive it. Saying 31 reassures us that the divine presence within our minds is hidden for a useful reason. Saying 32 predicts that the divinity within us will no longer be hidden after we have achieved wholeness. And Saying 33 announces that one who achieves this integration will become a light onto the whole world.

Jesus said: "Thou hearest with one ear, but the other thou has closed." (The Gospel of Thomas 33-A)

This passage is not found in the Coptic manuscript of the Gospel of Thomas found in Nag Hammadi, but does appear in the Oxyrhynchys Papyri, just after Saying 32.[50] It seems likely to have originally been a part of Saying 33 (see discussion to follow), which also addresses a distinction between our two ears. Unfortunately, that's where the Oxyrhynchys fragment ends, so this cannot be confirmed. In any case, its relevance to the BSD is obvious; one half of a person's spiritual being, the unconscious soul, hears the truth, but a human's other half, the conscious spirit, closes itself off from those messages. The remainder of Saying 33 posits a remedy to that problem.

Jesus said, "Whatever you hear in your ear, preach from the rooftops into your other ear. For no one lights a lamp and puts it under a basket, nor does he put it in a hidden place. Rather it is put on a lampstand so that all who enter and leave can see its light." (The Gospel of Thomas 33)

A person's mental being has two distinct sides that do not always communicate well with one another. This Saying encourages seekers to go to whatever lengths necessary to ensure that their one side communicates successfully with their other side. It does no good for the unconscious soul to generate messages of truth if they are not successfully transferred to the conscious spirit. For the soul to be constantly sending out messages that never reach conscious awareness, the Gospel of Thomas declares, is as pointless as lighting a lamp and covering it with a basket. But those who restore communication between the two halves of their being will become a blessing to the entire world.

Jesus said, "If a blind person leads a blind person, both of them will fall into a hole." (The Gospel of Thomas 34)

The East has long relied on direct one-to-one guru-to-student relationships to advance its religious traditions. This well-known passage in the Gospel of Thomas suggests that the earliest church believed something very similar, and may have provided its followers with far more than the simple theological teachings common to today's church. Christianity's various Gnostic factions consistently claimed that the original church also provided some of its members with a "secret baptism," a direct one-to-one transmission of Enlightenment, and those Gnostics insisted they had preserved that original mystical baptism and were still handing it down from person to person centuries after Christ. Both the Gospel of Thomas and the binary soul doctrine suggest, however, that, thanks to Christ's Resurrection, Christ's soul now lives within all our own souls, making Him immediately ready and available to teach and lead us Himself.

Jesus said, "It is not possible for anyone to enter the house of a strong man and take him by force unless he binds his hands; then he will move out of his house." (The Gospel of Thomas 35)

Who is the "strong man" here? *We* are. Who tied his hands? *We* did. Who is being evicted from his own home here? *We* are.

This ninth eschatological saying in the Gospel of Thomas seems to again refer to the coming Universal Resurrection of Judgment Day, when hordes of the dead resurface in the minds of the living, pushing the current occupants out of the way and taking over. This passage explains that the only reason these invaders will be able to overpower us at that time is because we have already tied our own hands before they even arrive. Being untrue to ourselves weakens our defenses. The more we repress parts of our own minds, the more our psychological energy gets tied up in fruitless little inner wars that achieve nothing except to neutralize our innate strength and potential. It puts a great drain on the mental system to keep it perpetually fighting against itself. Weakened by its engagement in these fights, the mind is left completely vulnerable to any attack that might be brought upon it, such as one by free radicals (reawakened past-life selves) within our own unconscious minds.

This saying refers to the same eschatological event spoken of in Sayings 21 and 37, in which Jesus suggests that it is in everyone's best interests to go along with this process and meekly allow the invading hordes to take back their domain without a struggle.[51]

Jesus said, "Do not worry from morning to evening and from evening to morning about what you will wear." (The Gospel of Thomas 36)

Since the subject of fashion does not tie in to the central theme of the Gospel of Thomas, the reader is forced to search for a symbolic interpretation, and this passage works quite well as a metaphor for reincarnation. Both this passage and the next discuss putting on and taking off clothes, a very useful symbol for repeatedly becoming embodied and disembodied. In that context, Jesus is advising us to be concerned neither about when we will die in this lifetime nor about what sort of a body we will have in our next incarnation.

His disciples said, "When will you appear to us, and when will we see you?"

Jesus said, "When you strip without being ashamed, and you take your clothes and put them under your feet like little children and trample them, then you will see the son of the living one and you will not be afraid." (The Gospel of Thomas 37)

The previous passage counseled us not to be anxious about our clothing, but this passage goes a step further, celebrating the ability to be unclothed without shame. To strip is a metaphor for removing the physical body. In this passage, Jesus seems to describe someone permanently discarding the body, trampling it underfoot as if it were no longer required. And instead of saying that everyone who dies gets to meet Him directly, Jesus adds another requirement: Only those who are not ashamed when they die will get to meet Him directly.

Near-death experiencers regularly describe having full memory-reviews of their lives after departing their bodies. They often feel extreme sadness, shame, and remorse. But Jesus maintains that only those who do *not* experience shame at death will see Him. How could anyone avoid that shame? No one manages to go through life without doing anything one is ashamed of later. So how could we not suffer shame when reminded of our misdeeds at death?

It's simple. Only unintegrated feelings are able to trip us up in the next world. By suffering through those feelings in life, we will not be embarrassed by them in death. What we allow ourselves to know about ourselves now will not be able to surprise us later; but what we hide from ourselves in this life can hurt us in the next.

Jesus said, "Many times have you desired to hear these words which I am saying to you, and you had no one else to hear them from. There will be days when you will look for me and will not find me." (The Gospel of Thomas 38)

This passage continues the theme of the previous saying, but instead of seeing Christ, the emphasis is now on hearing Him. The previous passage discussed how the disciples would eventually meet with Christ after He departed, indicating that they would not actually see Him again until they departed this world as well. This passage suggests, however, that even though they would be visually separated from Him after His departure, they would not be completely separated from His voice. Although "there will be days" after His departure when His voice might be difficult for them to hear, the language of this passage suggests that there would also be days after His departure when they *could* still hear His voice. The phrase "there will be days" suggests a temporary and even sporadic or intermittent condition. Thus these two passages together maintain that even though Christ's disciples would be fully separated from Him visually after His departure, they would only be partially separated from His voice.

This saying also contains one of many suggestions in the Gospel of Thomas that Jesus' teachings originally included a belief in reincarnation. Note that He did not say "long ago, your forefathers desired to hear these words I am saying to you now," but instead told His disciples that they *themselves* had, "many times," desired to hear these words. When did these desires occur? Had each of His disciples truly desired, "many times," to hear such teachings in their present lifetimes before finally meeting Him in Galilee? Perhaps a few of His disciples might have already tried on their own to explore some of the deeper mysteries of their Judaic faith before becoming acquainted with Jesus, but the majority of these "blue-collar workers" had probably devoted little if any time to such intellectual pursuits before meeting their miracle-working Teacher in the flesh. In fact, prior to meeting Him, the majority of Jesus' disciples had most probably not been interested in hearing the sort of spiritual teachings He came with at all, but instead had been hoping for a more politically oriented teacher who would lead them in a political revolution for independence from Rome. If this passage is to be taken literally, then, it is suggestive of reincarnation, indicating that His disciples had lived many past lives in which they'd thirsted in vain for these teachings. Much the same reincarnational message occurs again in Saying 92.

> *Jesus said, "The Pharisees and the scholars have received the keys of knowledge but have hidden them. They have not entered nor have they allowed those who want to enter to do so. As for you, be as wise as snakes and innocent as doves." (The Gospel of Thomas 39)*

Both this saying and its twin (Saying 102) inform us that Jesus believed that what He was teaching was not actually new to Judaism at all. These precious truths had been unconscionably hidden from the masses by intelligent but dishonorable men. Jesus advises His followers to be both wise and innocent, reflecting the binary soul doctrine's teaching that we possess two parts which must be united: a spirit, which provides rational intelligence; and a soul, which provides a heartfelt sense of right and wrong. By contrasting that formula with the unscrupulous scholars who hoarded the keys to the kingdom, Jesus emphasizes that mere intellectual knowledge of the path is not enough, and that integrity is the true key.

> *Jesus said, "A grapevine has been planted apart from the Father. Since it is not strong, it will be pulled up by its root and will perish."*
> *(The Gospel of Thomas 40)*

Both this passage and Saying 57 describe plants to be pulled up and destroyed. Since this uprooting occurs during the harvest in the later passage, it would seem that both passages refer to Judgment Day, when all the souls of the dead are to be harvested. Here we find the plant identified as a grapevine, a symbol encountered again in Saying 65. A grapevine is a very useful symbol for a person's string of past lives, all growing from the same line like grapes on a vine.

This passage contains a very somber warning: Entire lines of our past-life incarnations are corrupt, and all the unconscious souls we unceremoniously cast off from ourselves at the end of those incarnations are in danger of being completely obliterated at the Judgment Day harvest. While our conscious spirits will still continue to exist through Judgment Day and beyond, the souls from those incarnations, and all the memories they contain, risk being permanently and irretrievably lost.[52]

Fortunately, as we find elsewhere in the Gospel of Thomas, Original Christianity had a solution to this dilemma; the members of the church reached out toward their past-life selves, trying to extend their own salvation throughout the entire line of their past selves as well, saving the whole of their being from end to end.

> *Jesus said, "Whoever has something in his hand will receive more, and whoever has nothing will be deprived of even the little he has."*
> *(The Gospel of Thomas 41)*

In Saying 3, Jesus did not say the Kingdom of Heaven *will* be inside us if we only do this or that, but instead said that the kingdom is *already* inside us right now. Saying 41 explores that idea a bit more, explaining why the present existence of that kingdom inside us makes our attitude and perspective so important in life. While Saying 3 said, in effect, that we are already the children of God and have already inherited His kingdom, this passage suggests we are also already exercising the powers one would expect the heirs to the kingdom to possess.

Our inner attitude and perspective on life, this saying declares, truly do create and define our experience. The person who focuses on life's bounty will attract more of the same, while one who sees the glass as half empty will just attract poverty. Although we already possess these God-given abilities, Jesus teaches here, they unfortunately end up working against us much of the time because we don't realize the actual dynamics taking place. In many places in the Gospel of Thomas, Jesus declares that the physical universe itself will become our ready ally when we enter the Kingdom of Heaven; He said the same thing in the Gospel of Matthew, insisting that if we had the right attitude, no miracle would be beyond our ability. The earthshaking implications of these elements of Christ's original teachings have been all but erased from conventional Christianity, but the rediscovered Gospel of Thomas reminds us that those fantastic ideas were not peripheral to Christ's teachings, but instead were at the very heart of the revolutionary realization He was trying to share with us.

Jesus said, "Be passersby."[53] *(The Gospel of Thomas 42)*

This simple little passage sums up the entire message of the Gospel of Thomas in just two words, and in so doing it illustrates the common ground between Original Christianity and Buddhism. The Buddha taught his followers not to become attached to the things of this world. Jesus does much the same thing in the Gospel of Thomas, teaching His followers not to divide themselves in two by repressing their own mental content. Repression preserves and holds mental content. It is the *essence* of attachment. We all hold onto our repressed mental content. When we instead allow our feelings, emotions, and insights to flow naturally through us, however, they come and they go peacefully, and we can watch them do so as calmly and securely as a train passenger would watch the scenes of a town pass by the train window. Once this natural flow is restored, we become healthier, happier, and whole.

> *His disciples said to him: "Who are you to say this to us?"*
> *"Do you not realize from what I say to you who I am? But you*
> *have become like the Jews! They love the tree, but hate its fruit. Or they*
> *love the fruit but hate the tree." (The Gospel of Thomas 43)*

In this passage, Jesus uses His countrymen to illustrate humankind's spiritual duplicity. By the time the first century rolled around, the Jews had come simultaneously to delight in and resent their inherited covenant with God, a structure that produced fruit they both loved and hated. While they comforted themselves with the thought that they were God's chosen people, more often than not they regretted the political consequences that relationship brought about. They believed, for example, that their ancestors' unfaithfulness to God had caused their once-great nation to be occupied by foreign powers like Assyria, Greece, and Rome. And even though they loved thinking of themselves as God's elect, many Jews had come to hate the actual terms of their covenant with Him, feeling the 613 rules of the Mosaic Law to be an almost impossible burden. Nonetheless, those fortunate few within Judaic society whose social or economic position allowed them to observe dutifully the entire catalogue of the Mosaic Law still loved to lord it over their fellow countrymen, flaunting the exalted social status this technical perfection gave them. Thus they loved their covenant with God, but hated the political effects it had on their nation's international affairs, but at the same time they hated the terms of that covenant, even though they loved the status it could give an individual within Jewish society. In both cases, Thomas seems to suggest that the Jews of Jesus' day lacked true integrity, wishing to enjoy the legal, social, and political benefits of God's favor without honoring the true moral spirit of the law.

Jesus severely criticizes the Jewish people in this passage, presenting them as an example of what *not* to do and how *not* to be. He paints them as two-faced, wishing one thing on the inside while doing quite another on the outside. Jesus warns His disciples that they are acting the same way, wanting to be treated as if they had integrity without actually earning that right. So long as they keep lying to themselves in this way, Jesus suggests, they will never understand Who He really is.

In this passage, Jesus uses the Jews to symbolize humanity's spiritual disease, as if their entire race were a cautionary tale being told by God Himself, and the BSD makes the same metaphorical connection. The Jews of Jesus' day had a mental picture of themselves as a people who were tricked into slavery and then miraculously set free, passing through the Red Sea to ensure that freedom, then enduring great hardships on that path for a long time, and finally crossing a river to settle in the "Promised Land" at the Dead Sea.

The BSD reports much the same story, with but a single twist: It asks "What if we never really escaped, and are even now still slaves? What if that miraculous escape was just as big an illusion as the magical tricks performed by the Pharaoh's priests in that same story?" With the exception of that one twist, the stories of Exodus and the BSD are virtually the same. In the beginning,[54] according to the BSD, we violated our own integrity, which resulted in the repression and alienation of our souls. When communication was thus cut off between the conscious and unconscious, we became enslaved by the newly invisible forces operating in and from our unconscious minds. Just like the story of Joseph and his brothers, we thought that making this deal was a pretty clever move at the time, but in the end it backfired on us. Just as the Jews became slaves to Egypt, so too did humanity become completely controlled by its own unconscious slave-master. As the Gospel of Philip declares:

> We are its [the unconscious'] slaves. It takes us captive, to make us do what we do not want, and what we do want we do not do. It is powerful because we have not recognized it [because it remains hidden, being unconscious]. While it exists it is active. Ignorance [being unconscious of something] is the mother of all evil. (The Gospel of Philip 83:26–31)

To the Jews of Jesus' time, this would have been a very meaningful passage, since their whole cultural identity revolved around the idea of their having escaped slavery. The Jews believed they had escaped that fate, but here we find the early Christians, who still thought of themselves as Jews, maintaining that they are *still* slaves.

Just as the Jews suddenly found themselves set miraculously free from their slavery through no virtue of their own, so the spirits of the dead find themselves miraculously freed of their burdens when they split off from the soul at death, going on to reincarnate with a perfectly clean slate. And after the spirit splits off from the soul, thus escaping its burdens, it is reborn again in the ocean of humanity (a "Sea of Blood," i.e., the Red

Sea). And just as the Jews' self-image was completely refashioned during that passage through the Red Sea, so the spirit's self-image goes through a similar rebirth when it incarnates again.[55] And once the spirit has been reborn in that human ocean of blood and flesh, it must, like the Jews wandering in the desert, endure tremendous hardships and sorrows: all the miseries of another human lifetime. And just as the Jews wandered through that desert without a clue where they were going or why, so the reborn spirit wanders through its life without any sense of why it is there or what might be around the next corner. And just as the Jews finally crossed a great division at the end of their journey (a river) in order to enter the Promised Land, so the spirit suffers a division at the end of each incarnation's journey, seeing his own soul recede farther and farther away on the other side of death's dividing gulf.

The Jews' Promised Land has parallels to the destination of the divided soul. Once the Jews finally entered the land promised to them by the Dead Sea, they did not find the happiness they expected, but instead received nothing but misery, heartache, and strife. They anticipated finding a heavenly home in that place, but eventually it became clear that they were actually in hell. There was little peace in the land of Israel; everything seemed to go wrong all the time, and everyone seemed to be against them. In much the same way, the BSD suggests, those who cling to their hope of entering the heavenly realm of the dead at the end of their life's journey might also have a rude awakening in store for them. The Jews' Promised Land is near the Dead Sea, literally the lowest place on earth, which reminds us that those who divide at death also end up in a "Sea of the Dead" located in the deepest strata of the human psyche. And reminding us of the Jews' continuing failure to find happiness in the Promised Land, the binary soul doctrine warns those whose only earthly hope is to spend eternity in heaven that their expectations might also be disappointed. Instead of hoping merely for a postmortem existence in a realm of the dead, the BSD suggests, one ought instead to seek the Kingdom of Heaven while still alive. Anything else is just agreeing to the division.

> *Jesus said, "Whoever blasphemes against the Father will be forgiven, and whoever blasphemes against the son will be forgiven, but whoever blasphemes against the holy spirit will not be forgiven, neither on earth nor in heaven." (The Gospel of Thomas 44)*

A thorn in the side of many would-be theologians over the last 2,000 years, this curious distinction asks us to explain why one element of the Godhead should be treated any different from the others. The BSD provides an explanation, however, in that the Holy Spirit is the part of the Godhead that actually speaks to us inside our own minds. As I discussed in *The Division of Consciousness,* Jesus' death and Resurrection caused a part of His own mind to be strewn across the time-space universe, effectively bonding it to the unconscious minds of all people throughout history. This bond allows that part of His mind, which is now commonly called the Holy Spirit, to coexist in our minds, pointing out our errors and guiding us toward truth and wholeness.

It speaks to us. Unlike the other two parts of the Godhead, we personally experience the presence of the Holy Spirit, speaking to us as the voice of our own conscience. This is very different from our relationship with the Father and the Son, the other two elements of the Godhead, whom we do not experience as directly while we are still in a divided, corrupted spiritual state. The whole purpose of the Holy Spirit, indeed, is to guide us back to the point where we do again consciously experience our relationship with the Father and the Son. But until that mission is accomplished, the only voice of the Godhead we can hear is that of the Holy Spirit, and that is why the only one we are truly able to blaspheme is the Holy Spirit. While we remain divided, we do not really know or directly experience the Father or the Son, and so we cannot knowingly speak any lies about them.

The voice of the Holy Spirit is such an integral element of our minds that when we accept its judgments and insights instead of pushing them away, we automatically identify with those thoughts, claiming them as our own. In this way, our minds commune naturally with the Holy Spirit, and this is the process of how these two minds go about merging together and becoming one (this process is explored further in Saying 61). Thus, when we reject those judgments and insights from the Holy Spirit, we are at the same time rejecting our own minds' judgments, which the early church recognized to be the essence of sin itself: "Woe, woe unto the souls that despise their own judgment!" (The Epistle of Titus).[56]

When the Holy Spirit deposits thoughts, insights, or ideals within our minds, and we choose to deny having seen them pass through our minds, that *is* a lie, and it is a lie that we are never allowed to get away with. These lies are the blasphemies to which Saying 44 refers. Blasphemy is defined as a lack of reverence; denying we heard the voice of the Holy Spirit in our minds when we actually did would fit that definition. If we truly revered the voice of the Holy Spirit, we would wholeheartedly embrace and celebrate it whenever it spoke within our hearts, instead of ignoring its messages and denying ever hearing them as we are so accustomed to doing. We are always forced to confront those lies sooner or later; either we voluntarily admit them while we are alive, or we spend eternity stewing in the repressed pain we created for ourselves by denying what we ourselves knew to be true.

Jesus said, "Grapes are not harvested from thorn trees, nor are figs gathered from thistles, for they yield no fruit. Good persons produce good from what they've stored up; bad persons produce evil from the wickedness they've stored up in their hearts, and say evil things. For from the overflow of the heart they produce evil." (The Gospel of Thomas 45)

This passage needs little explanation for the student of the BSD. When we deny our own best thoughts and betray our own highest ideals, they do not suddenly disappear or cease to exist, but are simply submerged into our unconscious, where they remain and are preserved. In response to that choice to deny our best selves, our unconscious then generates self-critical insights and feelings, which we also repress, and this cycle goes around and around, generating ever more pain and self-criticism, which end up building up more and more inside our unconscious minds.

But the barrier between the conscious and unconscious is notoriously porous and leaky, and all that repressed self-condemnation in the unconscious always manages to seep out a little when we're not paying attention. It inevitably affects our moods, attitudes, and behaviors, often leaving us wondering after the fact why we acted so inappropriately in various situations. No matter how hard we try, this darkness within us cannot be firmly controlled, and the more of it we try to hold within, the darker and more evil we end up becoming on the outside, and the more our thoughts, speech, and behaviors involuntarily reflect the buildup of pain, rage, and self-hatred within us.

Thus it becomes harder and harder for us to produce "good" works in the world, in effect, to act like "good people," as long as we continue secretly to store and retain "evil" thoughts and feelings within our hearts. In the end, whatever we've stored in our hearts is what we reflect back to the world, whether we want to or not. As long as our hearts are full of grief, resentment, and self-condemnation, these feelings unconsciously sabotage our best efforts in the world. We indeed find, just as Jesus taught, that we cannot produce "grapes" when all we have inside are "thorns."

Knowing about this dynamic, however, is a great advantage. Those of us who always end up producing "thorns" in the world when we are trying to produce "grapes" will realize that our inner conflicts are secretly sabotaging our outer efforts in the world. Understanding and using these signals, we can accurately gauge the level and degree of our integrity. Employing such external gauges is essential on our spiritual paths, as people are always inclined to overestimate their own mental health and integrity.

> *Jesus said, "From Adam to John the Baptist, among those born of women there is no one so much greater than John the Baptist that his eyes should not be averted. But I have said that whoever among you becomes a child will recognize the Father's kingdom and will become greater than John." (The Gospel of Thomas 46)*

This familiar biblical passage takes on a whole new meaning within the context of reincarnation.

In early Christian scripture, a telling distinction is often made between "the son of man" and "those born of women," with the male representing wholeness and unity and the female representing division and duality. Thus John the Baptist is described here as being someone who is still divided, who has not yet achieved complete spiritual wholeness and integration. Anyone who *has* achieved such wholeness, the Gospel of Thomas indicates, would be able to reincarnate without any loss of memory. This would be the ultimate spiritual achievement; only one who had found the Kingdom of Heaven could accomplish it.

> *Jesus said, "It is impossible for a man to mount two horses or to stretch two bows. And it is impossible for a servant to serve two masters; otherwise, he will honor the one and treat the other contemptuously. No man drinks old wine and immediately desires to drink new wine. And new wine is not put into old wineskins, lest they split; nor is old wine put into a new wineskin, lest it spoil it. An old patch is not sewn onto a new garment, because a split would result." (The Gospel of Thomas 47)*

Both halves of our minds make demands on us, but we cannot honor both equally while they remain separate. If these two can be united into a single unit, then both *can* be honored at the same time. Time and again in the Gospel of Thomas, Jesus insists that we must "make the two one." This command does not refer, however, only to the union of our present-life soul and spirit, but also to the process of resurrecting our past-life souls. When a long-dead self reawakens in a person's mind, it will be impossible for both the past and present self to exist peacefully together unless they are integrated into a single self. Without that integration, two separate selves compete for control of the mind and body at the same time, and we are always forced to favor one over the other.

Such an integration, this passage warns, will not be easy. Both selves will believe they are already wholes unto themselves. Both will believe they alone are "the real person." Each will be compelled by his natural instinct for self-preservation to resist becoming a mere addendum to the other. Neither will be willing to play second fiddle.

This passage explores multiple possible approaches to integrating a present and past self, explaining why neither soul can be simply "added" unto the other like an afterthought. If a past-life self is resurrected in one's mind, that previous self (old wine) will not be keen to meet the new self (new wine) because it will be afraid of giving up its authority, autonomy, and sense of identity to that later incarnation. Similarly, the knowledge, memories, and experiences of the newer incarnation (the new wine) cannot simply be poured into the older soul (the old wineskin), for this would mark the older incarnation as the more authentic self, and the newer self as nothing but a supplemental afterthought. Nor can the knowledge, memories, and experiences of the older incarnation (the old wine) be poured into the mind of the new incarnation (the new wineskin), for this would mark the newer self as the dominant party. One can no more append an old soul unto a new one, this saying suggests, than one can sew an old patch onto a new garment.

The passage repeatedly warns that this second approach in particular is very dangerous, likely to result in ruin and spoilage (insanity). This makes psychological sense, for it would completely reverse our customary experience of cause and effect. After suffering blindly through the various events of our current life, we would find out only after the fact that many turns of fate in our life had been the effects of causes from a previously unknown earlier life. In that respect, at least, the alternative approach of adding the later memories onto the earlier soul would work better than vice versa, for effects would then be encountered after their causes, the way the mind is used to experiencing reality.

Nonetheless this passage insists that in the final analysis, neither of these methods of possible integration will be successful. Jesus' solution to this conundrum? As the Gospel of Thomas indicates in Sayings 8, 20, 23, 76, and 108, one must first choose to integrate one's soul with Jesus' soul, and only *then* do all those other integrations and resurrections succeed.

> *Jesus said, "If two make peace with each other in this one house, they will say to the mountain, 'Move away,' and it will move away."*
> *(The Gospel of Thomas 48)*

This is almost identical to Saying 106, which states, "When you make the two one, you will become the sons of man," and then one can order the mountain around. This obviously equates "two making peace in one house" with becoming "sons of man." The BSD declares that integrating the soul and spirit inside a person will turn that person into a Christ instead of merely a Christian, endowed with all the powers Jesus Himself displayed. Again, we see the Gospel of Thomas repeating the message that achieving unity and wholeness will allow one to inherit the kingdom, and all the empowerment that goes with it.

> *Jesus said, "Blessed are the single ones and the elect, for you will find the kingdom. For you are from it, and to it you will return." (The Gospel of Thomas 49)*

While we may currently find ourselves in a divided state, we did not start out that way. Our origins were in an undivided unity, and our destiny is to return to that same condition. Once we become whole and undivided again, we will enter the kingdom of God. Because the kingdom exists both within us and outside us, it is neither an event to be waited for nor a place to be entered. Instead, since it already secretly exists all around us, it merely needs to be found.

> *Jesus said, "If they say to you, 'Where have you come from?' say to them, 'We have come from the light, from the place where the light came into being by itself, established itself, and appeared in their image.'*

"If they say to you, 'Is it you?' say, 'We are its children, and we are the chosen of the living Father.'
"If they ask you, 'What is the evidence of your Father in you?' say to them, 'It is motion and rest.'" (The Gospel of Thomas 50)

Humanity's inner duality is presented with a variety of equal but opposite metaphor pairs in the Gospel of Thomas, such as above/below, inside/outside, male/female, and so on. In a number of instances, God Himself is also presented as a duality of light and image in Thomas' gospel. In this passage, the human reflection of that same divine duality is presented as motion and rest. Light and motion are apt metaphors for the conscious spirit, as image and rest are for the unconscious soul. This passage suggests that when we discover the wholeness within our duality, we will fully comprehend and appreciate the relationship between ourselves and our Creator.

The BSD does not shed light on the intended use of the dialogue in this passage. It may presume to provide readers with afterlife instructions, telling them what to say at specific stages in their afterlife journeys, or it may have just been misinterpreted as such by later Gnostic readers.[57] It is nonetheless clear that both God and humans are presented here as having similar dualistic compositions. When a person simultaneously possesses both motion and rest, this passage declares, he or she has achieved the human equivalent of divine perfection, and is a true Son of God.

In bringing up this duality, Jesus anticipated the work of a number of later philosophers, such as Kant, Hegel, Emerson, and Martin Buber, all of whom posited similar dualities in their works. In 1941, the American poet Eli Siegel founded his philosophical school of Aesthetic Realism on the premise that all reality can be viewed as the aesthetic oneness of opposites (much as Egyptians had believed 4,500 years earlier).[58] Music certainly follows this rule, with the silent, "still" spaces between the notes being just as essential as those "moving" notes themselves.

Human beings encompass this same duality; the person who gets up and moves around in the morning is the same one who slept the night before. Although one has moved and changed, one has in a sense at the same time remained still, continuing to be the same essential self one was before. One is, just as the Gospel of Thomas teaches, simultaneously motion and rest, change and sameness. The binary soul doctrine suggests that human beings are designed with two spiritual elements for just this reason, to facilitate and embody this duality. While our soul is like the ever-changing face of the moon, always growing or shrinking or shifting about, our spirit is like the eternally constant orb of the sun, always the same every time you see it. In Saying 50, the Gospel of Thomas indicates that the divine goal of the Christian religion is to preserve this duality, continuing to encompass both motion and rest. This concern, of course, suggests it must somehow be possible *not* to encompass both, which is precisely what the binary soul doctrine warned about. If the soul and spirit divide at death, one of them would then only know motion, the other, only rest.

Modern reports of afterlife phenomena reflect just such a situation. Near-death experiencers, who seem to describe the after-death experience of the soul, typically describe finding themselves in either a heaven or a hell, both of which are bursting with motion and activity. But past-life regression subjects, who seem instead to describe the after-death experience of the spirit, typically describe floating calmly alone in an empty black void after death, in a state of absolute rest and motionlessness.

> *His disciples said to him, "When will the rest for the dead take place, and when will the new world come?"*
> *He said to them, "What you are looking forward to has come, but you don't know it." (The Gospel of Thomas 51)*

This was the central point of Jesus' entire ministry; one did not have to wait until Judgment Day to enjoy the arrival of the kingdom, for it was here already:

> Jesus came into Galilee, preaching good news about God, saying, "The time has come, and the kingdom of God is at hand." (Mark 1: 14–15)

"The time *has* come," and is already here now, Jesus insisted. The BSD indicates the same thing: The prophesied events known as "the resurrection of the dead" and "the new world" are not events fixed at a certain point in future history, but instead are subjective experiences, shifts of awareness and consciousness, that can occur in a person at any point in time. Those who achieve soul-spirit integration will receive their own past-life selves as a reward of that accomplishment and will also then discover themselves to be living in a miraculous world without division, error, or death. Once our inner divisions are resolved, the rest of the world looks entirely different.

Of course, this is not to say that the Judgment Day/Harvest scenario (the resurrection of the dead and the second coming of Christ) will not occur to the many at a certain point in history, but only that the very same transformations that will occur to the majority on that day are already at hand now to any who would reach for them.

> *His disciples said to him, "Twenty-four prophets have spoken in Israel, and they all spoke of you."*
>
> *He said to them, "You have disregarded the living one who is in your presence, and have spoken of the dead." (The Gospel of Thomas 52)*

The Gospel of Thomas defines a theological perspective that is diametrically opposed to that of the official church, essentially undermining that church's entire claim to authority and ecclesiastical hierarchy. Truth is *not* to be sought first in the scriptures, nor in the opinions of others about those scriptures, Jesus says here, no matter what claims to authority they may seem to hold. Instead, truth is always to be sought first within one's own self. Again and again in the Gospel of Thomas, Jesus emphasizes that the key to the kingdom, and our only sure guide in this world, is to be found within our own souls.

Jesus' soul is within our own, this Gospel repeatedly reminds us. It is *always* in our immediate presence, and there is no better guide. The Living One within us holds all we need, including our whole self. He lacks nothing.

All other sources of information and guidance are secondary and supplemental. To look outward first is an error. If we look outward first, whether to science, or history, or religious scripture, we will miss the most important element of the picture, and thus fail to grasp fully the truth we seek. Outside of Christ, this world and all in it are dead and lifeless things that cannot aid the living. Instead, we must look inward and inquire of that Living One who resides within our minds and souls.

The Gospel of Thomas thus labels as dead all written rules and traditional guidelines.

> *His disciples said to him, "Is circumcision useful or not?"*
>
> *He said to them, "If it were useful, their father would produce children already circumcised from their mother. Rather, the true circumcision*

in spirit has become profitable in every respect." (The Gospel of Thomas 53)

This passage and the next carry the same message: the solution to humanity's spiritual dilemma involves some cutting back or limiting of the human spirit. Humanity's problem results from an imbalance between the soul and spirit, and this imbalance is ultimately the fault of the spirit, which, being stronger than the soul, represses it. This repression is the origin of all humanity's problems, from disease to war to death itself. The spirit represses the soul because it doesn't want its free-will decisions to be held back or be limited by the soul's memory or sense of right and wrong. Without the soul, the spirit has no moral compass and ends up sowing more and more injustice and disorder in the world. The solution to this problem—reuniting the soul and spirit—will require the spirit once again to honor the insights and guidance of the soul. This will require the spirit to make a personal sacrifice, however, giving up some of its autonomous free will.

This willingness to accept limits on our free will was symbolized in the Bible by the act of circumcision. Free will is the ability to be creative in our choices, and the physical symbol of man's creativity is the phallus. To circumcise the phallus voluntarily, then, is to symbolize the voluntary cutting back or reduction of one's free will. And since free will is the property of the spirit rather than the soul, it can be said that salvation involves a circumcision of the spirit.

Jesus said, "Blessed are the poor, for the kingdom of heaven belongs to you." (The Gospel of Thomas 54)

This familiar saying essentially condemns the riches of this world as having no real value and suggests that those acknowledging this have the best chance to recognize the invisible kingdom within which they live and move and have their being.

The word translated as "poor" here is better rendered as "destitute," indicating a person with neither money, nor home, nor family. This passage does not advocate the abandonment of earthly riches so much as it boldly declares that those who seem to have lost everything are actually society's most fortunate members. One reason the destitute are blessed is because fate has released them from all the normal cultural bonds that usually dictate behaviors and attitudes, putting them in the best position to honor their own vision of truth without compromise. This saying shares a radical perspective with many other passages in the Gospel of Thomas, turning many cultural perspectives upside down. The author rejected Jewish dietary laws, familial obligations, and even their traditional respect for the acquisition of material wealth. Those who have lost everything, the text suggests here, are uniquely able to pursue a life devoted to personal integrity, freed from the distractions of societal obligations and hypocrisies. Those who see this world's poverty for what it is will stop hoarding, protecting, and honoring its illusory values and will begin seeking out treasures of more substantial value.

This was obviously an authentic element of Christ's early teachings. When Jesus sent out His disciples in the Gospel of Matthew, they were similarly instructed to rely exclusively on God's providence during their journeys:

> As you go, preach this message: "The kingdom of heaven is already here." Heal the sick, raise the dead, cleanse those who have leprosy, drive out demons. Freely you have received, freely give. Do not take along any gold or silver or copper in your belts; take no bag for the journey, or extra tunic, or sandals or a staff. (Matt. 10:7)

Instead of acting on their fear that their earthly needs would go unmet on their journeys, Jesus insisted they go out empty-handed, so the true providence of the kingdom could be revealed to them. Jesus wanted to make sure that those who would be preaching His message that "the kingdom was already here" were themselves experiencing the presence of that kingdom both within their inner hearts and also out in the "real" world.

Jesus said, "Whoever does not hate father and mother cannot be my disciple, and whoever does not hate brothers and sisters, and carry the cross as I do, will not be worthy of me." (The Gospel of Thomas 55)

This passage, along with Sayings 99 and 101, discuss family relationships, and all three invert traditional ideas about the importance of family bonds. Like those passages condemning the world, business, and monetary wealth, these passages reject conventional attitudes and worldly behaviors, revealing Christianity to have originally been a very revolutionary movement. Jesus associates hatred of family members with the need to carry the cross, an obvious metaphor for the need to accept sacrifices when one's path requires it. These inversions emphasize that those seeking the kingdom of God cannot place any other value or obligation, no matter how customary or expected, above the demands of one's spiritual path.

Considering the later prominence of Jesus' own family members within the fledgling organization He founded (His brother James the Just became the leader of the Jerusalem Church after Jesus died, and His brother Judas Thomas took on a similar role among congregations in the East), this passage takes on even greater significance, reminding us of Mark 3:21 where Jesus' family is said to have thought Him insane. This passage's condemnation of familial bonds should be highlighted in the minds of all who realize that it was those very family members who relayed His message to the rest of the world after He was gone. Did He predict in advance in this passage that His message would ultimately be corrupted by His own family members?

Jesus seems here to warn His followers how impossible it will be to keep their families happy while they are trying to remain faithful to their own vision of truth. They could, for example, no longer willingly participate in perpetuating the various lies and falsehoods that family relationships often require. Much like a drunk who tries desperately to get his friend on the wagon to have "just one drink," those who are slaves to their self-betrayals usually feel very threatened by people who turn from that path to a new life of truth, honor, and integrity. Whenever we encounter those who are uncompromising in their struggle to be true to themselves, their wholeness and integrity tend to emphasize our own lack of same, and, in a flash, their integrity becomes threatening to us. The darkness in us is threatened by the light of others, for that light reminds us of what we could be and should be, and it angers us to be reminded of our own failings.

Now, that is the normal process, but when the two people in question are family members, a whole new dynamic enters the picture, and Jesus felt it was an important enough issue to warn us about it in advance. Seeing that our dedication to truth and integrity causes our family distress, those of us on the spiritual path are caught in a quandary, not wanting to hurt them but not wanting to sacrifice our salvation either. Jesus basically says here, "Do not sacrifice your own salvation just to make your family happy. You can't help them or yourself while you are still spiritually unhealthy." The whole world is caught up in this ancient conspiracy of spiritual self-betrayal, and we are all caught up in it together. Each time any of us manages to get free from this division, the whole world feels the impact, like a spider sensing motion anywhere on its web. But we are not emotionally bonded with the whole world in the same way we are with our family members, and so the pain our family feels from our success can be especially confusing and disturbing.

In a great twist that must have been even more surprising in that era than it seems today, Jesus obviously saw family bonds as part of the problem instead of the solution. In stark contrast to the "family values" emphasis of today's Religious Right, the Jesus of the Gospel of Thomas viewed these bonds as part and parcel of the whole web of concerns in this world that perform one function and one function only: diverting our attention and efforts away from our true goal—finding the Kingdom of Heaven. As long as all our time and attention keep getting bound up with family and/or business matters lifetime after lifetime, we never escape the insidious cycle of soul division and just keep retreading the same self-destructive life patterns incarnation after incarnation.

Jesus said, "Whoever has come to know the world has discovered a carcass, and whoever has discovered a carcass, of that person the world is not worthy." (The Gospel of Thomas 56)

Jesus' declaration that this world is nothing but a carcass reminds us of the view of Buddhism that the world is emptiness. When viewed from a long-term perspective, the origin of this seemingly pessimistic sentiment becomes obvious. This world is a kaleidoscope of images and forms that come and go quickly, ever changing. People, places, and things shift constantly, and nothing ever remains the same. The beauty of this world is fleeting, like the images in a dream, and when they are gone and no evidence of their existence remains, it becomes a very real question if they ever had any real value. Does the flower that bloomed for a day 65 million years ago have any value today? And if it doesn't have any value today, since this moment is the only moment that exists, did it ever have any true value?

This world, Jesus declares in the Gospel of Thomas, contains no objective value in and of itself. It is just a flat and empty screen on which various three-dimensional images are projected. If there is any true value to be found, it is not in the world, but within ourselves, and even then only if there is something within ourselves that will still exist when all else is gone. Those who realize this inherent emptiness of our physical world, Jesus teaches here, are themselves more valuable than that entire universe; and for them to spend their lives on worldly matters would be a waste and a self-betrayal.

> *Jesus said, "The Father's kingdom is like a person who has [good] seed. His enemy came during the night and sowed weeds among the good seed. The person did not let the workers pull up the weeds, but said to them, 'No, otherwise you might go to pull up the weeds and pull up the wheat along with them.' For on the day of the harvest the weeds will be conspicuous, and will be pulled up and burned." (The Gospel of Thomas 57)*

Planting seed in soil is an apt metaphor for the way the conscious mind deposits ideas and decisions in the fertile unconscious, and the student of the binary soul doctrine might at first assume that the relationship between these two is again the subject of this passage. That doesn't seem to be the case, however, since this passage is arguing *against* uprooting weeds, and other passages in the Gospel of Thomas support the immediate purge of undesired material in the unconscious.

This passage uses two well-known symbols: the planting of a crop and the harvest of the crop. This is one of the most obvious instances where the Gospel of Thomas refers to "the day of the harvest," a classic New Testament metaphor for the whole Judgment Day/Second Coming scenario. In Saying 9, the Gospel of Thomas also discussed planting seed, which in that case produced two separate crops. Both crops were from the same good seed, and both were good, even though one crop was better than the other, producing twice as much fruit. That "seed," of course, is traditionally identified in biblical exegesis as the teachings of the Christian church, and the two crops were the Orthodox and Gnostic branches of the early church. In this passage, however, we find two *different* kinds of seed being planted side by side, one good, the other bad. Both crops are allowed to continue to grow until harvest day, and only then will they finally be separated. Furthermore, if one prematurely tries to weed the garden of the undesired crop, the text declares, the preferred crop will be unnecessarily put in danger as well.

Given our previous identification of the "seed" metaphor in Saying 9 as factions or teachings of the Christian church, this passage predicted that, in addition to the two very different but equally good sets of teachings that arose in the early church, there would also eventually arise a third, evil set of teachings. Of course, this passage's prophecy was fulfilled in the fourth century, when Rome commandeered the church, transforming it into a tool of death and torture. At that time, in precise fulfillment of this scripture, the original teachings of the church were indeed compromised, adulterated with "bad seed."

Written long before Constantine, this passage prophesied that these alien teachings would so thoroughly intertwine themselves into the traditions and corpus of the church that it would be impossible to purge them without endangering the church's survival. This passage thus speaks directly to a belief held by fundamentalist Christianity today, which insists that the integrity of the Bible could never have been compromised or adulterated, because God would not have allowed it. But here we find that the Gospel of Thomas, written long before the formulation of the canon, not only prophesied that such corruption would eventually take place, but also explained why God allowed it to occur—because the survival of the faith itself would have been put at risk if Rome's unsavory influence had not been allowed to infiltrate the church.

Rome's autocratic ideology took firm root in the culture of the church and grew so strong over the centuries that, just like weeds, it repeatedly threatened to choke off the faith's purer attributes. The Gospel of Thomas indicates that Christianity's inauthentic elements will not be purged before "the day of the harvest." While such a prophecy might dampen the hopes of those looking forward to such a change, it also throws fear into the hearts of those who already see that change under way.

Jesus said, "Blessed is the man who has suffered and found life."
(The Gospel of Thomas 58)

This passage has the same message as Sayings 69 and 82. In order to "make the two one," we must experience and embrace *all* the messages coming from the soul, including all its negative messages, painful feelings, and self-recriminations. The human race has gotten into the habit of ignoring, denying, and rejecting those messages, but those who do not turn away from these painful self-recriminations will grow more whole and integrated, and will find the kingdom.

> *Jesus said, "Look for the living one while you are alive, lest you die and seek to look for him then and find you don't have the power to look." (The Gospel of Thomas 59)*

The binary soul doctrine explains why those who don't call on God in life will find themselves unable to do so in death. While we are alive, we possess both our autonomous free will and rational intellect (the possessions of the spirit) and our memories and sense of identity (the possessions of the soul). But if, when we die, our souls divide from our spirits, our souls will no longer possess free will or rational intellect and will be running on pure habit, doing and thinking the same things they did while alive. Those who do not develop the habit of thinking about and searching for their Creator while they are alive will be unable to change their behavior after death and so will not search for Him then either. After death, "all who call upon the Lord will be saved,"[59] but only those who habitually called on Him in life will also do so in death.

> *He saw a Samaritan carrying a lamb and going to Judea. He said to his disciples, "that person . . . around the lamb."*
> *They said to him, "So that he may kill it and eat it."*
> *He said to them, "He will not eat it while it is alive, but only after he has killed it and it has become a carcass."*
> *They said, "Otherwise he can't do it."*
> *He said to them, "So also with you, seek for yourselves a place for rest, or you might become a carcass and be eaten." (The Gospel of Thomas 60)*

Although this passage is incomplete, its missing text does not prevent us from grasping its main point. If we remain "alive" we will not be "eaten," but if we allow ourselves to die, we risk being "eaten." As the Gospel of Thomas teaches again and again, the way out of this dilemma is to find "rest"; if we find "rest," we will not die and so won't become a consumable. To find rest is thus equated with achieving "eternal life."

The word "carcass" was previously only used in Saying 56, when it was claimed that the world is itself a carcass, and the one who realized this was better than the world. Here it is suggested that those who do not realize this but instead relate to and identify with the world will become as much of a carcass as the world is, and as doomed to destruction.

Many ancient cultures held this notion that the souls of the damned would be eaten by some fearsome being on the other side of death's door. The Egyptians called this being "Ammit"; those souls who failed the after-death judgment were swallowed up by Ammit. Christian legends held that the souls of the damned were swallowed by the devil. Rudolf Steiner held that after the soul-spirit division, the souls of individuals eventually all merged or melted together into a great anonymous amalgamation on the other side of death's door, essentially being "consumed" by the collective. Emanuel Swedenborg also held that the souls of the dead entered such a collective, but he seemed to allow for at least some degree of continued independent identity within that collective.

In the Gospel of Thomas, Jesus portrays this fate as something that could be avoided:

> *Jesus said, "Two will rest on a bed: the one will die, and the other will live."*
> *Salome said to him, "Who are You, man, that You, as though from the One, have come up on my couch and eaten from my table?"*
> *Jesus said to her, "I am He who exists from the Undivided. I was given some of the things of my Father."*
> *Salome said, "I am Your disciple."*
> *Jesus said to her, "Therefore I say, if he is undivided, he will be filled with light, but if he is divided, he will be filled with darkness."*
> *(The Gospel of Thomas 61)*

As in so much of the Gospel of Thomas, the theme here is nothing but division and more division. The first sentence defines the very essence of the binary soul doctrine: if our souls and spirits are not united while we are alive, then when we pass away, one part will survive to live again, while the other will die, becoming trapped in the realm of the dead. This problem is then contrasted with its solution—Jesus—who is undivided. If we are undivided, the text suggests in the last lines, we will be just as immortal and enlightened as Jesus is; but if we are divided, then not only will we die, but we will also suffer all sorts of miseries and ignorance in both life and death.

The text prompts the reader to wonder "what does it mean to be 'undivided' in the way Jesus is 'undivided'?" and then proceeds to answer that question with an example. Jesus comes up on Salome's couch and eats from her table, precisely as if Jesus were pretending to *be* Salome. And indeed, the text suggests, this is exactly what it means to be undivided. Just as Jesus is not divided within Himself, so too He is not divided from her, either, but actually lives *within* her and therefore shares in all her earthly experiences. Jesus, the text reports, was given some of the things of His Father, apparently including Salome herself, since right after He claims receipt of some possessions, Salome declares *herself* to be one of His possessions. Jesus' ownership of Salome, however, is not merely a philosophical or ideological matter, but complete and utter possession of every facet of her existence. In this passage, Jesus is shown actually living in and through her, lying on her couch when she lies, and eating from her table when she eats. This passage is thus connected with Saying 108, which says this same thing, that Jesus and His followers actually merge together, becoming one and the same being.

> Jesus said, "I disclose my mysteries to those [who are worthy] of [my] mysteries. Do not let your left hand know what your right hand is doing." (The Gospel of Thomas 62)

At first, this seems to promote and encourage division. It actually highlights the difference between division and differentiation, however. If all there was in this passage were the left and right hands doing incompatible things, that would be a symbol of division. But the two hands are both being controlled by a single master, their separate tasks being coordinated and integrated to serve a common cause. This is a perfect symbol of the type of unity and integration sought by the binary soul doctrine. The soul and spirit do not need to become the same in order to achieve their integration. Instead, they retain their separate natures, working together to achieve a common purpose.

This passage also suggests that there were two separate sets of teachings at the dawn of early Christianity, of equal value and necessity, both serving to forward a common goal. The idea that Jesus had one set of teachings for one group of followers and a separate set for the rest was a familiar and fundamental element of Christ's original teachings, also found in Luke 8:9–10, Matthew 13:10–11, and Mark 4:10–12.

> *Jesus said, "There was a rich person who had a great deal of money. He said, 'I shall invest my money so that I may sow, reap, plant, and fill my storehouses with produce, that I may lack nothing.'*
>
> *"These were the things he was thinking in his heart, but that very night he died. Anyone with ears had better listen!" (The Gospel of Thomas 63)*

We are reminded here of the inevitability of our own physical mortality. Original Christianity emphasized the vanity and foolishness of seeking one's treasure in the physical world. In Saying 27, Jesus instructs us to fast from the world, and in Saying 56, He declares that the physical universe has no more value than a dead carcass. This passage points out that since this earthly life is fleeting, our true concerns ought to revolve around our more long-term welfare. This theme takes an interesting twist in subsequent passages, however, where it starts to be suggested that *all* selfish efforts to promote one's own personal agenda, physical or otherwise, will ultimately meet with failure.

> *Jesus said, "A person was receiving guests. When he had prepared the dinner, he sent his slave to invite the guests. The slave went to the first and said to that one, 'My master invites you.'*
>
> *"That one said, 'Some merchants owe me money; they are coming to me tonight. I have to go and give them instructions. Please excuse me from dinner.'*
>
> *"The slave went to another and said to that one, 'My master has invited you.'*
>
> *"That one said to the slave, 'I have bought a house, and I have been called away for a day. I shall have no time.'*
>
> *"The slave went to another and said to that one, 'My master invites you.'*
>
> *"That one said to the slave, 'My friend is to be married, and I am to arrange the banquet. I shall not be able to come. Please excuse me from dinner.'*
>
> *"The slave went to another and said to that one, 'My master invites you.'*

"That one said to the slave, 'I have bought an estate, and I am going to collect the rent. I shall not be able to come. Please excuse me.'

"The slave returned and said to his master, 'Those whom you invited to dinner have asked to be excused.'

"The master said to his slave, 'Go out on the streets and bring back whomever you find to have dinner.'

"Buyers and merchants [will] not enter the places of my Father."
(The Gospel of Thomas 64)

This passage's last line is not found in its more familiar biblical versions. By adding "buyers and merchants will not enter the places of my Father," it is no longer a simple condemnation of people who turn away from their religious or spiritual obligations to take care of worldly issues. By condemning all the guests as "buyers and merchants," the passage now condemns what "buyers and merchants" do, which is simply to get the best deal they can. In Jesus' day, merchants were not well respected, believed to cheat their customers as much as they could. For example, one of the sorest points in Jewish culture revolved around the money changers at the temple. The people had to buy their pigeons and other sacrificial animals at the temple, because they were not allowed to bring their own. But they were not allowed to buy them with their own money and had to have their money changed first into temple money. This made them feel they were getting doubly cheated at the temple, both by the money changers and then again by the animal sellers, neither of whom could be bartered with, since they had a monopoly on those markets.

Thus the addition of this one line transforms this well-known passage into an encompassing condemnation of everyone who makes their own advantage their first priority in any given situation. This sentiment is very much in keeping with what we know about Original Christianity from other sources. What has come down to us from the lost Gospel of the Hebrews, for instance, informs us that the familiar biblical story about the rich man who was told to give away all his money to the poor originally had another element to it. When the rich man told Jesus he had faithfully kept the law and the prophets, Jesus challenged him on that, pointing out that if the rich man had really "loved his neighbor as himself," he would recognize no financial distinctions between himself and others, but would share with them all that he had. It is well known that the early church was very communal in nature, with all believers sharing their possessions in common, and this passage reflects that same attitude, condemning those who put their own profit before that of others.

Such an attitude, such a priority, is essentially the hallmark of the division between the soul and spirit. Whenever the conscious spirit determines that the messages trying to rise up from the unconscious soul are not to its liking, it rejects and represses them. In doing this, it is behaving exactly like a merchant trying to profit from a trade, trying to get more than it is giving. The spirit gives everything it has to the soul but does not accept everything in return. The soul receives, processes, and stores all mental input coming from the conscious mind, but the conscious mind edits and censors the material the unconscious tries to send back in exchange. In order for the conscious spirit to reject the messages from the unconscious soul, it has to lie to itself, saying either that those messages don't exist or that they have no value. In much the same way, when a merchant buys or sells an item, his whole profit results from a lie. He profits by exchanging something of lesser value for something of greater value, but only accomplishes this by convincing the other party that they are getting a fair exchange. Here and elsewhere, the Gospel of Thomas suggests that the act of seeking one's own advantage in life involves this same unequal internal exchange.

Finding this teaching in the Gospel of Thomas speaks to the authenticity of this scripture. The Didache, the Epistle of Barnabas, and Acts all carry this early Christian message as well, counseling against seeking personal profit or individual advantage, advising Christians to "share all things with your brother, and do not say that they are your own." The Epistle of Barnabas even goes so far as to condemn pursuing any recompense for one's work. Conventional Jewish thought during that era held a similar opinion about profit. The Mishnah, which records Jewish teachings during the first and second centuries, advocates a radical utopian economic system that condemns all profit via business or financial transactions:

Every negotiation or business transaction ends up with the involved parties no better or worse off than they were before. No party in the end may have more than what he did at the outset, and none may emerge as the victim of a sizable shift in fortune and circumstance. What is forbidden, in other words, is not just usury (an unfair profit) or interest (a fair profit) but any profit at all. The model is friends or associates exchanging equal objects in a commonly agreed barter. The end is to ensure equal exchanges in all transactions. . . . The Mishnah . . . found profit incompatible with holiness.[60]

The existence of Judaism's Mishnah supports the idea that Christianity originally contained two separate traditions, two equally valid and complementary sets of teachings. Judaism also contained twin traditions in the first centuries of the church; Rabbinical Judaism has always held that the books of the Old Testament were transmitted alongside an equally important oral tradition, a second set of teachings that supplemented the written scriptures. According to rabbinic sources, this Oral Law was given to Moses at Mount Sinai and passed down from generation to generation. For centuries, it had been forbidden to put the Oral Law in writing because it was thought that any writing would be incomplete and subject to misinterpretation. But amid the political tumult of the second century, concerns arose that the Oral Law might be lost, so the ancient restriction against committing it to print was lifted.

Rabbi Judah HaNasi, the eventual compiler of the Oral Law, was born shortly after Israel's disastrous Bar Kochba revolt of 135 A.D., growing up in a devastated and defeated land with its cities in ruins and a pagan temple standing on the site of the destroyed Jewish temple. With Jews banned from even entering the holy city of Jerusalem and the center of Jewish culture shifting more and more toward the Diaspora, the preservation of Judaism's ancient traditions seemed in grave danger. Compiled by HaNasi around the year 200 A.D., the Mishnah records Judaic Oral Law during the first centuries of the church, throwing great light on Jewish thought during that era. In much the same way that the Gospel of Thomas records Jesus' secret oral teachings, the Mishnah records Judaism's oral teachings. In the same general era, then, the secret oral traditions of both Judaism and Christianity were committed to writing.

Jesus said, "A . . . person owned a vineyard and rented it to some farmers, so they could work it and he could collect its crop from them. He sent his slave so the farmers would give him the vineyard's crop. They grabbed him, beat him, and almost killed him, and the slave returned and told his master.

"His master said, 'Perhaps he didn't know them.'

"He sent another slave, and the farmers beat that one as well. Then the master sent his son and said, 'Perhaps they'll show my son some respect.'

"Because the farmers knew that he was the heir to the vineyard, they grabbed him and killed him. Anyone here with two ears had better listen!" (*The Gospel of Thomas* 65)

As we have seen, grapes provide a useful metaphor for a person's string of past lives. And much like a farmer, the conscious spirit plants the seeds of its ideas in the ground of its own unconscious soul, which grows and develops and brings forth the fruit of those ideas. If one's conscious ideas and choices in life are good and nourished well, one's unconscious is enriched by them, growing full and sweet, bringing one much inner joy. But if those ideas and choices are evil, the soul they form is hard and bitter.

In this parable, these farmers are merely renters; the crop they grow belongs not to them, but to their landlord, just as the souls we form and build during our lives (our identities, memories, and personalities) do not really belong to us, but to our Maker. In this saying, the farmers did not want their lives' fruit to be delivered up to the landlord and tried to prevent that from happening by violently turning his messengers away whenever they came calling. In much the same way, when God sends His own messengers—thoughts, feelings, and insights—into our minds, we often respond with extreme prejudice, violently attacking and rejecting them. If we were to embrace those messages instead of turning them so discourteously away, they would guide us toward making the healthy choices and decisions in life that would ultimately result in our souls reaching God's kingdom. Those messengers would have succeeded in delivering the renters' crop to the landlord.

This parable warns us that just as those messengers are sent to us, so too will Jesus enter our lives, by way of the thoughts and feelings spontaneously arising and circulating in our own minds. This parable symbolizes the rejection and turning away of those messages with the image of slave messengers who are beaten up and turned away. The parable meaningfully distinguishes, however, between those slave messengers who are merely beaten up, and another sort of messenger, symbolized in this parable by the vineyard owner's son, who is actually killed. In the context of Christianity, of course, this son must be recognized as Jesus Himself, which leaves the parable ending on a truly ominous note. It suggests that when we persistently reject these messages, we effectively "murder" (permanently extinguish) Jesus' voice within our souls, turning down the volume on these messages so much that we don't ever hear them in our minds again. This is precisely what occurs in criminals and sociopaths who have gotten so good at ignoring the voice of their own consciences that they no longer seem to have any conscience at all.

Emphasizing the gravity of this possibility with the words "Anyone here with two ears had better listen!" the Gospel of Thomas warns in this passage that it is possible for people to permanently block out the voice of God in their hearts, virtually guaranteeing their soul division at death.

Jesus said, "Show me the stone the builders rejected. That one is the cornerstone." (The Gospel of Thomas 66)

This quotation from the Old Testament (Ps. 118:22) is unquestionably authentic. Besides the Gospel of Thomas, it is found in Matthew, Mark, Luke, Acts, and 1 Peter.[61] The binary soul doctrine, of course, would identify that rejected cornerstone as the unconscious soul itself.

With its memory, personal identity, and sense of right and wrong, the unconscious soul was originally intended to be the very foundation of the self. People were meant always to recall their past choices and experiences, so they could enjoy a permanent, continuous, and incorruptible sense of self-identity. That grand design, however, was circumvented in Eden. In the event called the Fall of Man, the natural checks and balances of the system were overridden, allowing great evil to be done. When the conscious spirit[62] chose to violate its covenant with its partner, disassociating from the unconscious soul[63] in Eden, it caused a whole universe of division and corruption to come into existence. Generations upon generations of selves (souls) were created and later abandoned to hell because of that betrayal, while their conscious spirits reincarnated again and again, free as a lark, suffering nothing but memory loss from that lie. Still, memory loss was punishment enough. Humanity became trapped in a prison of self-alienation and forgetfulness, doomed to revisit the same unsuccessful behaviors lifetime after lifetime:

From that fate came forth every sin and injustice and blasphemy and the chain of forgetfulness and ignorance and every difficult command and serious sins and great fear. And thus the whole creation was made blind . . . And because of the chain of forgetfulness their sins were hidden. (The Secret Book of John 28:21–33)

Recall, however, that in the original biblical quote, the rejected cornerstone returns again, this time as the uppermost point of the whole building:

> The stone the builders rejected has become the capstone; the Lord has done this, and it is marvelous in our eyes. (Ps. 118:22–23)

As we will see in Saying 81, the Gospel of Thomas arrives at the same conclusion, expecting that same rejected unconscious soul to be given eventually the uppermost position in the kingdom of the psyche, ruling over the conscious spirit.

Jesus said, "Those who know all, but are lacking in themselves, are utterly lacking." (The Gospel of Thomas 67)

Jesus implies here that knowledge has no real value unless it can make a person completely whole again. No matter how much someone knows, no one can hope to comprehend the truth about oneself, one's universe, or one's God while still incomplete. This was a common theme in early Christian literature:

> Truly I say to you, no one will ever enter the kingdom of heaven at my bidding, but only because you yourselves are full. . . . Therefore I say to you, become full and leave no space within you empty. . . . Become filled, that you may not be in want. . . . he who has been filled, in turn, attains due perfection. (The Secret Book of James 2:30–4:14)

Jesus said, "Blessed are you when you are hated and persecuted; and no place will be found, wherever you have been persecuted." (The Gospel of Thomas 68)

This is the first of three back-to-back passages that sing the praises of those who willingly endure persecution. In the first, the source of this persecution is undefined, but in the second, it is shown to come from within our own being, and in the third, it is made clear that allowing this material to rise up within us is the key to our salvation.

When we allow the voice of our own conscience to speak openly in our mind, and take it to heart when it points out our sins and mistakes, enduring these self-criticisms keeps our minds healthy and balanced. But if we repress this inner voice, it just continues to attack and berate us on an unconscious level, slowly poisoning our self-esteem by flooding our psyche with barrages of self-hatred and self-contempt.

When we finally acknowledge our errors and allow ourselves to experience fully the painful disappointment we caused ourselves by betraying our highest ideals, the pressure, force, and charge of those criticisms are then completely released. As paradoxical as it sounds, enduring this inner persecution and self-hatred is a blessing. Once we have done so, the persecution itself disappears entirely, leaving behind nothing but a healthy mind that is finally at peace with itself. Our inner pain is transformed and our self-condemnation extinguished, no longer being found anywhere within us after that. Admitting our mistakes neutralizes those guilty feelings; once they are fully processed, they no longer have any place in us to hide, nowhere to call home, no foothold in our psyche from whence they can continue to throw out their poisonous barbs. Once we stop resisting our own mental content, the natural restorative processes of the psyche take over, flushing this inner persecution completely out of our systems.

Jesus said, "Blessed are those who have been persecuted within themselves; they are the ones who have truly come to know the Father. Blessed are those who go hungry so the stomach of the one in want may be filled." (The Gospel of Thomas 69)

Although this passage seems to have two parts, both relay the same message. In fact, it seems that all passages in the Gospel of Thomas follow this same general rule; no matter how many elements it may seem to have or how convoluted its text seems to be, each passage has but a single point to make. The first part of this passage revisits the theme of the previous passage, but then adds that such a baptism in grief and self-condemnation will provide authentic knowledge of God Himself. In effect, Thomas declares that a person who is psychologically whole and healthy will eventually become one with God. While the second part of this passage seems to take quite a different direction, it actually continues the same message. Being one with God, individuals will naturally feel deep brotherhood with their fellow humans and so will instinctively respond to the needs of others rather than selfishly putting their own interests first.

Jesus said, "When you bring forth what is within you, what you bring forth will save you. If you do not have that within you, what you do not bring forth will kill you." (The Gospel of Thomas 70)

While the previous passage celebrates our efforts to achieve integration, this one warns of the consequences of failing that endeavor. We must stop repressing psychological material within the unconscious soul, this passage insists, and bring this material forward into the light of our conscious minds. The stakes could not be higher. If we consciously experience and integrate this material, its psychological charge will be released and thereby neutralized, leaving us whole and healthy. But if we do *not* bring forth this material, it will cause disease and disharmony in our lives and eventually bring about our complete destruction when our soul and spirit divide at death.

In the context of reincarnation, Saying 70 seems to strongly promote the practice of past-life regression. Those early Christians who believed in reincarnation would naturally read this passage as a command to seek out their past-life souls and bring them forward as well. And indeed, it seems that many in the primitive church did read this passage in that context, as we will see in other early scriptures in chapter 6.

Jesus said, "I shall destroy this house, and no one will be able to build it." (The Gospel of Thomas 71)

What "house" is Jesus speaking about here? Being Jews, the earliest Christians would have known that the very first letter of the Hebrew Bible, the first letter of the first word of the first chapter of Genesis, is *bet*—the second letter of the Hebrew alphabet. In Hebrew, letters have their own meanings, and the meaning of the letter *bet* is "house" and what a house does and represents. A house divides inside from outside, and so this letter inherently suggests the division between what is inside and what is outside. This same idea of division is the primary theme of the Gospel of Thomas, and so the play of words in this passage probably would not have been overlooked by the Jews reading this early gospel. Being the second letter, *bet* implies duality and therefore division, but the parallels to the binary soul doctrine go far deeper than that.[64] The division implied by the symbolism of a house has much in common with the division between the conscious and unconscious in the human psyche.

In this saying, Jesus promises to destroy this "house," the dividing structure that separates the soul from the spirit, echoing similar statements in other early Christian scriptures: "For this reason faith came—it did away with the division" (The Gospel of Truth 34:29); and "He himself is our peace who has made the two one and has destroyed . . . the dividing wall of hostility" (Eph. 2:14–16).

With three early Christian scriptures emphasizing the same point again and again—the idea that Jesus' mission had something to do with ending a division between two elements by destroying a wall dividing them—it is clear that this idea held great meaning and currency in the theology of the earliest church.

> *A man said to him, "Tell my brothers to divide my father's possessions with me."*
> *He said to him, "O man, who has made me a divider?"*
> *He turned to his disciples and said to them, "I am not a divider, am I?" (The Gospel of Thomas 72)*

This saying seems to have been included in the Gospel of Thomas purely to help identify and further emphasize its primary theme: that division itself is the enemy, something to be avoided at all costs. Throughout Thomas' gospel, Jesus behaves as if division and duality are humanity's primary spiritual problems, presenting that same message in passage after passage.

> *Jesus said, "The crop is huge but the workers are few, so beg the harvest boss to dispatch workers to the fields." (The Gospel of Thomas 73)*

This is the last of five passages in the Gospel of Thomas[65] that refer to the harvest. In Christian symbolism, the theme of the harvest refers to Judgment Day, when all the world's dead are to be resurrected for a great reckoning. Appearing here in the Gospel of Thomas, this theme demonstrates that the theology in this work does *not* deny or ignore the primary theme of official Christianity, as some interpreters have suggested. The entire promise of the original church revolved around the idea of a coming Universal Resurrection. Jesus rose from the dead, and because He did it, we too could hope to beat death. Even though we might die, we could hope to live again. This theology has long been contrasted with the focus of the Gnostic Church, whose members sought instead to inherit the kingdom in their present life, *before* they died. Whereas the Jesus of the Gospel of Thomas taught His followers that they could and should aspire to reach the kingdom before they died, however, He also taught that the clock was ticking and the day of the harvest was approaching. Those who could not completely avoid death by satisfactorily "living in Him" in this life could still hope to be resurrected by virtue of faith alone at the Last Day.[66] The Gospel of Thomas may be the only extant church document that straddled this line, embracing and defending both positions.

In this passage, it is noted that there are many souls ready to be harvested, but not enough workers around to facilitate that harvest. As we saw in Saying 65, the "crop" to be harvested is humanity's unconscious souls, while those "farmers" who work the fields are humanity's conscious spirits. Since each conscious spirit has, presumably, reincarnated many times, each now possesses many unconscious souls hidden deeply away within itself. If so, it is true that a very large crop indeed now exists to be harvested. But unless those conscious spirits come down to earth and incarnate once again in physical bodies, their souls cannot be harvested. These souls can only be brought back from the dead, or reawakened, by reuniting with their original conscious spirits, and numerous BSD sources indicate that such a reunion can only occur in a physical body.[67] So in order for the harvest to occur, all of humanity's reincarnating spirits must return to incarnate in physical bodies on earth at the same point in history. Given this necessity, it is perhaps more than merely curious that the world is in the middle of a completely unprecedented population explosion.

He said, "Lord, there are many around the drinking trough, but no one is in the well." (The Gospel of Thomas 74)

This passage refers to two very different kinds of vessels. The first, a drinking trough, is a shallow vessel usually used by dumb animals and presumably contains standing water that is probably stale and possibly even filthy and fetid. A well, on the other hand, is deep, is only used by intelligent human beings, and contains fresh water. The trough stands right out in the open and is visible to all, while the well is hidden deep inside the earth. These two vessels, of course, symbolize the two branches of Original Christianity. Like the stagnant water in a drinking trough, the teaching of the Orthodox Church was fixed and unchanging and, although it had little depth, Thomas reports that the majority of people still gathered around that vessel. Meanwhile, the Gnostic Church's teaching, like the water in a well, was deeper, hidden, fresh (evolving), and life-giving, but far fewer people came to it. This passage says that no one could be found in the bottom of the well, which reminds us of Jesus' frustration that none of His followers ever fully understood His deeper teachings:

> Christ said this also: They that are with me have not understood me. (Acts of Peter 10:15)

> At first I spoke to you in parables and you did not understand. Now I speak to you openly, and you still do not perceive. (The Secret Book of James 7:2–6)

Indeed, if there was no one "in the well" as this passage suggests, it comes as no surprise that the Gnostic branch of the church fared more poorly than its orthodox brother as history progressed. Unfortunately, since the contents of troughs are only proper for beasts, this passage suggests that of the two, only the Gnostic Church was actually able to provide the living waters needed by the sons of men.

Jesus said, "Many are standing at the door, but it is the solitary who will enter the bridal chamber." (The Gospel of Thomas 75)

This passage again emphasizes the primary theme of the Gospel of Thomas, that achieving a state of unity, wholeness, and singleness is the only solution to humanity's spiritual dilemma. Here Jesus suggests that only those who have "made the two one," overcoming their inner divisions, self-contradictions, and self-betrayals to become a single, integrated self, will enter the kingdom of heaven. Those who are still two separate selves, continuing to receive conflicting messages from the left-brain conscious mind and the right-brain unconscious mind, will be unable to enter.

Jesus said, "The Father's kingdom is like a merchant who had a supply of merchandise and found a pearl. That merchant was prudent; he sold the merchandise and bought the single pearl for himself. So also with you, seek his treasure that is unfailing, that is enduring, where no moth comes to eat and no worm destroys." (The Gospel of Thomas 76)

The Father's kingdom is like a merchant, and so are we. Perpetually occupied with life's various trades, we are always exchanging this for that, trying to get the most we can in each transaction. Every choice we make is a trade of one kind or another. Every time we choose to acquire one thing, we have to give up something else in exchange. In order to get married, we have to give up the single life. In order to give our best to our careers, we may have to give up having a family (or vice versa). In order to take one job, we may have to give up another. Every choice carries its price and, like merchants always looking for the best deal, we spend our lives calculating those prices and choosing the trades that seem in our best interest.

The things we own in life are what we exchange in these trades. The least of these is our actual physical possessions; we also trade our interests, hopes, loves, memories, idiosyncrasies, careers, dreams, families, and even our very identities. But all of these things are taken away from us when we die, according to the binary soul doctrine. When our souls split apart from our spirits, everything is erased from our memories, leaving us to start again with a clean slate. Everything we struggled a lifetime to acquire, everything we fought to learn both about ourselves and our world is wiped away, leaving us to stumble blindly up that craggy mountain all over again.

In this passage, Jesus tells us that there is one trade we can make that is unlike all others. Something altogether extraordinary exists, an available treasure entirely unlike anything else we might spend our lives trying to acquire, only to give up at death. This treasure is described as a "single" unity, as whole, complete, and indivisible as a pearl. If we manage to acquire this treasure of unity and wholeness before we die, it can never be taken from us afterward. Unlike everything else we toil to acquire in life, this one treasure is not temporary. The catch is, however, that we have to trade away everything else we possess in order to acquire this treasure.[68] It is only by valuing this treasure above all else in our lives that we will find it.

> *Jesus said, "I am the light that is over all things. I am all: from me all came forth, and to me all attained. Split a piece of wood; I am there. Lift up the stone, and you will find me there." (The Gospel of Thomas 77)*

The original Christians were convinced that Jesus had managed to envelop the whole of creation within Himself. We see this report both here in the Gospel of Thomas, and also in the New Testament: "He who descended is the very one who ascended higher than all the heavens, in order to fill the whole universe" (Eph. 4:10).

The careful reader will note that Ephesians 4:10 does not say that, like "God the Father," Jesus *always* had the entire universe within Himself. Although Acts 17:28 suggests that the whole of creation has always "lived and moved and had its being" inside of God the Father, this was apparently not always the case for Jesus as well. Instead, it would seem from the text of Ephesians 4:10 that there was a time when Jesus did not yet "fill the whole universe," and He intentionally did something "in order to" change that. This passage suggests that Jesus personally evolved and changed over time, a teaching that the early church fought furiously over and which the official church ultimately condemned at Nicaea.

Nonetheless, with Jesus' soul within our own souls, and with Jesus' soul also simultaneously present within every other particle and fragment of reality as well, the full promise and miraculous potential of the message in the Gospel of Thomas that "the kingdom is inside of you, and it is outside of you" can finally begin to be appreciated.

> *Jesus said, "Why have you come out to the countryside? To see a reed shaken by the wind? And to see a person dressed in soft clothes, like your rulers and your powerful ones? They are dressed in soft clothes, and they cannot understand truth." (The Gospel of Thomas 78)*

The people streaming into the countryside to see John the Baptist were surprised at his appearance. They expected him to be soft and weak, traits Jesus condemns here as belonging to the ruling class. The BSD explains why Jesus made a special point of condemning these traits. Humankind's whole problem, according to the binary soul doctrine, is that we have sacrificed truth for personal comfort, and this has made us very weak indeed. Instead of suffering the pains of our own conscience, we repress those unpleasant thoughts and feelings, choosing our immediate comfort over our integrity and wholeness. But this tactic has backfired on us, rendering us weak and vulnerable. Our minds are now self-programmed to avoid the pain of this inner criticism at all costs, which causes us to sacrifice continually more and more pieces of ourselves, nullifying more and more of our inherent strength, potential, and potency.

> *A woman in the crowd said to him, "Blessed are the womb that bore you and the breasts that fed you."*
>
> *He said to her, "Blessed are those who have heard the word of the Father and have truly kept it. For there will be days when you will say, 'Blessed are the womb that has not conceived and the breasts that have not given milk.'" (The Gospel of Thomas 79)*

In Jesus' era, conventional Jewish thought associated having children with good fortune; if a married couple gave birth to children, they were considered blessed by God. But in this saying, Jesus turns that belief on its head by suggesting that those *without* children will eventually be recognized as the more truly blessed. Both those who have kept the word of the Lord and those who have remained childless are "blessed" in this passage, suggesting that those who keep God's word will not have children. Of all the different ways Jesus reversed traditional Jewish perspectives, none could have possibly seemed more radically alien than this teaching. Nonetheless, it was not without precedent; in fact, this connection between blessedness and barrenness was an ongoing theme in both the Old Testament and the lost scriptures of the Christian Gnostics.

The spiritually perfect have long been characterized as unable to produce offspring; even Osiris, the legendary savior of ancient Egypt, was depicted without any genitals. When he died, according to legend, Osiris was violently ripped into pieces; but when those pieces were eventually reunited, he found himself restored to eternal life, becoming a symbol of spiritual perfection that inspired the Egyptian people for thousands of years. His phallus was never returned to him, however, and this detail is very telling. Although Osiris was a classic BSD symbol of the wholeness needed to acquire eternal life, he lacked the ability to sire offspring after being restored to wholeness, and his missing phallus reflects that inability.[69]

The same theme is also preserved in some of the oldest biblical traditions. Those very patriarchs said to possess God's blessing paradoxically found themselves unable to have children. Adam and Eve, Abraham and Sarah, Isaac and Rebekah, and Jacob and Rachel were all mysteriously barren at first, which is just the opposite of what one would expect for people blessed by God. In fact, it was only after each of these couples sinned, and so presumably *lost* God's blessing, that they finally had children.[70] The consistency of this pattern in the lives of the patriarchs suggests that this recurring barrenness is a symbolic message that those enjoying God's blessing will *always* be barren.

This theme appears not only in the Gospel of Thomas, but also in other early Christian scriptures:

> The heavenly man has many more sons than the earthly man. If the sons of Adam are many, although they die, how much more the sons of the perfect man, they who do not die but are always begotten. The father makes a son, and the son does not have the power to make a son. For he who has been begotten has not the power to beget, but the son gets brothers for himself, not sons. (The Gospel of Philip 58:17–26)

Traditional biblical scholarship has never been able to explain this mysterious connection between holiness and barrenness, but the binary soul doctrine does. Those who are perfect and whole, those who live in God's grace, do not divide at death and so never reincarnate as independent and alienated generations of themselves. With no memory loss, the continuity of self-awareness is not broken, and so no generation gap arises between one's past, present, and future incarnations. When memory is retained between incarnations, one does not create a later "generation," but merely other selves of equal rank and value. Such people produce no spiritual offspring, just as the legend of Osiris, the tales of the biblical patriarchs, and the Gospels of Thomas and Philip all report.

Those of us who have not yet overcome our divisions, however, do produce these alienated generations of ourselves when we reincarnate. Just as the early church once taught, it indeed is through sin that we create "children" for ourselves. Our own self-betrayals cause us to reincarnate without memory, creating our own alienated spiritual offspring. This insight seems to have been misunderstood by the Orthodox Church, which taught that the physical sex act of one's biological parents was itself sin, and thus that all people are brought into this world through sin. The second and third century Acts of John, Acts of Paul, Acts of Peter, Acts of Andrew, and Acts of Thomas all "took sexual continence to be an essential feature, or sometimes indeed the essential content, of the Christian message."[71] The BSD suggests, however, that it was not the errors of our parents that brought us into this world, but our *own* errors. The original insight behind that corrupted tradition, that our *own* past sins caused our current amnesiac incarnations, was buried and forgotten when the Orthodox Church decided to eliminate all references to reincarnation from its legacy. The original church, as it turns out, was not antisex at all, even though later authors certainly made it seem that way. It is only through the rediscovery of these lost texts that the original vision in those ancient teachings can again be appreciated.

Jesus said, "Whoever has come to know the world has discovered the body, and whoever has discovered the body, of that one the world is not worthy." (The Gospel of Thomas 80)

This passage is identical to Saying 56, except it exchanges the word "body" for the word "carcass." Just as Jesus declared the physical world to be devoid of value in Saying 56, He likewise dismisses the worth of the physical human body here as well. In fact, throughout the Gospel of Thomas, He consistently denies any substantial value to the body, also declaring it to be a worthless poverty in Saying 29. In both Sayings 21 and 37, He implies that willingness to discard the physical body is necessary to finding the kingdom, and in Saying 36, he advises us not to worry about what bodies we have, assuring us that God will provide whatever we need. And in Sayings 87 and 112, Jesus specifically warns us not to rest our hopes on the physical body.

This theme, undoubtedly an authentic element of early Christianity, came to be interpreted almost entirely as antisex by the official church. But in these early Christian passages from the Gospel of Thomas, we find no reference to sex whatsoever, suggesting that the official church's interpretation was incorrect.

The binary soul doctrine suggests that these teachings were, instead, a corrective reaction to inaccurate expectations about the promised Universal Resurrection. Although the resurrection of the dead could only occur in physical bodies, the acquisition of those bodies was not in and of itself the primary goal of that resurrection. Since soul and spirit were originally separated while still in the flesh, they can only be reunited in the flesh.[72] But once that reunion was accomplished, they would not necessarily have any further need for the flesh. In short, Jesus was telling His followers not to pin their hopes for eternal life on the physical body they would reacquire at their resurrection, a warning also given in later Gnostic works:

> Some are afraid lest they rise naked. Because of this they wish to rise in the flesh, and they do not know that it is those who wear the flesh who are naked. . . . I find fault with the others who say that it will not rise. Then both of them are at fault. You say that the flesh will not rise. But . . . it is necessary to rise in this flesh, since everything exists in it. (The Gospel of Philip 56:26–57:19)

As Jesus makes clear in the Gospel of Thomas, the physical human body is a great poverty and, as such, its simple reacquisition cannot be the ultimate goal of the resurrection. As the BSD makes clear, reacquiring that body is not the end, but merely our means to a far more important end: restoring the original wholeness of the self.

Jesus said, "Let the one who has become wealthy reign, and let the one who has power renounce." (The Gospel of Thomas 81)

This passage refers to two elements, one that currently does not hold power but ought to, and another that does have power but ought to give it up. Ever since the Fall of Man, the spirit has used the power of free will to repress the unconscious soul, thus maintaining control over the kingdom of the self. The soul, however, has recently (relatively speaking) enjoyed a change of fortune, becoming rich, thanks to the fact that Jesus' own soul bonded with it at the time of His Resurrection. Thanks to that new development in the organizational structure of the human psyche, the soul is now in a better position to control and direct the overall functioning of the psyche.

This revolutionary transfer of power within God's creation will occur; Jesus' Resurrection made that a certainty. The only question is how and when. Each individual can allow this inner transfer of power to proceed gently and gracefully over time, or the inner transfer will occur abruptly and violently on Judgment Day.

Jesus said, "He who is near me is near the fire, and he who is far from me is far from the kingdom." (The Gospel of Thomas 82)

This passage carries the same meaning as Sayings 58 and 69. Although the messages from our souls are often painful and self-critical, they must be accepted and embraced as corrective input that our Creator designed our souls to generate for us.[73] A similar sentiment is also found in another Gnostic scripture: "Accept correction from me and save yourselves" (The Secret Book of James).

If, however, we reject this psychologically painful guidance, we cannot hope to find heaven or enjoy eternal life. In order to grow close to Jesus, one must be willing to accept and embrace the input from one's own soul, for to reject the one is to reject the Other as well.

Jesus said, "Images are visible to people, but the light within them is hidden. The image of the Father's light will be disclosed, but His image will be hidden by His light." (The Gospel of Thomas 83)

God and Man, according to the Gospel of Thomas, both contain a duality within themselves. In this passage, the text refers to God's duality as "image and light." The unconscious soul was often referred to as one's "image" in ancient religious scriptures because it contains all one's personal memories, including one's entire self-image. Similarly, the conscious spirit was frequently associated with "light" in religious literature because it contains both the light of conscious awareness and the spark of life.

While both God and Man possess this duality within themselves, the Gospel of Thomas suggests in this passage that people experience their own duality differently from God's. For example, when people discover their own past-life souls via past-life regression, they usually encounter at first what seems to be an inert image. They see the image but not the light. The past-life soul seems to have an intact identity and memory but not independent will or autonomous consciousness. Not currently making new decisions or actively asserting its will, it seems to be nothing more than a dead recording at first, an inert memory. Via the slow process of past-life integration, these old selves can begin to reanimate themselves in a person's mind, functioning again as living, revitalized, dynamic beings.

When one encounters God, the Gospel of Thomas suggests in this passage, the exact opposite dynamic occurs. In *that* encounter, one is confronted *first* with His light (i.e., the commanding power of God's free will intent), while His image, His personality and sense of self-identity, hides in the background, invisible behind the blinding display of His light. In other words, when you meet God, at first you don't get to see Who He Is as much as you get to find out What He Wants.

> *Jesus said, "When you see your image, you rejoice. But when you see your images which came into being before you, and which neither die nor become manifest, how much you will have to bear!" (The Gospel of Thomas 84)*

More evidence that Original Christianity not only believed in preexistence but subscribed to an unorthodox version of reincarnation, this passage discusses the continuing existence and activity of past-life souls in one's psyche. While we have a current self-image (soul) in this life, Jesus taught that we also possess others from our past, which came into being long before this life and still live (exist and function) within us but don't manifest themselves. The binary soul doctrine says the same thing. Jesus makes the eschatological prediction that we will find ourselves confronted with a number of those past-life selves one day, which He describes as a traumatic and challenging event. This, of course, also ties in with the binary soul doctrine's expectation that our past-life souls will be resurrected inside our conscious minds on Judgment Day.

> *Jesus said, "Adam came from great power and great wealth, but he was not worthy of you. For had he been worthy, he would not have tasted death." (The Gospel of Thomas 85)*

The last line here reminds us of the first passage in the Gospel of Thomas, which promised that if we discovered the meaning of Thomas' Gospel, we would not taste death. This is one of just a very few passages in the text that harken back to the Old Testament, and here it points to the Old Testament's promise that those who were perfect would not die. In the Old Testament, people were thought capable of living forever, and it was considered their own fault if they did not: "All . . . those who cannot keep themselves alive" (Ps. 22:29).

Enoch and Elijah are the only Old Testament examples of those perfect enough to "never taste death," but they are sufficient to demonstrate that Jesus' second promise, "those who live and believe in me will never die," was even in effect *prior* to His death and Resurrection. This is, again, dramatically different from His first promise, which simply guaranteed that if someone believed in Jesus, they would be resurrected at some future date after they had died. Enoch and Elijah never died at all. And what they did, Jesus taught, we can *all* do. This is the remarkable promise given by Jesus in John 11:26, the same promise the Gospel of Thomas and other Gnostic works focused on, the promise later ignored and denied by the official church: It was possible to reach the Kingdom of Heaven in *this* life, and those who did would *never* die.

This passage mentions a relationship between Adam and the people of Jesus' era. Adam died, the Gospel of Thomas maintains, because he had not been worthy of living on to see that later generation. Adam *could* have seen that later generation, the BSD suggests, if he hadn't violated his own integrity and caused his own soul division. He could have consciously reincarnated as a member of Jesus' generation, living among those people with his memory completely intact, knowing that he had been the "Adam" of the Bible. But he did not do this, the Gospel of Thomas declares, and the BSD explains why. Adam lost his memory at death because he betrayed his integrity. If he had not, his worthiness would have been so great he would have been able to incarnate again and again without any memory loss. Here again is the concept immortalized in Genesis, the *Epic of Gilgamesh,* and the legends of Egypt, all of which insist that a human being can live for many hundreds and even thousands of years.

> *Jesus said, "Foxes have their dens and birds have their nests, but human beings have no place to lay down and rest." (The Gospel of Thomas 86)*

This saying can also be translated ". . . but the Son of Man has no place to lay down and rest." Which of the two is the correct translation has long been argued, and both sides have their advocates. The binary soul doctrine suggests that in this case, however, the term in question refers to human beings in general rather than to Jesus Christ. If so, then this passage can be seen as continuing the theme that human beings cannot find anything of true value in this world. Unlike the natural animal world, humanity is fundamentally ill, spiritually divided. And as long as we remain in this crippling state of division, as long as the two halves of our being continue to war with each other within us, we will know no rest or comfort.

> *Jesus said, "How miserable is the body that depends on a body, and how miserable is the soul that depends on these two." (The Gospel of Thomas 87)*

In Saying 112, the Gospel of Thomas declares that the soul who depends on the flesh is damned, and Jesus seems to elaborate on that sentiment here, specifically condemning those whose happiness depends on the flesh. It is not surprising to find such sentiments in a gospel claiming to contain Christ's original teachings; in fact, it would have been more surprising if the subject had not come up. There can be little doubt that Christ specifically addressed sexual behavior; His brother James the Just, who ruled the fledgling church from 33 A.D. until about 62 A.D., was famous for remaining sexually abstinent all his life, and the apostle Paul also promoted lifelong chastity. Indeed, many second- and third-century apocryphal works put so much emphasis on the issue that it almost seemed the core message of the faith. According to this passage in the Gospel of Thomas, however, those later works missed the actual point Christ was trying to make. The Jesus speaking in this passage does not directly condemn sexual behavior itself, but simply the effect this instinct has on the human psyche. He merely condemns *depending* on sex, and the binary soul doctrine explains why He would be so concerned about this natural instinct. The soul whose happiness revolves around sex, according to the BSD, is only setting himself up for ruin. Those whose lives and thoughts revolve around sex will find themselves in a sorry state on the other side of death's door. The physical urges they spent so much time thinking about while alive will then be permanently hardwired into their thought patterns, and even though they will no longer be able to satisfy those physical desires, sex will remain all they can think about. Such souls will find themselves in a hellish state indeed after death, eternally focused on getting what is no longer available.

The Christ of this gospel recognized our sexual instinct to be one of the greatest challenges on the Christian path, and this has certainly proven to be the case in the centuries since the text was originally written. How many otherwise sincerely devoted Christian leaders have been tripped up by their inability to control their sexual behaviors? But even as powerful as this stumbling block has proven to be in our era, the issue would have been even more pronounced in Christ's day, when the average life span was so short that most people never outlived their peak hormonal years. In emphasizing the challenge of not letting ourselves be controlled by our sexual instincts, Christ anticipates Freudian psychology by almost 2,000 years. And while the scientific community no longer fully endorses Freud's theories about the sexual instinct being the underlying drive of all human behavior, the advertising industry seems to disagree, putting their money firmly behind the assumption that sex can be reliably used to manipulate behavior.

Jesus said, "The angels and the prophets will come to you and give you what belongs to you. You, in turn, give them what you have, and say to yourselves, 'When will they come and take what belongs to them?'" (The Gospel of Thomas 88)

As God's servants, angels and prophets do His work and act in His name. When we finally achieve soul-spirit integration and rediscover our authentic selves, God returns our past-life souls to us as our inheritance. In return, we will then be obligated to remain pure and undivided, no longer repressing any mental input from the unconscious soul, instead allowing its messages to flow naturally through us. Once we have achieved spiritual wholeness, we will no longer desire selfishly to keep any of this material for ourselves, wishing instead only that it move effortlessly through us, returning to the universe that spawned it. By giving it freely back to the universe, we avoid alienating and dividing ourselves anew. By emptying ourselves in this way, we are filled with the natural flow between our souls and spirits, discovering an unimaginably richer and more abundant existence.

Even after we have received our lost past-life selves and have learned how to live in harmony with our own souls, however, we will still long to be closer still to God, waiting for the day when our Creator will send for us and we will be taken up into paradise.

Jesus said, "Why do you wash the outside of the cup? Do you not realize that he who made the inside is the same one who made the outside?" (The Gospel of Thomas 89)

This passage is obviously related to Saying 22's statement that the king-dom can only be found by one who makes "the inside like the outside." In this passage's criticism of those who only concern themselves with the outer elements of the self and disregard the inner elements, Jesus makes it clear that the key to wholeness and integration is to clean that inner ele-ment as well, purging it of all its poisonous built-up repressed content.

> *Jesus said, "Come to me, for my yoke is comfortable and my lord-ship is gentle, and you will find rest for yourselves." (The Gospel of Thomas 90)*

A close parallel to Matthew 11:25–30, this passage demonstrates that the earliest teachings in Christianity included the classic religious concept of a "yoke" being essential for salvation. The word "yoke," of course, is related to the Hindu word *yoga*, both of which actually point to the same concept: joining or coupling two things together. The Greek term trans-lated in the Bible as "yoke" literally refers to the beam of a balance that connects the two sides of a scale. Of course, such a symbol fits in perfectly with the BSD's teaching that one's soul and spirit must be joined together in a perfectly balanced state in order to achieve salvation.

> *They said to him, "Tell us who you are so that we may believe in you."*
> *He said to them, "You examine the face of heaven and earth, but you have not come to know the one who is in your presence, and you do not know how to examine the present moment." (The Gospel of Thomas 91)*

This passage has the same message as Saying 52. People spend their lives looking for truth in the universe outside their skin. But neither ancient scriptures and holy books, nor search into various scientific fields, nor other arenas, is able to answer the questions that drive them; none is able to fill the inner void.

Jesus' soul resides within our own, the Gospel of Thomas declares, and provides those who find it with an eye that sees true. This was a major theme in Original Christianity: "What you seek and search for, look, it is within you" (The Dialogue of the Savior 9:3); "Be on your guard that no one deceives you by saying 'Look over here!' or 'Look over there!' For the

Son of Man exists within you. Follow it! Those who search for it will find it" (The Gospel of Mary 4:3–6).

Those who have found Jesus within themselves, the Gospel of Thomas suggests, understand this world with a clarity, depth, and focus that no independent, external search can begin to match. But as long as we remain ignorant of the One Who resides within, we will continue to stumble around this world like blind men.

> *Jesus says: "Seek and you will find. But the things you asked me about in past times, and what I did not tell you in that day, now I am willing to tell you, but you do not seek them." (The Gospel of Thomas 92)*

Much like Saying 38, this passage indicates that His disciples had asked Him questions prior to His ministry. Given that Jesus is supposed not to have met His disciples prior to the beginning of His ministry in first-century Israel, this seems to say that they had dealings with one another prior to that period, in previous lives.

Jesus' soul now resides within our own, the Gospel of Thomas declares, a great resource that has been made available to us. If we seek His knowledge, wisdom, and guidance, we cannot help but find them, because they already exist within us. If, on the other hand, we still find ourselves stumbling around in this world, it is only because we have never asked for the guidance available to us.

> *"Don't give what is holy to dogs, for they might throw them upon the manure pile. Don't throw pearls [to] pigs, or they might . . . it. . . ." (The Gospel of Thomas 93)*

Although part of the text of this passage is missing in the Coptic manuscript, what remains is enough to determine that Jesus' original teachings, according to the Gospel of Thomas, included the principle that not all of Jesus' teachings were suitable to all people. This, of course, reinforces the long-held theory that the early Church possessed two separate and distinct sets of teachings. One set, of course, ultimately came to enjoy the favor of the political authorities, and so survived history; the other did not, until now.

> *Jesus said, "One who seeks will find, and for one who knocks it will be opened." (The Gospel of Thomas 94)*

This familiar biblical passage promises that the division between the soul and spirit is no longer insurmountable, that Jesus has built a dependable bridge between the two. The lines of inner communication have been reopened. If we seek the lost psychic material hidden within the deeper levels of our minds, we will find it. If we work to recall and repent our sins, we will not fail to remember them. If we pray for our integrity, wholeness, and unity, we will rediscover it. If we listen for the voice of Christ within, we will hear it.

> *Jesus said, "If you have money, don't lend it at interest. Rather, give it to someone from whom you won't get it back." (The Gospel of Thomas 95)*

Again and again, Jesus seems to denigrate the value of the material world in the Gospel of Thomas. Here He suggests we stop wasting our time being concerned about matters of no ultimate consequence. When we are able to cheerfully give away our money without hope or expectation of making a profit or even getting back our original capital, when we have rejected the apparent riches of this world, we will be ready for the true riches of the kingdom of God. Many early Christian scriptures taught this lesson: "When you leave behind the things that cannot follow you, then you will rest" (The Dialogue of the Savior 25:4).

To do this, we need first to foster the same attitude in the relationship between the soul and spirit. When the conscious mind is finally willing to engage in open exchanges with the unconscious soul, the interactive communication between them can become healthy and fully productive. As long as the conscious spirit continues to view every potential exchange between them as an opportunity either to profit or to minimize its losses, it will continue to restrict and repress the unconscious. Only when the spirit ceases to insist on controlling all the exchanges with its unconscious soul, and demonstrates a willingness to enter into a true partnership based on mutual respect and equality, will it find the rest and security for which it longs.

> *Jesus said, "The kingdom of the father is like a certain woman. She took a little leaven, concealed it in some dough, and made it into large loaves. Let him who has ears hear." (The Gospel of Thomas 96)*

This passage carries the same message as Sayings 47, 70, 76, and 108, reinforcing the idea that once one's soul bonds with Jesus' soul, that bond will then spread throughout one's entire system, automatically transforming, saving, and eventually resurrecting all one's past-life souls as well. Jesus is the "person who understands" of Saying 21 Who will make all the difference if He is "in one's midst," as well as the pearl of Saying 76 and the treasure of Saying 109; His presence and influence, if acquired, will save and transform all of one's being, from one end of one's personal history to the other.[74]

Jesus said, "The kingdom of the father is like a certain woman who was carrying a jar full of meal. While she was walking on the road, still some distance from home, the handle of the jar broke and the meal emptied out behind her on the road. She did not realize it; she had noticed no accident. When she reached her house, she set the jar down and found it empty." (The Gospel of Thomas 97)

Here we find yet more evidence that reincarnation was a key element of Jesus' original teachings. This saying warns that although we go through our lives assuming that we are safely carrying our valued possessions along with us, when we get to the end of our journey, we discover they are all gone. This is precisely how the BSD describes the memory loss that takes place in reincarnation. This passage indicates that this loss occurs continuously throughout our journey, although we don't realize what has been going on until the end. As we proceed through our lives, the binary soul doctrine maintains, we unknowingly repress some of our feelings, insights, and memories, with every passing year pushing away, rejecting, and disassociating a little more of our mental content. This constant habit of self-rejection and self-betrayal causes our souls and spirits to become ever more alienated as the years pass and, at the end of life, the final result of this habit becomes apparent when our souls and spirits divide completely, causing us to lose all our memories. This passage in the Gospel of Thomas is entirely in line with the BSD's teaching on gradual and ongoing soul loss and memory loss *during* life as well as *between* lives, both of which stand in sharp contrast with conventional teachings on reincarnation that do not acknowledge the occurrence of any memory loss during life, but only after death.

This saying stands as more evidence that Jesus focused on the significance of memory loss, and is strongly indicative of a pro-reincarnational theology. It is also worth noting that this passage indicates that the kingdom of God recognizes the occurrence of this memory loss, and, since so many other passages in the Gospel of Thomas associate the kingdom with wholeness and restoring what has been lost, it must be concluded that Jesus expected all these lost memories to be restored in the kingdom.

> *Jesus said, "The kingdom of the father is like a certain man who wanted to kill a powerful man. In his own house he drew his sword and stuck it into the wall, so that he would realize that his hand would be strong inwardly. Then he slew the powerful man." (The Gospel of Thomas 98)*

This passage is related to Saying 3, in which Jesus explained that the spiritual seeker would go through a period of astonishment before finally arriving at the kingdom. The "powerful man" in this passage seems to be a metaphor for the dividing wall between the soul and spirit. Spiritual seekers must destroy this wall before they can enter the kingdom, but since the wall is filled with all the repressed contents of their unconscious, they have an automatic reaction of fear and revulsion every time they contemplate approaching it. Discovering its existence, seekers consciously want to destroy this wall, but this automatic reaction makes them question their courage and ability to do so. But when seekers practice confronting their own repressed material a little at a time, they discover they are able to work their way through this barrier. Once they learn not to fear the wall, they attack it vigorously, integrating all the repressed material in their psyches. Destroying the wall, they thus also destroy their false self-image, that "powerful man" who had been created out of fear of the wall.

> *The disciples said to him, "Your brothers and your mother are standing outside."*
> *He said to them, "Those here who do what my Father wants are my brothers and my mother. They are the ones who will enter my Father's kingdom." (The Gospel of Thomas 99)*

Although this passage presents a hard teaching, it seems to reflect accurately realities under the binary soul doctrine. Continuing the revaluation of personal relationships He began in Saying 55 (and returns to again in Saying 101), Jesus emphasizes here that the only relationships that truly matter in life are those of the kingdom. Any relationships in our lives that are not consistent with wholeness, truth, and integrity, the BSD suggests, will disintegrate and cease to exist in the end. People who devote themselves to the lies and betrayals of dishonest relationships just end up losing their memories at the end of each life, and the loss of memory tends to undermine a person's relationships, as any amnesiac will testify. Ever the pragmatist, Jesus seems to encourage us not to waste our resources on relationships doomed to failure. Many relationships in this world, even between family members, can be built on dishonest foundations, and Jesus warns us that such relationships are not only a waste of our time because they won't survive our passing, but also because they increase our spiritual illness instead of our health.

In much the same way, our relationships with our own past-life selves seem slated to follow the same rule. We have no real relationship with them when we don't remember them. If we can recall them and reintegrate them into our psyche, we can build permanent relationships with our past selves. But as the Gospel of Thomas has made clear, that integration requires both our past and present souls first to be brought into the kingdom. This, again, explains why early Christianity originally strove to raise and baptize the dead.

The Bible, the Gospel of Thomas, and the BSD all declare the same hard truth: All who stand outside God's perfection, failing to reembrace their original wholeness and integrity, will eventually disappear as completely as if they never existed. While their living spirits will continue on, they will be as erased chalkboards; their souls, containing all their personalities, senses of identity, and memories of everything they've done and every relationship they've had, will not survive. As Paul warned in 1 Corinthians 3:14–15, while they themselves will survive the fiery restoration of Judgment Day, their "works" will not.

> *They showed Jesus a gold coin and said to him, "The Roman emperor's people demand taxes from us."*
> *He said to them, "Give the emperor what belongs to the emperor, give God what belongs to God, and give me what is mine." (The Gospel of Thomas 100)*

This passage is particularly interesting, for it depicts Jesus emphasizing a distinction between Himself and God, a concept the official church struggled hard to minimize. But the student of the binary soul doctrine will recognize something else in this passage—the familiar idea that a person possesses three different things that might eventually be divided up and sent off in three different directions. In the alternate version of this passage that appears in the Bible, the three-part division is revised into a two-part division, thus masking the original relevance and meaning of this passage.

The coins given to the emperor obviously represent the physical world and, by extension, one's physical body, which the Roman emperor could also claim to possess and take away if he chose. But what of the other two possessions? Jesus claims here that people possess something that belongs to Him but not to God, and something else that belongs to God but not to Jesus. This distinction makes no sense to conventional Christianity, but one's own spirit, of course, belongs to God, returning to Him after death, according to Ecclesiastes 12:7. One's soul, Jesus claims here, belongs not to oneself, but to Jesus.

> *Jesus said, "Whoever does not hate father and mother as I do cannot be my disciple, and whoever does not love father and mother as I do cannot be my disciple. For my mother . . . , but my true mother gave me life." (The Gospel of Thomas 101)*

Although the first part of this saying is a variation of Saying 55, Jesus distinguishes between two distinct sets of parents here, an earthly set and a heavenly set, and advises us to use two different ways of dealing with these two sets of parents. With two sets of parents and two sets of instructions, it seems clear that one set of instructions is meant be applied to one set of parents, and the other set of instructions to the other set of parents. The text is fragmentary, but the BSD suggests the missing words are "gave me mortality," or "gave me death," or something along those lines. Throughout the Gospel of Thomas, Jesus bemoans the emptiness of the physical world and the physical body, and this passage clearly contrasts that corrupt physical world with its more perfect spiritual counterpart.

In the teachings recorded in the Gospel of Thomas, Jesus attempted to reintroduce a controversial idea into Judaic theology: that the Creator God had an equal but opposite feminine counterpart, or, perhaps more accurately, the idea that what we think of as "God" is Itself a dynamically integrated pair of equal opposites. Although God possesses perfect whole-ness and unity, many ancient BSD cultures believed Him to be a unity that contains a duality within itself, a unity that has parts but is still greater than the sum of those parts. In the Old Testament, God's nature is described with the words "The Lord our God, the Lord is one." The word for "one" in this famous Hebrew passage is *echad*, which specifically refers to a com-pound unity, a whole made up of parts. A great many cultures' Creation legends describe the universe being created when a Primordial Being divided into two separate selves that then began interacting with one another (the Gnostics saw the Adam and Eve story as a variation on that theme). The two divine halves mated, and the world we know today is the fruit of that union. While there indeed was a divine Father, these cultures believed, there was also a divine Mother as well.

The microcosm is said to reflect the macrocosm. Atoms are shaped like solar systems. Hurricanes are shaped like galaxies. It was once even believed that man was shaped in God's image. BSD cultures held that, like human beings, God also possesses two distinct elements to His being, both a soul and a spirit, and Israel was once a member of an extensive fraternity of nations that believed this. Old Testament passages and archaeological finds both mention a female counterpart to the Hebrew God.[75] Indeed, the divine Mother is well represented in Judeo-Christian scripture, appear-ing in the Old Testament as Sophia, the divine personification of Wisdom Itself. In the New Testament, the divine feminine found a fresh new sym-bol in Mary, the "Mother of God."

God's masculine aspect seems to have been depicted in the Old Testament, whereas its counterpart held court in the New Testament. Like the conscious spirit, the Old Testament focused on left-brain issues like strength, order, justice, and the differences between people. The New Testament, on the other hand, was more oriented toward the opposite val-ues of the right-brain unconscious, such as love, faith, acceptance, forgive-ness, and the connections between people. It is appropriate that Jesus introduces the concept of the heavenly Mother in the Gospel of Thomas, for His entire ministry could be described as an effort to reintroduce the feminine aspect of the Godhead.

In Saying 101, Jesus says that His heavenly Mother gave Him His eter-nal life, a sentiment the BSD would agree with. Although the conscious spirit cannot die, the unconscious soul possesses memory, and without memory, no one would *know* they had eternal life, even when they did.

> *Jesus said, "Damn the Pharisees! They are like a dog sleeping in the cattle manger: the dog neither eats nor lets the cattle eat." (The Gospel of Thomas 102)*

In a passage similar to Saying 39, Jesus confirms that the Jewish religion already contained the secrets to the kingdom of heaven. He does not seem to believe He was introducing new teachings but was reinvigorating material already familiar to Israel's religious tradition. This does indeed seem to be so; the binary soul doctrine is readily apparent within the entire body of the Old Testament, as I demonstrated in both *The Division of Consciousness* and *The Lost Secret of Death*.

Hypocrisy is the one sin Jesus criticizes the most in early Christian scripture. Here, He condemns Israel's religious leaders, the Pharisees, for secretly doing the very opposite of what they publicly claim to do, inhibiting the religious development of the very people they are supposed to be serving.

> *Jesus said, "Blessed is the man who knows in which part the brigands are going to enter, that he may arise, muster his kingdom, and prepare himself before they enter." (The Gospel of Thomas 103)*

By leaving it unclear which "part" the robbers are going to enter, this passage has inspired modern commentators to speculate that it may refer to a certain place in the house, or perhaps a certain time of day. But the BSD makes it clear that the "part" in question is neither of these, but rather a part of the person being attacked: the unconscious. Jesus was a spiritual teacher and the invasion he warned of is a spiritual invasion. These invaders are not attacking our countries or homes, but our very souls.

The Coptic word translated here as "brigands" can also be translated as "rebels" or "robbers." These rebellious robbers are our own past-life souls who will reawaken en masse inside our psyches at Judgment Day unless we heal the dangerous ruptures inside our minds before these past-life selves are able to slip through and overpower us. By helping the reintegration of these lost pieces of our beings to occur in a safe and controlled manner, we can prevent an uncontrolled and chaotic invasion of our past-life souls and the catastrophic mental breakdown that would otherwise ensue.

They said to Jesus, "Come, let us pray and fast today."
Jesus said, "What sin have I committed, or how have I been
undone? Rather, when the groom leaves the bridal suite, then people
will have to fast and pray." (The Gospel of Thomas 104)

This passage seems to introduce a striking distinction between the Jesus of the Gospel of Thomas and the Jesus of the New Testament, but that distinction is an illusion. Thomas' Jesus claims that He has no need to fast or pray, while the New Testament portrays Jesus praying often. This apparent discrepancy, however, is merely the result of clumsy translation. The Bible translates seven very different Greek words all as "prayer." The Greek word *proseuchomai* alone accounts for 121 of the 166 times that some form of the word "prayer" appears in the New Testament. This word means "to worship attentively," and the Bible records Jesus doing this in at least 18 different verses. The Greek word *deesis,* however, which means "to beg, petition, or request," is also translated as "prayer" and, just as Thomas maintains in the passage cited here, the Bible does not report that Jesus indulged in *this* sort of "prayer" at all. In fact, the Bible's variation on this passage seems to specifically *deny* that Jesus or His disciples engaged in that sort of prayer:

> They said to him, "John's disciples often fast and pray [*deesis*], and so do the disciples of the Pharisees, but yours go on eating and drinking."
> Jesus answered, "Can you make the guests of the bridegroom fast while he is with them? But the time will come when the bridegroom will be taken from them; in those days they will fast." (Luke 5:33–35)

The beginning of this passage emphasizes something religions often overlook: that solutions are for problems. Religious practices are supposed to be the solution, or at least part of the solution, to humanity's problem. In the Gospel of Thomas, Jesus portrays Himself *as* that solution in its entirety, as uncompromised perfection and wholeness itself, the very perfection and wholeness that the whole of creation is searching for. And as such, He Himself has no need of any redemptive religious practices; having no problem, He has no use for any solutions. He contrasts His own needs (or lack thereof) with our own needs, however. While Jesus is with us, the Gospel of Thomas teaches, it is possible for us to share in His wholeness. If we take advantage of this opportunity, we will find that, like Him, we will then have no need for any other solution or redemptive religious practice. Just like that, our problem will be solved.

This passage begs the question "When *would* Jesus leave us?" Under what circumstances, in other words, would He become unavailable to us? The binary soul doctrine suggests that if we pass through death's door in a state of division, it will be too late then to ask for Jesus' help. The problem is not that Jesus would not be willing to respond to a request if we made one then, but that we will no longer even be capable of making such a request. Without the rational conscious mind, we will not possess the ability to comprehend our situation, nor the free will initiative to do anything about it even if we did understand it. With our minds ripped apart, we will no longer have the *presence of mind* to respond appropriately or creatively to any challenges or dilemmas. Instead, after the second death, our unconscious souls will automatically find themselves both "fasting" and "praying" just as the Gospel of Thomas predicts. Lacking the conscious spirit, they will indeed have to "fast," forced to do without everything the conscious spirit had previously provided them. And just like those who "pray" by mindlessly mumbling the same words and phrases over and over again, so too will our unconscious souls find themselves engaged in endless repetitive behaviors, automatically reviewing the same memories and retreading the same thoughts and emotions.

> *Jesus said, "Whoever knows the father and the mother will be called a son of a whore." (The Gospel of Thomas 105)*

Those who have found the kingdom of God within, rediscovering their own wholeness, must expect to be persecuted by the world, because their success is a direct threat to the whole world system. Healthy, spiritually integrated people behave in ways that conflict with the expectations of the divided. They seem a "peculiar people," standing out in ways the spiritually dead cannot tolerate. In the early church, those who embraced both these elements were said to "know" both mother and father:

> When we were Hebrews we were orphans and had only our mother, but when we became Christians we had both mother and father. (The Gospel of Philip 52: 21–24)

In a very real sense, integrity is the enemy of this world; a great many social and political systems would crash if everyone insisted on being completely honest and refused to compromise their principles. Feeling threatened whenever anyone chooses integrity over corruption, the whole system seems programmed to persecute such rebels wherever they are found.

> *Jesus said, "When you make the two one, you will become the sons of man, and when you say, 'Mountain, move away,' it will move away." (The Gospel of Thomas 106)*

Clearly related to Saying 46, this saying promises that those who successfully reunite and integrate their two halves will be made whole again, becoming a Christ rather than merely a Christian. They will find themselves filled with the omniscience and omnipotence exhibited by Jesus Christ Himself. This was a familiar theme in Original Christianity: "Anyone who has faith in me will do what I have been doing. He will do even greater things than these" (The Gospel of John 14:12); and "This person is no longer a Christian but a Christ" (The Gospel of Philip 67:25).

The salvation described here does not come from one's hopes for an eventual resurrection to wholeness at some future moment, but from a resurrection into wholeness in the present.

> *Jesus said, "The Father's kingdom is like a shepherd who had a hundred sheep. One of them, the largest, went astray. He left the ninety-nine and looked for the one until he found it. After he had toiled, he said to the sheep, 'I love you more than the ninety-nine.'" (The Gospel of Thomas 107)*

This familiar passage[76] seems to be a variation on Saying 8, the one about the big fish found among the catch of many fish. In both cases, the big find is preferred to the others, which are discarded or left behind. Here, however, one's past-life selves are symbolized as sheep instead of fish. Thanks to our multiple incarnations, we each have many of these selves, but each of them ends up getting tossed aside when we die. Of course, we only abandon these small selves because the biggest self, the original self, was lost, having "gone missing" long ago. When we finally find that biggest self again, we discover that we love it more than all the rest of them put together.

Jesus said, "He who will drink from my mouth will become like me. I myself shall become he, and those hidden will be revealed to him." (The Gospel of Thomas 108)

Here we find Jesus openly declaring what He only implied in Saying 61, where He seemed to have actually become Salome, taking her place on her couch and eating her food from her table. The BSD explains this dynamic. Due to the natural dynamics of the unconscious, if Jesus' soul were awakened inside one's own soul, the barriers and boundaries between the two souls would eventually dissolve, and they would, in time, indeed become one.[77] After this union, the two minds would be forever psychically connected, and each would partake of the experiences of the other. How is Jesus' soul resurrected within one's own mind? By first having faith that He is there, and then constantly requesting His guidance, perspective, and insights. To "drink from his mouth" in this way is to "live in Him," a phrase used both in the New Testament and also in the Gospel of Thomas.

This saying also indicates, as have other passages in Thomas' gospel, that if one first bonds with Jesus' soul in this way, all of one's long-lost past-life souls, "all those hidden," will subsequently be resurrected in one's mind without difficulty or complication.

Jesus said, "The kingdom is like a man who had a hidden treasure in his field without knowing it. And after he died, he left it to his son. The son did not know (about the treasure). He inherited the field and sold it. And the one who bought it went plowing and found the treasure. He began to lend money at interest to those he loved." (The Gospel of Thomas 109)

The binary soul doctrine suggests that Christ's soul was strewn throughout time and space at His Resurrection, mingling in the process with the unconscious souls of all humanity.[78] If so, this would have enabled Him to share in the psychological experience of every man, woman, and child throughout history. Discovering all our minds floating around inside His own, Jesus would have found Himself face to face with all our repressed soul pain, and sooner or later He would have realized the world-shaking potential of that discovery.

Everything we'd repressed inside our souls was essentially a debt we owed ourselves, a huge unpaid psychological obligation. We had gone through lifetime after lifetime piling up ever more psychological debt against ourselves that never went away, but just continued to accumulate, waiting to be paid off. This buried debt (buried treasure) was invisible to us, but in each new lifetime, we inherited all the debt from all our previous selves and then unknowingly added even more to it.

When Jesus looked into the depths of His psyche ("went plowing") after His Resurrection and discovered this debt, He would have realized He was now in the ultimate position of power. Everything we had collectively rejected, denied, ignored, and just plain refused to experience consciously inside our psyches, He was now in a position to influence. He was not only able to see into our minds, but also able to make subtle changes there as well. Before Jesus entered the picture, the relationship between each of us and our own soul debt had always been a completely private affair, but now a third party had become involved. Jesus could manipulate that buried material in our minds. He could nudge it, shift it, rock it, and, if He wanted to, completely expose it. He could help us continue to hold it back or He could activate it and release it. It was all up to Him. His new-found ability to influence the delicate balance in our minds could restore us to wholeness, or, if He preferred, cast us into mental chaos. He could release all of humanity's repressed pain, buried memories, and rejected insights if He wished, opening the floodgates to allow all of it to sweep through our minds.

Even though it was our psychological property, we had no say in the matter because we didn't even realize this material existed within us. Jesus was now in a position where He could reap what He had not sowed (Luke 19:21–22); He had not created the debt He now controlled, but now that He *was* in control of it, He could use it in any way He pleased. Archimedes, the discoverer of the lever, said that if he only had a place to stand, he could move the entire world. Jesus' Resurrection had given Him just such a place to stand. Finding His finger on the one stimulus to which we were most sure to respond, our own soul pain, Jesus had effectively become Lord and Master of the entire human species, able to lead us around as easily as a shepherd leads his sheep, and able to favor and assist whomever He pleased.

Jesus said, "Let one who has found the world, and has become wealthy, renounce the world." (The Gospel of Thomas 110)

As Saying 27 says, the kingdom can only be found by fasting from this world. A person who sees this world for what it truly is, Jesus says again and again in the Gospel of Thomas, recognizes it as an empty corpse of no inherent value. Everything in this world changes, dies, and disappears sooner or later, and grasping for such things is just grasping at empty air. Most people waste their entire lives grasping at illusions, only to find their hands empty. One thing of genuine and lasting value does exist, however, and those who discover that treasure will find themselves to be wealthy indeed. When we find this solitary white pearl, and contrast it with the black emptiness of the world, we will have no trouble rejecting the one and embracing the other.

> *Jesus said, "The heavens and the earth will roll up in your presence, and whoever is living from the living one will not see death."*
> *Does not Jesus say, "Those who have found themselves, of them the world is not worthy"? (The Gospel of Thomas 111)*

In the last 30 years, the world has received thousands of reports of near-death experiences (NDEs), consistently reporting a dark tunnel. Subjects commonly describe leaving their bodies only to find themselves caught up suddenly in what seems to be a swiftly moving tunnel. First the earth, and then all of space itself, seems to rush by them at incomprehensible speed, just as if it were rolling up like a scroll. After that, subjects often describe a wholly different experience in which they enter a realm of light bustling with activity and emotion. In *The Lost Secret of Death*, I explain how these two NDE phases suggest that the two halves of the human psyche are operating independently of each other during these experiences. The dark tunnel experience is exactly what one would expect the conscious mind to experience after it has separated from the unconscious, and the Realm of Light experience is just what one would expect the unconscious to experience if it is separated from the conscious.

In Saying 111, Jesus promises that it is possible to pass through the doors of death without suffering such a self-destructing division, but only if one is "living from the living one." This phrase reminds us once again of the two foundational promises of Original Christianity:

> Jesus said to her, "I am the resurrection and the life. He who believes in me will live, even though he dies; and whoever lives and believes in me will never die." (John 11:25–26)

Unlike the official church, which focused on the promise of resurrection through faith, this passage speaks of the far older promise of life through life, salvation through wholeness and perfection. If we restore our original integrity by fully embracing our own souls, we, at the same time, fully embrace Jesus, Who lives within each of our souls. Jesus Himself then lives in and through us and, as Saying 108 declared, the two individuals then merge together to become one Self.

Jesus said, "Damned is the flesh that depends on the soul. Damned is the soul that depends on the flesh." (The Gospel of Thomas 112)

The body *does* depend on the soul, and *is* damned. The body stops functioning and starts to disintegrate as soon as the soul leaves it at death, and since the soul's departure is inevitable, the physical body is essentially doomed right from birth.

The BSD indicates, however, that the soul who depends on the body is no less doomed. If a soul identifies too deeply with its physical body in life, that perspective will be permanently hardwired into its mental processes at death. The soul who was completely focused on bodily needs and physical pleasures during its life will find itself locked into an after-death mentality where it is always fretting about physical concerns it can no longer satisfy. Both the Gospel of Thomas and the BSD agree: All who worship their bodies in life, both those who abandon themselves to physical appetites as well as those who painstakingly craft their physiques into perfect physical specimens, are setting themselves up for ruin. When their bodies are taken away at death, their minds won't be able to adjust to the change.

His disciples said to him, "When will the kingdom come?"
Jesus said, "It will not come by looking outward for it. It will not be a matter of saying 'here it is' or 'there it is.' Rather, the kingdom of the father is spread out upon the earth, and men do not see it." (The Gospel of Thomas 113)

Again, the Gospel of Thomas explains that the kingdom of heaven is not something that won't exist until some future date, but something that exists now, in the present. When Jesus began His ministry by announcing that "The kingdom of heaven is at hand," the text suggests, He didn't mean that it was going to arrive in the near future, but that it was already here for the taking. This passage has the same message as Saying 3, which says that the kingdom is already inside us and outside us, and also Saying 41, which says that we are already exercising the powers of heaven in our lives, but just don't realize the dynamic that is taking place.

> *Simon Peter said to him, "Let Mary leave us, for women are not worthy of life."*
> *Jesus said, "I myself shall lead her in order to make her male, so that she too may become a living spirit resembling you males. For every woman who will make herself male will enter the kingdom of heaven."*
> *(The Gospel of Thomas 114)*

This passage has led many to suspect a sexist element to the Gospel of Thomas, but, as in so much else in this gospel, these terms are but metaphors for the two equal but opposite halves of the human psyche. The conscious spirit is often said to possess masculine qualities, and the unconscious soul has likewise been associated with feminine qualities. In later Gnostic scriptures, the male is directly associated with the spirit, and the female with the soul.[79]

Taken at face value, this passage is worse than meaningless, but seen as metaphor, its message falls right in line with the ancient binary soul doctrine. Can a woman be turned into a man? Physically? Perhaps today, with our advanced medical techniques. Certainly not in first-century Israel. But can something unconscious be made into something that is conscious? Yes, and this is not only Jesus' recipe for entering the kingdom of heaven, but it was also the recipe of the ancient Egyptians, Chinese, and others for surviving the death transition. And of course, it is also the recipe of modern psychology for a person becoming happy, healthy, and whole.

The classic sexual symbolism discussed earlier—"man" as a symbol for wholeness and unity and "woman" as a symbol for division—is also applicable here. Using those symbols, it is easy to see that this passage says the very same thing the rest of the Gospel of Thomas does, that the salvation Jesus proclaims can only be found by leaving a state of inner division and becoming united, integrated, and whole.

6

The Other Half of the Bible: Resurrection and Redemption in the Nag Hammadi Scriptures

For this reason, God came: to destroy the division.

—The Gospel of Truth

By the fourth century, the official church was burning books, demolishing meeting places, and terrorizing everyone associated with pagan art, religion, or philosophy. It burned Alexandria's library to the ground in 391 A.D., unconscionably destroying the greatest collection of wisdom literature in the ancient world. All potential rivals of the church were converted, exiled, or slaughtered, including neoplatonists, Jews, Gnostics, and all "heretical" Christian sects within the empire. By the time the fifth century rolled around, the Gnostic version of Christ's original message had been all but erased from human memory.

For the next 1,500 years, all that the world was taught about the Gnostics' beliefs was what the group responsible for their genocide saw fit to report. But that changed in 1945 when long-forgotten scriptures from the earliest years of Christianity were unearthed in a little town in Egypt. When these texts were finally published in 1978, a startling realization raced through Christian academia: The message of salvation that these mysterious Gnostics had once preached sounded an awful lot like modern psychology. In fact, the most famous Nag Hammadi passage, the Gospel of Thomas 70, seemed to be nothing less than an injunction to enter psychoanalysis! ("Jesus said, 'When you bring forth what is within you, what you bring forth will save you. If you do not have that within you, what you do not bring forth will kill you.'") And since it has long been known that the Gnostics believed in reincarnation, it seems they were concerned that humanity's immortal minds were suffering from some sort of sustained mental illness. Unfortunately, even though this same psychological undertone characterized the majority of texts found at Nag Hammadi, the specific theology of these works remained uncertain for many years after their publication.

A comparison of these scriptures with the ancient world's binary soul doctrine, however, has demonstrated a truly extraordinary fit. Of the 40 newly discovered early Christian texts in the Nag Hammadi library, 17 of them (The Gospel of Thomas, The Book of Thomas, The Gospel of Mary, The Gospel of Philip, The Gospel of Truth, The Secret Book of John, The Secret Book of James, The Tripartite Tractate, The Hymn of the Pearl, The Teachings of Silvanus, The Apocalypse of Adam, The Treatise on the Resurrection, The Dialogue of the Savior, The Second Apocalypse of James, The Revelation of Adam, The Exegesis on the Soul, and The Thunder, Perfect Mind) reflect the same theological perspective as the BSD. Together, these 17 works seem to have once constituted a formidable Gnostic counterpart to the official church's New Testament.

Gnostic Christianity has been accused of originally being a loose hodgepodge of eclectic and incompatible teachings whose only common denominator was their rejection by the official church. The fury with which the official church attacked its Gnostic counterpart belies that implied weakness, however. The ferocity of Rome's response to Gnosticism testifies to just how substantial a threat it was judged to be. The genocidal desperation the official church brought to bear against the Gnostics mirrors the terror the Gnostic movement inspired in the orthodox authorities. It was obviously viewed as a powerful and awesome adversary.

Furthermore, a comparison of these Nag Hammadi texts with the BSD demonstrates that claim of eclecticity to be untrue; the Gnostics were, in fact, united by a common theology far more sophisticated than that of the official church. The Gnostics developed and expounded on the story of Christian redemption—not introducing an alternate version of events, but providing a supplemental report that added greater depth to the biblical account, explaining many mysteries of the faith that the official church left unclear. Instead of disputing the orthodox vision of Christ's life, death, and Resurrection, it supported and enhanced that report. Instead of denying Christ's sacrificial gift, the Gnostics celebrated it as being even more magnificent than the official church suspected. Instead of refuting the Resurrection, it insisted that the salvation Christ provided was so perfect and complete that no waiting was required. The kingdom of heaven, they rejoiced, was *already* at hand for the true Christian! One didn't have to wait until the end of time to receive the resurrection Christ promised, these scriptures insisted, but could acquire and enjoy eternal life immediately.

These supplemental insights into the deeper mysteries of the faith were not for everyone, but had to be held in reserve for the exclusive few who demonstrated their readiness by perfecting and purifying themselves. As different as the two branches of early Christianity were, they agreed on one thing: The distinction between their two sets of teachings had to be maintained: "The knowledge of the secrets of the kingdom of heaven has been given to you, but not to them" (Matt. 13:11). "Take care not to recount this book to many—this which the Savior did not desire to recount to all . . ." (The Secret Book of James).

From the very beginning, the Gnostic branch of the church insisted on a clear line of demarcation between their two sets of teachings. As we read in chapter 2, Clement of Alexandria, Origen, and many other early church fathers held this same view; there was one set of teachings for novices in the faith, and quite another for the more advanced. The Gnostics seem to have viewed these two sets of teachings as complementary, each needing the other for its own completion. Each set of teachings was thought to be essential, but they were to be kept distinct from one another, presumably so the separate dignity of each could be preserved.

The Gnostics took great care not to share their teachings too openly or broadly, employing a variety of tactics to accomplish this goal. For one, they tried to make sure that they only shared their oral and written teachings with students who passed certain criteria. Many Gnostic groups only revealed their secret teachings to pupils after many years of initiation. Even so, these early Christians realized that anything they put down in writing was still liable to end up in the hands of people who were not prepared for that advanced level of revelation, so they also shrouded their works in a sort of literary obscurity. The closer their written discussion came to the central mystery of their faith, the more they relied on symbolism, metaphor, and allegory. This proved a very effective strategy. Those who were not already familiar with their underlying theological assumptions could study these scriptures as long as they wanted and still only gain a very murky sense of what was being said, often completely misunderstanding the author's true message. Even the most famous of the Nag Hammadi scriptures, the Gospel of Thomas, starts out with this premise; one had to know the central secret of the Gnostics' theology in advance in order to appreciate what their books were elaborating on. Without the depth provided by that all-important context, the texts of these scriptures remained inscrutable. In effect, these works were locked and needed a key.

That key, it now appears, was the binary soul doctrine. These Gnostic scriptures were utterly saturated with classic BSD themes like ignorance versus knowledge, forgetfulness versus memory, unconsciousness versus consciousness, emptiness versus fullness, incompleteness versus completeness, division versus wholeness, and so on. Duality, division, and double-mindedness are regularly and consistently condemned in the Nag Hammadi texts, while the virtues of wholeness, perfection, fullness, completion, and undividedness are brought up again and again, always being associated with divinity, redemption, and salvation.

Soul Duality at Nag Hammadi

These scriptures emphasize one point again and again. The spiritual being of humans has a binary structure, comprised of two equal but opposite elements (which were often, but not always, identified as the soul and the spirit), and the relationship between these two elements is the core issue of salvation:

> Man is a mixed formation and a mixed creation, and a deposit of the left and the right, and a spiritual word whose attention is divided between each of the two substances from which he takes his being.[1] (The Tripartite Tractate 106:19–25)
>
> The soul of Adam came into being by means of a breath. The partner of his soul is the spirit. (The Gospel of Philip 70:22–25)
>
> I saw myself; though we derived from one and the same, we were partially divided . . . I saw two beings, but there existed a single form in both, one single royal token consisting of two halves. (The Hymn of the Pearl 112:77–81)

I said to Him, Lord, how does he who sees the vision see it, through the soul or through the spirit? The Savior answered and said, He does not see through the soul nor through the spirit, but the mind between the two is what sees the vision. (The Gospel of Mary)

But before everything (else), know your birth. Know yourself, that is, from what substance you are, or from what race, or from what species. Understand that you have come into being from three races: from the earth [the physical], from the formed [the soul], and from the created [the spirit]. (The Teachings of Silvanus)

Without the soul the body does not sin, just as the soul is not saved without the spirit. But if the soul is saved when it is without evil, and if the spirit also is saved, then the body becomes sinless. For it is the spirit that animates the soul. (The Secret Book of James)

In many Gnostic scriptures, this duality was figuratively associated with the human sexes, and often with the legend of Adam and Eve:

Whereas in this world the union is one of husband with wife— a case of strength complemented by weakness—in the eternal realm, the form of the union is different, although we refer to them by the same names. (The Gospel of Philip 76:6–9)

Just as the Gnostics believed that each individual possessed body, soul, and spirit, so too they divided humanity into three classes: the Pneumatics, those in whom the spirit, or *pneuma*, was strongest; the Psychics, those in whom the soul, or *psyche*, was strongest; and the Hylics, those in whom the physical body was strongest.[2]

Death and Madness: The Wages of Sin at Nag Hammadi

Death did not exist, nor will it exist at the end. (The Teachings of Silvanus)

In the beginning of Creation, the Gnostics agreed, death did not exist. They believed death was the consequence of an error, a mistake that was introduced into the original perfection of the divine system. It was only after the primordial division of "Adam" and "Eve," symbols for the conscious spirit and unconscious soul, that death was introduced into human experience: "When Eve was still with Adam, death did not exist. When she was separated from him, death came into being" (The Gospel of Philip 68:22–26). "If the woman had not separated from the man, she should not die with the man. His separation became the beginning of death" (The Gospel of Philip 70:10–22).

This deadly division, however, was not actually blamed on third parties. The Christian Gnostics viewed "Adam" and "Eve" as symbols for elements within our own being. This mortal alienation was our own fault:

> Since you cast from yourself God, the holy Father, the true Life, the Spring of Life, therefore you have obtained death as a father and have acquired ignorance as a mother. They have robbed you of the true knowledge. (The Teachings of Silvanus)

The Gnostics viewed the division of Adam and Eve, not their subsequent expulsion from paradise, as the primary consequence of sin. They believed that the expulsion was just a consequence of their division. Splitting them did far more than usher death into the human experience, according to the Gnostics; it destroyed the original perfection and integrity of the minds of humans, causing a catastrophic memory loss that has been the source of all humankind's trouble ever since:

> Then God, the ruler of the aeons and the powers, divided us in wrath. Then we became two eternal realms. And the glory in our hearts left us, me and your mother Eve, along with the first knowledge that breathed within us. And glory fled from us . . . After those days the eternal knowledge of the God of truth withdrew from me and your mother Eve. Since that time we learned about dead things, like men. (The Apocalypse of Adam 64:21–31)

The Gnostics believed that this primordial amnesia stripped us of our rightful possessions: "He passed through those who had been stripped naked by forgetfulness . . ." (The Gospel of Truth 20:36).

Humanity had become, they believed, woefully incomplete. All our troubles in life could be traced back to this incompleteness, all because our rightful possessions had been scattered:

Where there is envy and strife, there is an incompleteness; but where there is unity, there is completeness. . . . now their works lie scattered. In time unity will make the spaces complete. By means of unity each one will understand itself. By means of knowledge it will purify itself from diversity to unity, devouring . . . death by life. (The Gospel of Truth)

We lacked possessions that were rightfully ours, and we needed to recover them in order to ensure our salvation: "The Father . . . knows the things that are yours, so that you may rest yourselves in them" (The Gospel of Truth).

These possessions were not merely things that we owned, but things that we had ourselves created, and then somehow lost. These possessions still secretly existed within us, yet we did not know how to find them:

That which came into being on your account, is it not yours? Does not that which is yours exist with you? Yet, while you are in this world, what is it that you lack? This is what you have been making every effort to learn. (The Treatise on the Resurrection)

Our amnesia and unconsciousness were our downfall: "End the sleep which weighs heavily upon you. Depart from the forgetfulness which fills you with darkness" (The Teachings of Silvanus).

Ignorance enslaved us, generating evil in our hearts and ultimately bringing about our deaths:

As for ourselves, let each one of us dig down after the root of evil which is within one, and let one pluck it out of one's heart from the root. It will be plucked out if we recognize it. But if we are ignorant of it, it takes root in us and produces its fruit in our heart. It masters us. We are its slaves. It takes us captive, to make us do what we do not want; and what we do want, we do not do. It is powerful because we have not recognized it. While it exists it is active. Ignorance is the mother of all evil. Ignorance will result in death. (The Gospel of Philip 83:19–32)

Blinding and enslaving the whole world, this forgetfulness was viewed as the sole cause of all human misfortune. The wheels of cause and effect that we set in motion in previous lives, the Gnostics believed, always came back again to direct the course of our later lives:

> From that fate have come all iniquity and injustice and blasphemy, the bondage of forgetfulness, and ignorance, and all burdensome orders, weighty sins, and great fears. And thus has all creation been blinded. . . . Because of this chain of forgetfulness, their sins have been hidden. They have been bound with dimensions, times, and seasons, with fate the master of all . . . In this way all creation was forever enslaved, from the beginning of the world until the present day. (The Secret Book of John)

Since these possessions we lost were memories, our own psychological data, the only way to restore them was through knowledge:

> They receive knowledge about themselves . . . If one has knowledge, he gets what belongs to him and draws it to himself. For he who is ignorant is deficient, and it is a great deficiency, since he lacks that which will make him perfect. . . . It is necessary for . . . each one to get the things which are his. (The Gospel of Truth 21:5–24)
>
> It is possible for you all to receive the Kingdom of Heaven [but] unless you receive it through knowledge, you will not be able to find it. (The Secret Book of James)

Jesus came to reverse this forgetfulness:

> That is the gospel of him whom they seek, which he has revealed to the perfect through the mercies of the Father as the hidden mystery, Jesus the Christ. Through him he enlightened those who were in darkness because of forgetfulness. (The Gospel of Truth)

This memory loss, the Gnostics believed, was not something that had merely occurred once, long ago, but something that was occurring continually. As long as we continued to jettison our memories at the end of each life, the Gnostics believed, humanity was condemned to make no progress, always finding ourselves right back where we started again at the beginning of each new life, wiped freshly clean of all memory and identity. Unable to retain any learning from one life to the next, we were unable to advance:

> An ass which turns a millstone did a hundred miles walking. When it was loosed, it found that it was still at the same place. There are men who make many journeys, but make no progress toward any destination. . . . In vain have the wretches labored. (The Gospel of Philip 63:13–22)

The Gnostics felt we betrayed our original knowledge, and that the unconsciousness within us was self-indulgent self-deception, insanity we willfully brought upon ourselves:

> This is why you get sick and die, for you love what deceives you. Anyone with a mind should use it to think! (The Gospel of Mary 3:7–9)
>
> They rejoice in the fire, and love madness and derangement, because they are fools. They pursue this derangement without realizing their madness. (The Book of Thomas 141:38–39)
>
> O you wretched! O you unfortunates! O you dissemblers of the truth! O you falsifiers of knowledge! . . . Do you even now dare to sleep, when it behooved you to be awake from the beginning, in order that the Kingdom of Heaven might receive you? (The Secret Book of James)

Afterlife Conceptions at Nag Hammadi

Believing in reincarnation, the Gnostics viewed the living not as being in danger of dying, but as individuals who had *already* died many deaths, and who desperately needed to correct those past catastrophes and find a way to avoid dying again: "And the Life died for you when he was powerless, so that through his death, he might give life to you who have died" (The Teachings of Silvanus). "They will find me and live, and they will not die again" (The Thunder, Perfect Mind).

The early Christians believed we had literally turned ourselves into tombs, places where our own dead were buried: "You were a temple, (but) you have made yourself a tomb" (The Teachings of Silvanus). "You hypocrites! You are like whitewashed tombs, which look beautiful on the outside but on the inside are full of dead men's bones and everything unclean" (The Gospel of Matthew 23:27).

Death was understood by the ancient Gnostics as bringing a dissolution or disintegration of the self, just as it was by so many other BSD cultures. This dissolution was viewed as the ultimate enemy of man and would defeat all but the most fortunate:

> Light and darkness, life and death, right and left, are brothers of one another. They are inseparable. Because of this neither are the good good, nor evil evil, nor is life life, nor death death. For this reason each one will dissolve into its earliest origin. But those who are exalted above the world are indissoluble, eternal. (The Gospel of Philip 53:15–23)

At death, these early Christians thought, our two halves are ripped apart; one half returns to God while the other half suffers eternal punishment:

> The flesh shall be judged together with the soul and the spirit, and the one part shall rest in heaven and the other part be punished everlastingly yet living. (The Epistle of the Apostles)

Even though the early Christians believed that human beings possessed both soul and spirit, only one of these was in danger after death; only the soul needed to be protected: "You are receiving the goal of your faith, the salvation of your souls" (1 Peter 1:9).

In the Book of Thomas, another work which stood alongside the Gospel of Thomas in the Thomas tradition, the classic BSD process of soul division is described without using the terms "soul" and "spirit." This work distinguishes between two different spiritual elements that human beings possess while they are alive: a visible part that can be seen (an object), and an invisible part that sees (a subject). These, of course, are elegant descriptions of the conscious and unconscious; the conscious left-brain spirit, the part of the human mind that is right out in the open and easiest for its owner to observe, has a more *objective* perspective, while the unconscious right-brain soul, the part of the human mind that is more hidden from view, has a more *subjective* perspective. At death, the Book of Thomas declares, these two elements divide:

> The visible parts of people will depart—their fleshly body will perish, and when it is dispersed it will come to reside among visible things that are seen. And then the visible fire will torment them because of the faithful lover they formerly possessed. They will be gathered back to the realm of the visible. Meanwhile, in the absence of their first lover the invisible parts who see will be ruined by concern for the present life and the scorching of the fire. Only a little while longer, and the visible parts will depart; then shapeless shades will emerge, and in the midst of tombs they will forever dwell upon the corpses in pain and corruption of soul. (The Book of Thomas 140:5–16)

Obviously discussing the subject of what happens after death ("their fleshly body will perish, and when it is dispersed . . ."), this brief passage manages to present a concise synopsis of the entire binary soul doctrine. Both the visible and invisible elements are described as suffering after they divide from one another at death, and in both cases this suffering is blamed on the loss of their partner. The conscious spirit, the "visible" part of the psyche we consciously perceive, departs at death because it has lost its other half, the "faithful lover" that had kept it company all through life. After departing, this "visible" half of the self eventually reincarnates into the physical realm, returning to the "visible realm." Meanwhile, the "invisible" part of a person, the unconscious soul, also suffers after death, and for the same reason—from the absence of the loving partner it had in life. Without that partner, it finds itself obsessing over its memories and emotions of its past life, "ruined by concern" for the life it just left. When one's visible part departs, then one's previously "invisible" soul emerges into view as a shapeless shade, eternally suffering its own inner pain and corruption. This pithy passage even places blame correctly; it identifies the invisible part that sees as having been a "faithful partner," but since the partnership is breaking up, the other partner must be the guilty party.

According to these Gnostic scriptures, even Jesus Himself had to suffer this division: "'My God, my God, why, O Lord, have you forsaken me?' It was on the cross that he said these words, for it was there that he was divided" (The Gospel of Philip 68:27–29).

This division was understood to destroy the self completely, dissolving it and "bringing it to naught." Much as in modern psychology, the ancient Gnostics seem to have understood the self to be an "emergent quality" created by the union of the two halves of the psyche. Thus death was the ultimate enemy, for it disintegrated that precious, all-important union. The body fell, the spirit fled, and the soul was left weakened and alone:

> When the time of dissolution arrives, the first power of darkness will come upon you. (The Dialogue of the Savior)
>
> [Jesus] said: Verily I say unto you, the resurrection of the flesh shall come to pass with the soul therein and the spirit. And we said unto him: Lord, is it then possible that that which is dissolved and brought to nought should become whole? . . . He said unto us: That which hath fallen shall rise again, and that which was lost shall be found, and that which was weak shall recover. (The Epistle of the Apostles)

Death turned our souls into fugitives and exiles, forcing them to abandon their rightful places alongside their living spirits:

> Why are you troubled when you oust yourselves of your own accord and depart from your city? Why do you abandon your dwelling place of your own accord, readying it for those who desire to dwell in it? O you exiles and fugitives! Woe to you, because you will be caught! (The Secret Book of James)
>
> He has turned many from error. He went before them to their own places, from which they departed when they erred. (The Gospel of Truth)

In further agreement with the BSD, the Gnostics also believed that the souls of the dead would lose their ability to reason logically after the dissolution of the second death: "It is not good for any man to fall into death. For a soul which has been found in death will be without reason" (The Teachings of Silvanus).

These early Christians believed that people are the authors of their own fate, in charge of their own fortune or misfortune in life and death. They did not believe that God judges our souls after death. Instead, they thought we judge ourselves, usually with harsh self-criticisms that imprison us. When we die, they believed, we finally confront and repent the choices we made in life, but that repentance is then too late, no longer able to bring us any benefit:

> No one will persecute you, nor will any one oppress you, other than you yourselves. (The Secret Book of James)
>
> He will not judge you for those things that you did, but will have mercy on you . . . But you have judged yourselves, and because of this you will remain in their fetters. You have oppressed yourselves, and you will repent, but you will not profit at all. (The Second Apocalypse of James 59:7–18)

Like the binary soul doctrine, the Gnostics believed that the pain suffered in hell is not intentionally inflicted by God, the devil, or any other outside agency, but instead is the natural consequence and experience of one's own inner nature: "They will be thrown down to the abyss and be afflicted by the torment of the bitterness of their evil nature" (The Book of Thomas 141:32–34).

Also agreeing with the BSD, the Gnostics taught that our unconscious souls find themselves confined in a deep dark place after soul division, unable to move or act, experiencing steady and unrelenting bitterness:

> [He will be cast] down to the abyss, and he will be imprisoned in a narrow dark place. Moreover, he can neither turn nor move on account of the great depth of Tartaros and the heavy bitterness of Hades that is steadfast . . . (The Book of Thomas 142:32–39)

While one part of our being is eternally imprisoned in this realm of the dead, the Gnostics believed that our other half could still reincarnate. Some not only believed in reincarnation, but also, like the Hindus, feared that we might even find ourselves being reborn as animals in our next lives:

> If you become horse or ass or bull or dog or sheep, or another of the animals which are outside or below, then neither human being nor spirit nor thought nor light will be able to love you. Neither those who belong above nor those who belong within will be able to rest in you, and you have no part in them. (The Gospel of Philip 79:6–12)

And so, again like Hinduism and Buddhism, these Gnostic Christians viewed future incarnations in the flesh as something best to be avoided:

> Watch and pray that you not come to be in the flesh, but rather that you come forth from the bondage of the bitterness of this life. (The Book of Thomas 145:8–10)

The Nag Hammadi authors painted the relationship between soul and spirit as absolutely crucial. Like the BSD, the Gnostics blamed the spirit for the soul's misfortunes, believing that the spirit's choices in life formed, developed, and defined the soul, but at the same time brought about the soul's doom at death, causing it to suffer imprisonment in the afterlife:

> Those who have gone astray, whom the spirit begets, usually go astray also because of the spirit. Thus, by one and the same breath, the fire blazes and is put out. (The Gospel of Philip)
>
> I said, "Master, where will their souls go when they leave the flesh?" He laughed and said . . . "The spirit lays a heavy burden on the soul, leads her into evil, and hurls her down into forgetfulness. After the soul leaves the body, she is [bound] with chains and throw[n] into prison." (The Secret Book of John)

Redemption at Nag Hammadi

> Redemption takes place in the bridal chamber. (The Gospel of Philip 70:26)

The Gnostics who wrote the Nag Hammadi scriptures did not believe, as the official church did, that Jesus' promise of salvation revolved exclusively around the delayed prospect of being resurrected at the Last Day. Instead, they believed that Christ had provided a far more perfect salvation that was *immediately* available. While their vision of God and His salvation was thus more glorious than that of their counterparts, it may have also been (from today's perspective, at least) somewhat less miraculous, as it did not necessitate the replication of their original earthly bodies.

Nonetheless, the Gnostic salvation was first and foremost a *restoration*. The Gnostics believed that everything people had lost psychologically and spiritually throughout all their many reincarnations, Jesus had made available to be immediately restored. The Gnostics of Nag Hammadi believed that their savior had *already* freed them from the revolving wheel of soul division, that, thanks to Him, their original identities and primordial integrity had *already* been restored. There was no need to wait until the end of time to witness or experience the salvation He provided. This more immediate salvation Jesus offered was a solution wrought of self-knowledge, and through the saving revelation He so graciously made available, all that had once gone wrong within each of us could finally be set right. To the Gnostics, Jesus' salvation was one of restored memory, identity, integrity, wholeness, and perfection.

More to the point, these early Christians believed that Christ had made it possible for each of us to reintegrate all the lost fragments of our eternal souls:

> I was crowned by God, by a living crown. My lord justified me. He is my sure salvation. He freed me from myself and [my own self-] condemnation. . . . He glorified me by kindness and lifted my thoughts to truth and showed me his way. I opened closed doors [within myself], shattered bars of iron. My own shackles melted. Nothing appeared closed because I was the door to everything. I freed slaves, left no man in bonds. I spread my knowledge and love and sowed my fruits in hearts and transformed them. I blessed them. They lived. I gathered them and saved them. They became the limbs of my body and I was their head. (Ode 17 of the Odes of Solomon)

> I have come to be acquainted with myself; I have collected myself from everywhere. I have not sown children for the ruler, but have eradicated its roots and collected the scattered members. If the soul is found to have produced a child, it is restrained below until it can get back its own offspring and return to itself. (Saint Epiphanius, quoting the Gospel According to Philip)

> I am the first who descended for my portion of what was left behind: the spirit in the soul. . . . And I went down to those who were mine from the first, and reached them and broke the first strands that enslaved them. Then everyone in me shone, and I made a pattern for those lights that are ineffably in me. (The Revelation of Adam)

Through Jesus, they believed, we can recover our lost souls, raise our dead, free our prisoners, and release our captives, thereby reclaiming our rightful inheritance as the children of God:

What the father possesses belongs to the son, and the son himself, so long as he is small, is not entrusted with what is his. But when he becomes a man, his father gives him all that he possesses. (The Gospel of Philip 60:2–6)

The Gnostics believed that once we reassembled all our lost parts, death would have no further power over us. But the Primordial Division between the human soul and spirit had to be fully overcome. Only after our two halves were reunited and the contents of the unconscious soul had been assimilated into the conscious spirit would we know true immortality:

When Eve was still with Adam, death did not exist. When she was separated from him, death came into being. If he enters again and attains his former self, death will be no more. (The Gospel of Philip 68:22–26)

Our dead selves had to reawaken *within* the present self, being resurrected through our present souls:

I said, Master, how can the soul become younger and return into its mother's womb, or into the human? [He said] this soul will be made to follow another [soul] in whom the living spirit dwells, and she is saved through that one. (The Secret Book of John)

Then when she [the soul] becomes young again, she will ascend, praising the father and her brother [the spirit], by whom she was rescued. Thus it is by being born again [reincarnated] that the soul will be saved. (The Exegesis on the Soul)

Not only was this inner work the true resurrection, according to the Gnostics, it was the duty of every true Christian:

Raise up those who wish to rise, and awaken those who sleep. (The Gospel of Truth 33:6)

Light the light within you. Do not extinguish it! . . . Raise your dead who have died, for they lived and have died for you. Give them life. They shall live again! . . . Knock on yourself as upon a door, and walk upon yourself as on a straight road. (The Teachings of Silvanus)

Now it is fitting that the soul regenerates herself and become again as she formerly was . . . so that she might be restored to the place where originally she had been. This is the resurrection from the dead. This is the ransom from captivity. This is the upward journey of ascent to heaven. (The Exegesis on the Soul)

This long-censored conception of the Christian salvation embraced and restored the whole of one's psychological and spiritual being, including all the long history of one's past lives and past selves. But there was a catch: One's restoration had to be absolutely perfect to achieve true salvation. No parts of one's psychological being could still be missing:

> He said on that day in the thanksgiving, "You who have joined the perfect light with the Holy Spirit, unite the angels with us also, the images." . . . No one will be able to go in to the king if he is naked [if he is not clothed with all his own past-life souls]. (The Gospel of Philip 58:11–17)
>
> Truly I say to you, no one ever will enter the Kingdom of Heaven if I bid him, but rather because you yourselves are full. . . . Therefore I say to you, become full and leave no place within you empty. . . . Those who are diminished, however, will not be saved. For fullness is good and diminution is bad. (The Secret Book of James)
>
> The All which we are, we are saved. We have received salvation from end to end. Let us think in this way! Let us comprehend in this way! (The Treatise on the Resurrection)

Although this emphasis on personal wholeness may seem an alien teaching to modern Christians, it should not, for the Bible also records that Jesus viewed perfect wholeness as a prerequisite for salvation: "Be ye therefore perfect, even as your Father which is in heaven is perfect" (Matt. 5:48).

The Greek word used in this passage, *thamîm*, is usually translated as "perfect," but it actually means "fully whole and complete": "Be perfectly whole and complete, as your Father in heaven is perfectly whole and complete" (Matt. 5:48).

By recovering all the memories of our past lives, we would not only learn of our past, but also gain a better understanding of the karmic forces currently in play in our lives, as well as the karmic forces that await us in our future: "He who is to have knowledge in this manner knows where he comes from and where he goes" (The Gospel of Truth 22:14–16).

When we reincarnate after each soul division, we automatically inherit all the dead souls from our past lives, unknowingly hosting their continuing dreams, desires, fears, and nightmares within our unconscious minds. Because the psychological barrier between the conscious and unconscious in our minds tends to leak, the hidden sickness, self-betrayal, and self-loathing of those lost souls eventually infect and corrupt our present minds as well, causing us in our turn to follow along their same doomed path of self-destruction. Through this inner psychological process, the sins of our past generations are revisited on their future generations again and again,[3] keeping us unknowingly imprisoned in a cyclical replay of self-destructive behaviors lifetime after lifetime:

> It will blind them . . . and burn their souls and become for them like a stake stuck in their heart which they can never dislodge. And like a bit in the mouth it leads them according to its own desire. . . . They fulfill the lusts of their fathers. (The Book of Thomas 140:25–31, 141:33)

By restoring these past-life souls to consciousness within us, however, the Gnostics believed we could correct those ancient imbalances in our psyches. Such a restoration would simultaneously resurrect and heal our own past dead, while also immunizing us against suffering the second death again in this present lifetime:

> Those who are heirs to the dead are themselves dead, and they inherit the dead. Those who are heirs to what is living are alive, and they are heirs to both what is living and the dead. The dead are heirs to nothing. For how can he who is dead inherit? If the dead inherit the living, the living won't die and the dead will live again. (The Gospel of Philip 52:7–15)

Surviving death was only thought possible by restoring this "disconnect" within our psyches, reestablishing communication between the two halves of our being: "These do not die, nor do they perish, for they knew their consorts" (The Dialogue of the Savior 125:14–15). This is only possible by "making the two one," by integrating our two halves so perfectly that they function together with a common purpose and effect:

> If both of the orders, those on the right and those on the left, are

brought together with one another by the thought which is set between them, which gives them their organization with each other, it happens that they both act with the same emulation of their deeds, with those of the right resembling those of the left and those of the left resembling those of the right. (The Tripartite Tractate 108:14–21)

The ultimate goal is to restore the original integrity and unity that our minds possessed before the Primordial Division: "For the end we receive a unitary existence just as the beginning . . . The restoration of that which used to be is a unity" (The Tripartite Tractate 132:21–25).

This restoration was made possible by Jesus' sacrifice, which He used to ransom the whole of humanity from the clutches of death:

> [Jesus] descended to the underworld. He released the children of death . . . And when all the powers had seen him, they fled so that he might bring you, wretched one, up from the abyss, and might die for you as a ransom for your sin. (The Teaching of Silvanus 104:11–14)
>
> He was to . . . ransom those who had fallen ignorant of the father. . . . He knew that his death would mean life for many. (The Gospel of Truth 16:38; 20:14)
>
> End the sleep which weighs heavy on you. Depart from the forgetfulness which fills you with darkness. If you were unable to do anything, I would not have said these things to you. But Christ came in order to give you this gift. (The Teaching of Silvanus 88:24–27)

Jesus was thought to have reversed the original division symbolized by the legend of Adam and Eve, thus reuniting all the souls and spirits that had been separated since that first division:

> If the woman had not separated from the man, she should not die with the man. His separation became the beginning of death. Because of this, Christ came to repair the separation, which was from the beginning, and again unite the two, and to give life to those who died as a result of the separation, and unite them. But the woman is united to her husband in the bridal chamber. Indeed, those who have united in the bridal chamber will no longer be separated. Thus Eve separated from Adam because she never united with him in the bridal chamber. (The Gospel of Philip 70:10–22)

This inner process relied upon Jesus, and could not be done independent of Him. At Jesus' Resurrection, the Gnostics seem to have thought that His soul swallowed up the whole universe, incorporating all the souls of humanity into Himself:

> He went before them to their own places, from which they departed when they erred. (The Gospel of Truth)
> He who descended is the very one who ascended higher than all the heavens, in order to fill the whole universe. (Eph. 4:10)
> The Savior swallowed up death . . . He transformed himself into an imperishable eternal realm and raised himself up, having swallowed the visible by the invisible, and he gave us the way of our immortality. (The Treatise on the Resurrection)

This effectively preserved all the souls of humanity's dead in their original condition:

> He retained their perfection in himself, giving it to them as a way to return to him and as a knowledge unique in perfection. (The Gospel of Truth)

The souls of all humanity were then inextricably interconnected with Jesus' soul:

> He discovered them in himself, and they discovered him in themselves. (The Gospel of Truth)
> On that day you will realize that I am in my Father, and you are in me, and I am in you. (The Gospel of John 14:20)

This union, the Gnostics believed, produced an experiential merging or blending of identity of His soul and the souls of all humanity since the beginning of time. He experienced our lives through our own eyes, learning exactly what it felt like to be each and every one of us: "How many likenesses did Christ take on because of you!" (The Teachings of Silvanus). "It was not only when he appeared that he voluntarily laid down his life, but he voluntarily laid down his life from the very day the world came into being" (The Gospel of Philip 53:6–10).

He would thus know, experience, and contain all the contents of our psyches, including all the repressed guilt and grief in our present-life souls as well as our past-life souls, none of which we allow ourselves to feel:

> He knows the things that are yours, so that you may rest yourselves in them. (The Gospel of Truth)
>
> Accept Christ, the narrow way. For he is oppressed and bears affliction for your sin. (The Teachings of Silvanus)
>
> This is the book which no one found possible to take, since it was reserved for him who will take it and be slain. No one was able to be manifest from those who believed in salvation as long as that book had not appeared. For this reason, the compassionate, faithful Jesus was patient in his sufferings until he took that book, since he knew that his death meant life for many. . . . For this reason Jesus appeared. He took that book as his own. (The Gospel of Truth)

One of the chief complaints the official church raised against the Gnostics was that they shifted the focus of the faith from a God-oriented religion to a self-oriented religion. These Nag Hammadi scriptures, however, reveal those criticisms to have been unfounded. These early Christians still sought God, in the person of Jesus, just as the official church did, and were every bit as passionate about this search. The Gnostics were pragmatists, however, and went about this quest in the most efficient way available. Understanding Jesus' soul to have "filled the whole universe," they reasoned that if one wished to search for God, one need look no further than one's own inner self, for God was as much there as He was anywhere. Thus sheer pragmatism shifted their focus from an external to an internal orientation.

Since Jesus had already risen from the dead, and all of humanity's souls were thought to be already contained within Jesus' risen soul, the Gnostics considered that each of us have already technically risen as well. In the Gnostics' view, then, the phenomenon of resurrection is not actually the rising of the souls of the dead, but merely the display, or presentation, or realization of those who have *already* arisen: "What, then, is the resurrection? It is always the disclosure of those who have risen" (The Treatise on the Resurrection).

Everything humanity lacks and needs, the Gnostics thought, Jesus already contains within Himself and makes freely available to us. Thus they viewed our salvation as depending totally on Jesus. The only way we could reacquire our lost wholeness was through Him:

> Since the perfection of the All is in the Father, it is necessary for the All to ascend to him. Therefore, if one has knowledge, he gets what belongs to him and draws it to himself. For he who is ignorant, is deficient, and it is a great deficiency, since he lacks that which will make him perfect. Since the perfection of the All is in the Father, it is necessary for the All to ascend to him and for each one to get the things which are his. (The Gospel of Truth)

The road to our wholeness, these original Christians believed, passes directly through Jesus. Through Him, they thought, one could rediscover and reintegrate all his own lost past-life selves, seeking out his own dead and raising them back up to full consciousness:

> Truly I say to you, none will be saved unless they believe in my cross. But those who have believed in my cross, theirs is the Kingdom of God. Therefore, become seekers for death, just as the dead who seek for life, for that which they seek is revealed to them. (The Secret Book of James)
>
> Is it not necessary for all those who possess everything to know themselves? Some indeed, if they do not know themselves, will not enjoy what they possess. But those who have come to know themselves will enjoy their possessions. (The Gospel of Philip 76:16–22)
>
> Again I reprove you. You who are, make yourselves like those who are not, in order that you may come to be with those who are not. (The Secret Book of James)

The Mystery of the Bridal Chamber

> Great is the mystery of marriage! For without it, the world would not exist. (The Gospel of Philip 64:33)

A number of these Nag Hammadi scriptures mention a mysterious sacrament called the "bridal chamber." The Gospel of Philip discusses the soul joining with its other half in an "imaged bridal chamber," which seems to join them in a unified state of spiritual androgyny. The famous

Gnostic teacher Ptolemy also described a second self or "angel" with which one's soul would unite in a "mystery of the bridal chamber." This would seem to be where the marriage of the long-alienated spiritual halves of a human took place:

> Once they unite with one another, they become a single life. Wherefore the prophet said concerning the first man and the first woman, "They will become a single flesh." For they were originally joined one to another when they were with the father before the woman led astray the man, who is her brother. This marriage has brought them back together again and the soul has been joined to her true love, her real master [the spirit]. (The Exegesis on the Soul)

The most important of the five sacraments of the Gnostic Church, the marriage in the bridal chamber was thought to provide immediate entrance to the kingdom of heaven while one was still alive:

> The chrism is superior to baptism, for it is from the word "Chrism" that we have been called "Christians," certainly not because of the word "baptism." And it is because of the chrism that "the Christ" has his name. For the Father anointed the Son, and the Son anointed the apostles, and the apostles anointed us. He who has been anointed possesses everything. He possesses the resurrection, the light, the cross, the Holy Spirit. The Father gave him this in the bridal chamber; he merely accepted (the gift). The Father was in the Son and the Son in the Father. This is the Kingdom of Heaven. (The Gospel of Philip 74:12–24)

The mystery of the bridal chamber seems to have provided revelations about one's identity and true nature that were so dramatic they were characterized almost as a second birth:

> O soul, persistent one, be sober and shake off your drunkenness, which is the work of ignorance. . . . When you entered into a bodily birth, you were begotten. Come into being inside the bridal chamber! Be illuminated in mind! (The Teachings of Silvanus)

This sacrament, a prerequisite for the resurrection of one's past-life souls, had to be received while one was still alive. After death it was too late. Once one received the mystery of the bridal chamber, all past-life souls were guaranteed salvation:

> When it is revealed, the perfect light will flow out on every one. And all those who are in it will receive the chrism. Then the slaves will be free and the captives ransomed. . . . Those who are separated will be united and will be filled. Every one who will enter the bridal chamber will kindle the light. . . . If anyone becomes a son of the bridal chamber, he will receive the light. If anyone does not receive it while he is here, he will not be able to receive it in the other place. . . . And again when he leaves the world, he has already received the truth in the images. The world has become the Aeon (eternal realm), for the Aeon is fullness for him. (The Gospel of Philip 85:25; 86:15)

This sacrament was specifically called an "imaged" bridal chamber, which reminds us that many BSD cultures referred to one of the binary souls as one's spiritual twin, double, or image. This term also suggests that the marriage occurring in this bridal chamber is primarily a psychological event involving the union or integration of mental images. This sacrament may have brought about a comprehensive mental review of all one's past souls and memories, possibly similar to the instantaneous "panoramic life review" often described in near-death experiences (NDEs), but surveying dozens or even hundreds of past incarnations instead of just one. In NDEs, this life review is said to occur in a single moment; if all the memories of an entire lifetime can be scanned in an instant, then reviewing multiple lifetimes should not take appreciably longer. And simply by catching a glimpse of those lost memories, it seems, one would automatically begin the fuller process of recovering and consciously incorporating those previous selves and identities back into one's psyche:

> It is not possible for anyone to see anything of the things that actually exist unless he becomes like them. This is not the way with man in the world: he sees the sun without being a sun; and he sees the heaven and the earth and all other things, but he is not these things. This is quite in keeping with the truth. But you saw some-

thing of that place, and you became those things. You saw the Spirit, you became spirit. You saw Christ, you became Christ. You saw the Father, you shall become Father. So in this place you see everything and do not see yourself, but in that place [the bridal chamber] you do see yourself—and what you see you shall become. (The Gospel of Philip 61:21–36)

Such a panoramic life review would probably not fully integrate and resurrect each of those past-life selves, but it would at least provide some initial acquaintance with one's past selves, and that is, indeed, how the early Christian Gnostics referred to themselves, as those who had "gnosis," or self-*acquaintance.* These images and memories of one's past selves had to resurface through one's present-life soul. In this way, the two halves of one's being could be firmly bonded together, and when one had achieved this state of perfect wholeness, one would then be equal to Christ. Not only would one receive all one's own lost possessions, but one would also receive Christ:

It is certainly necessary to be born again through the image. What is the resurrection? The image [the past soul] must rise again through the image [the present soul]. The bridal chamber and the image must enter through the image into the truth: this is the restoration. . . . But one receives the unction of the . . . power of the cross. This power the apostles called "the right and the left." For this person is no longer a Christian but a Christ. (The Gospel of Philip 67:14–26)

If you do the Father's will, I say that he will love you and will make you equal with me . . . (The Secret Book of James)

Every scriptural student who becomes a disciple of the kingdom of heaven is like a homeowner who brings new treasures out of his storeroom as well as old. (The Gospel of Matthew 13:52)

Repentance as Baptism

And so John came, baptizing in the desert region, preaching a baptism of repentance for the forgiveness of sins. (The Gospel of Mark 1:4)

While this inner marriage was the ultimate goal of the Gnostic Church, it required advance preparation. One's present-life soul had to be healed of its diseases and divisions before it would be capable of assimilating any other soul material stored on deeper levels of the psyche:

> When you rid yourselves of jealousy, then you will clothe yourselves in light and enter the bridal chamber. (The Dialogue of the Savior)
> The cleansing of the soul is to regain the newness of her former nature and to turn herself back again. That is her baptism. (The Exegesis on the Soul)

Before one could resurrect one's past-life souls, one first had to restore one's present-life soul to optimum functionality by purging it of repressed psychological material. Such a purge can only be done by dredging up all one's repressed material and making it conscious; only then can it be discharged from the system of the psyche. Since most of the material we tend to repress is unpleasant, this psychological process is painful:

> This bringing back is called repentance. (The Gospel of Truth)
> Repentance takes place in distress and grief. (The Exegesis on the Soul)

By purging all this repressed grief and despair, the Gnostics thought we could restore our souls to greater health and wholeness. Viewing this as but an essential first step in the far greater process of achieving total salvation, the early Christians formalized it as the sacrament called "baptism," which seems to have originally been a psychological process similar, at least in intent, to modern psychoanalysis. There was one huge difference, however. Although this process involved a great deal of private soul-searching, it also rested on the implicit assumption that Christ was already present within one's psyche and would actively guide the practitioner on this inner quest toward wholeness, honesty, and integrity:

> Open the door for yourself, that you may know the One who is. Knock on yourself, that the Word may open for you. . . . If you have Christ, you will conquer this entire world. That which you

open for yourself, you will open. That which you knock upon for yourself, you will knock upon, benefitting yourself. (The Teachings of Silvanus)

Those who are to be taught . . . learn for themselves, receiving instructions from the Father. (The Gospel of Truth)

Beseech the Father. Implore God often, and he will give to you. . . . Take reproof from me and save yourselves. (The Secret Book of James)

Do not flee from the divine and the teaching which are within you, for he who is teaching you loves you very much. (The Teachings of Silvanus 87:21–25)

The Gnostics' salvation theology seems to have been internally consistent and based on sound psychological principles. When Jesus' soul united with humanity's souls, He would have experienced all the contents of our psyches, including all the repressed feelings and emotions we refuse to allow ourselves to confront and process. Knowing we would have to seek out and release this repressed material before we could move on to the next step in our salvation, He encouraged us to do so. The same inner psychological walls that prevented people from accessing their own grief kept them locked out of His Kingdom. To be "one with Jesus," the Gnostics seem to have concluded, an individual would first have to be "one with" everything else inside his own psyche, including all his own inner grief and mourning:

I remember your tears, your mourning, and your grief. They are far from us. You who are outside the father's inheritance, weep when you should, mourn, and preach what is good. (Secret Book of James)

He who does not possess all is unable to know Christ. (The Teachings of Silvanus)

The sacrament of the bridal chamber, which initiated the return of all one's past-life souls, was the final seal of salvation, but it first required that one's soul be perfect and complete in this present life. Only those whose present-life souls were free of divisions and defects could receive the salvation of the bridal chamber:

> They . . . speak about Christ in their midst so that they may
> receive a return and he may anoint them with the ointment. The
> ointment is the pity of the Father, who will have mercy on them.
> But those whom he has anointed are those who are perfect. For
> the filled vessels are those which are customarily used for anoint-
> ing. (The Gospel of Truth)

The Gnostic concept of "perfection" did not require one to be sinless
or without guilt. It merely required that one fully recognize all one's personal failings, and completely accept and process one's soul's reactions to
them. While the official church focused on acquiring faith, it seems the
Gnostic church focused more on acquiring psychological health and
wholeness. It was not perfect sinlessness they preached, but perfect self-
honesty. Many Gnostic works, such as the Second Treatise of the Great
Seth, were specifically addressed to an audience of these "perfect and
incorruptible ones."

The Resurrection Debates

> Those who say they will die first and then rise are in error. If
> they do not first receive the resurrection while they live, when they
> die they will receive nothing. (The Gospel of Philip 73:1–5)

By the middle of the second century, the Roman Empire was ablaze
with theological debate over proper Christian doctrine. One of the most
contentious and passionately disputed topics concerned the correct
understanding of Christianity's promised resurrection. The Gnostic and
orthodox branches of the church had very different ways of looking at this
issue. The Gnostics explained this discrepancy by arguing that even Jesus'
closest apostles didn't fully understand everything he was trying to get
across to them: "I first spoke with you in parables, and you did not understand. Now, in turn, I speak with you openly, and you do not perceive"
(The Secret Book of James).

While the official church believed the resurrection was something that
was going to happen to everyone at the same time in the final dramatic
conclusion of history, the Gnostics felt the resurrection could take place
on an individual basis at any point in time and pointed to Lazarus as the
proof of that possibility. Many religious scholars have noted an apparent

connection between Lazarus and the legendary Egyptian god Osiris, whose name was actually pronounced "Ausar." In Egyptian, the phrase "the Osiris" (L'Ausar) would sound remarkably similar to "Lazarus." Since both Osiris and Lazarus were reportedly raised from the dead, one might wonder if this was more than coincidence, but the explanation may be nothing more than a colloquialism. If Jesus had raised someone from the dead during His ministry, that person would surely have been a topic of conversation in the community for years to come, and with Israel and Egypt being next-door neighbors, the general populace might well have informally referred to him as another "Osiris." If this is so, then "Lazarus" was not his name, but his *nickname.*

The truly curious thing about the Lazarus story is that according to virtually every early Christian source, both orthodox and Gnostic, resurrection was originally considered the "be-all-end-all" of salvation. Once someone was raised from the dead, he would thereafter possess eternal life. In Jesus' day, people didn't expect their resurrection to occur until Judgment Day. But in the eleventh chapter of John, in the middle of the very story where Jesus raises Lazarus from the dead, He disputes this preconception, suggesting instead that eternal life can be given to an individual at *any* time. When Mary is grieving for Lazarus' death and admits she doesn't expect him to be raised until the Last Day, Jesus corrects her, saying that He can give life to a person whenever He chooses.

In any event, if Lazarus already received the resurrection, early Christian doctrine would suggest that the chains of death would have no further hold over him after that. He would be *immune* to death. Just as Jesus promised in John 11:26, he would never die. As the Gospel of Thomas promised, he would never taste death. Interestingly, the end of the Gospel of John reports that someone in the nascent Christian community *was* rumored to possess such an immunity—the apostle John himself, "the one whom Jesus loved":

> Peter turned and saw that the disciple whom Jesus loved was following them. . . . When Peter saw him, he asked, "Lord, what about him?" Jesus answered, "If I want him to remain alive until I return, what is that to you? You must follow me." Because of this, the rumor spread among the brothers that this disciple would not die. . . . This is the disciple who testifies to these things and who wrote them down. (The Gospel of John 21:19–24)

Earlier in John's gospel, it was reemphasized *three times* that Jesus greatly loved Lazarus:

> Now a man named Lazarus was sick. He was from Bethany, the village of Mary and her sister Martha. . . . the sisters sent word to Jesus, "Lord, the one you love is sick." . . . Jesus loved Martha and her sister and Lazarus. . . . Jesus wept. Then the Jews said, "See how he loved him!" . . . Jesus, once more deeply moved, came to the tomb. (The Gospel of John 1–38)

Lazarus, whom Jesus greatly loved, received the resurrection and so presumably would thereafter be immune to death. Is this the same person we know as the apostle John, whom Jesus also greatly loved, and who indeed was rumored to be immune to death? Does this new "Osiris," the author of the Gospel of John, still walk our planet today?

Whereas the official church expected the resurrection to occur after they died, the Gnostics felt instead that it was a sacrament one preferably received *before* death. The Gnostics even believed that Jesus had to receive this sacrament before He died. Receiving this sacrament was the whole key to eternal life; one who received the resurrection would not suffer the second death:

> Those who say that the Lord died first and (then) rose up are in error, for he rose up first and then died. If one does not first attain the resurrection, will he not die? (The Gospel of Philip 56:16–19)

This sacrament brought about the final and permanent union of one's soul and spirit:

> The Lord did everything in a mystery, a baptism and a chrism and a eucharist and a redemption and a bridal chamber. . . . he said, "I came to make the things below like the things above, and the things outside like those inside. I came to unite them in the place." (The Gospel of Philip 67:27–34)

This "resurrection" that occurred while one was still alive was not merely a different interpretation of the Old Testament prophecy of a

Universal Resurrection occurring at Judgment Day, but an entirely different event thought capable of preempting that later occurrence on an individual basis. It was, they argued, vastly preferable. While the Universal Resurrection would occasion the reawakening of all humankind's unintegrated souls in a climactic conclusion to history, the Gnostics believed there was another resurrection one could opt for in advance, which would make that later event unnecessary for the individual who chose it. The Gnostics believed there was also a resurrection of the spirit, which would make the resurrection of the soul at Judgment Day unnecessary: "This is resurrection of the spirit, which swallows up resurrection of the soul along with resurrection of the body" (The Treatise on Resurrection 45:39–42).

Those fortunate enough to have received the resurrection before death would avoid the second death, remaining whole and perfect. Those who had not would still suffer the second death, after which their separated unconscious souls would remain trapped in a dreamlike netherworld experience of their own imaginations' making until the eventual arrival of Judgment Day. And since there are literally no limits to the human imagination, the horrors one might have to endure in that dreamlike realm could far exceed the worst atrocities humankind comes up with on this side of death's door:

> And so he dwells either in this world or in the resurrection or in the middle place. God forbid that I be found in there! In this world, there is good and evil. Its good things are not good, and its evil things not evil. But there is evil after this world which is truly evil—what is called "the middle." It is death. While we are in this world, it is fitting for us to acquire the resurrection, so that when we strip off the flesh, we may be found in rest and not walk in the middle. (The Gospel of Philip 66:7–21)

There was vehement disagreement in the early church over whether the Universal Resurrection would occur in the flesh or out of it:

> Some are afraid lest they rise naked. Because of this they wish to rise in the flesh, and they do not know that it is those who wear the flesh who are naked. It is those who . . . to unclothe themselves who are not naked. "Flesh and blood shall not inherit the kingdom of God." What is this which will not inherit? This which is on

us. . . . I find fault with the others who say that it will not rise. Then both of them are at fault. You say that the flesh will not rise. But tell me what will rise, that we may honor you. You say the spirit in the flesh, and it is also this light in the flesh. (But) this too is a matter which is in the flesh, for whatever you shall say, you say nothing outside the flesh. It is necessary to rise in this flesh, since everything exists in it. (The Gospel of Philip 56:27–57:22)

In this passage, Philip condemns both those who say the resurrection will occur in the flesh as well as those who feel it will occur outside the flesh. From the perspective of the BSD, he seems to be pointing out that while the Universal Resurrection will indeed witness the souls of the dead reawakening inside physical bodies, they won't be the original bodily forms those souls possessed in their earlier incarnations, but instead the body of their spirit's current incarnation. Thus the Gnostics viewed the orthodox tradition that the Universal Resurrection would be a bodily resurrection as technically correct, but not correctly understood by the orthodox.

Indeed, the Gnostics condemned the official church's understanding of resurrection as *doubly* mistaken. The orthodox, they said, erroneously expect their current physical bodies to provide their salvation at the Last Day, when they won't, and, at the same time, they erroneously expect something else *not* to be there when it actually will:

> Woe to you, godless ones, who have no hope, who rely on things that will not happen! Woe to you who hope in the flesh and in the prison that will perish! How long will you be oblivious? And how long will you suppose that the imperishables will perish too? Your hope is set upon the world, and your god is this life! You are destroying your souls! . . . "You love the garment that is put upon you, although it is filthy, and you are gripped by a groundless hope. You have believed in what you do not know." (The Book of Thomas 143:8–40)

This is all in line with the BSD, which suggests that instead of refitting each dead soul with a whole new body at the Universal Resurrection, the dead will simply reawaken inside the already-existing bodies of their current incarnations. And whereas the bodies that the orthodox await won't be delivered in quite the fashion they expect, the Gnostics hinted, they *will* receive something else at that time instead, something they are not expecting and probably assumed didn't even exist anymore: all their own past mental content. All this lost material, the Gnostics insisted, was actually imperishable, poised to take the orthodox by surprise at Judgment Day. It would emerge within them at the very moment of their expected deliverance, dashing their naive hopes for an effortless and painless salvation.

A Church Divided

Every kingdom divided against itself will be ruined." (The Gospel of Matthew 12:25)

To the untrained eye in the early years of the faith, the Gnostics who wrote these 17 scriptures believed the same things Christians did. Both groups believed that humanity suffered from sin inherited from our ancestors, and that our souls would go to hell after our deaths because of those sins. Both believed that Jesus willingly suffered crucifixion, giving His life to rescue us and save our souls from that fate. Both believed that Jesus rose from the dead with a promise to resurrect also the souls of everyone who followed His teachings. Both believed that Jesus possessed a perfection the rest of us had lost, and that He had made it possible for us to partake of that perfection, and that, if we did, we would be saved and our resurrection guaranteed.

Beyond this common framework, the two groups believed quite different things, but those differences seem to have stemmed from a single fundamental distinction: One group believed in reincarnation whereas the other did not. Adding reincarnation to the Christian message required the full reinterpretation found in the Gnostic Church. Or perhaps it would be more correct to say that subtracting reincarnation from the Christian message required the drastic reinterpretation found in the official church. In either case, all their subsequent differences seem to have stemmed from that one original distinction.

The debate between these two groups seems to have been tolerated in the nascent Christian community for a considerable time before they parted company. Once these two split from one another, however, the differences between them fell into sharper relief, and everything went downhill after that. The official church ended up focusing more on developing its massive political organization than on nurturing the spiritual development of its individual members. It tried to impose societal belief autocratically from the top down. Meanwhile, the Gnostic Church did the opposite, focusing on the subjective experience of the individual at the expense of their group's objective standing in society.

Just as the division between official and Gnostic Christianity led the official church into its millennia-long orgy of murder and terrorism, so too did this division send the Gnostic church into its extensive conjectural fantasies known as the Gnostic creation mythology. In the later years of the Gnostic Church, its members indulged in ever more intricately detailed conjecture about the processes God employed to create the universe. In the end, these seemingly meaningless yet confoundingly elaborate creation myths contributed to Gnosticism's political downfall, being used as evidence of Gnosticism's unsound theology. In fact, until the Nag Hammadi scriptures were recovered, many modern historians had viewed these labyrinthine creation myths, rather than the psychological process of inner revelation that feature so prominently in these 17 scriptures, as the defining signature of the entire Gnostic movement. This skewed perspective seems to have been manufactured by the censorship campaign of the official church.

In the end, it seems that both these fragments of Christ's original church failed to pass on the gift that had been handed down to them. Once the two halves of Christ's church split off from one another, each found itself terminally crippled by the other's absence, and their equally tragic histories reflect that disappointing reality.

Single Standards and Twin Traditions: Echoes of Our Lost Inheritance

He says to his mother,
"Don't cry. I am returning to my Father, and to eternal life.
Here is your son! This man will take my place."
Then he says to his disciple, "Here is your mother!"
Then, bowing his head, he gave up his spirit.
—A variation on John 19:26–30 in Codex evangelii Johannei Templariorum

Although the official church succeeded in stifling the public activities of the Gnostic Church, it was never able to shut it down completely or totally eliminate its teachings about humanity's binary soul. By receding into the shadowy fringes of Western culture, the BSD was able to survive the world's transition into Christianity. In much the same way that the Mesopotamians believed in two souls (the *napistu* and the *zaqiqu*) two thousand years before Christ, and the Canaanites believed in two souls (the *nps* and the *th*) one thousand years before Christ, so too the Jews, Manichaeans, Mandaeans, Muslims, Cathars, and Templars continued to do so long after Christ.

Long before Jesus appeared on the scene, the binary soul doctrine was deeply ingrained in Judaism, and signs of that ancient connection saturate the history and culture of the Jewish people.[1] From God creating the world through division,[2] to the Jewish legend that Adam originally had two faces,[3] to the first human children (Cain and Abel) being twins, to the twin two-faced cherubim standing on either side of the Ark of the Covenant, to the twin pillars standing on either side of the entrance to Solomon's Temple, to the Abrahamic Covenant being consummated by slicing animals down the middle and arranging their halves opposite each other,[4] to the legend of Isaiah dying by being cut in two with a saw,[5] to the two goats of the Yom Kippur atonement sacrifice, it is clear that duality and division were fundamental themes in Judaism long before Jesus arrived on the scene. This didn't end with the advent of Christianity. In fact, evidence suggests that the BSD was well known among the general Jewish population in Jesus' day. For example, one popular book at the time was credited to Enoch, one of only two people in history, according to Judaic teaching, who had never suffered the second death: "I created man from visible and invisible nature. From both comes his death, his life, and his image" (Book of the Secrets of Enoch[6]).

Centuries later, Judaism's mystical school of Kabbalah was openly teaching the binary soul doctrine, declaring that one's soul and spirit must *both* be perfected before one could achieve salvation:

> The soul (nephesh) stands in intimate relation to the body, nourishing and upholding it; it is below, the first stirring. Having acquired due worth, it becomes the throne of the spirit (ruah) to rest upon, as it is written, "until the spirit be poured upon us from on high." And when these two, soul and spirit, have duly readied themselves, they are worthy to receive the "supersoul" (neshamah). (The Zohar, from the Jewish Kabbalah)

As we saw in the previous chapter, Enoch's theme of mixing of visible and invisible elements was also explored in the Book of Thomas. The unification of equal opposites seems to have been such a fundamental element of early Christianity, in fact, that the notion was incorporated into both of Christianity's primary logos: the cross, obviously, but also the fish, or *Ichthys* symbol. For millennia, humanity has wondered, "What does Christianity have to do with a fish?" But to the Gnostic Christians, this logo would have served as an elegantly subtle reminder of Jesus' injunction to "make the two one." If the two arcs of the Ichthys symbol are continued, they form two perfect circles overlapping one another, a perfect representation of an integrated duality.

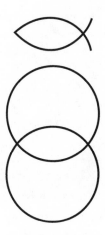

In the East, the BSD continued to be a consistent feature of religious movements founded after Rome embraced Christianity. The Mandaean religion (which is still followed by certain tribes in Iraq and Iran) claims to have originated in Judea around the time of Christ, and to this day it teaches a doctrine of two souls that divide at death. Every Mandaean believes himself to possess both a soul (*nishimta*) and a spirit (*ruha*). At the time of death, one's soul is weighed on a scale. If found worthy, it is permanently united with its spirit in the afterlife, entering a world of light. If found unworthy, it is eternally divided from its spirit, becoming imprisoned in a realm of the dead.[7]

Obviously, this same train of thought was still in circulation two hundred years later when Manichaeism came on the scene, also teaching a doctrine of dual souls. Its legendary founder Mani was said to have always been accompanied by his own Syzygus, or "Divine Twin."[8] When Islam arrived on the scene four hundred years after that, it too seems to have originally subscribed to the binary soul doctrine. Written in the late sixth or early seventh century, the Koran declares that people possess two spiritual elements, the *nafs* and the *ruh,* both of which leave the body at death. While the *nafs* is taken by God and said to have died, the person's other half is said *not* to have died, but instead is sent off to complete other tasks. One part of man, then, was thought in early Islam to be "ordained to die," while the other part was believed to continue living:

> God takes to Himself the souls [*al-anfus,* plural of *nafs*] at their deaths, and that which has not died [He takes] in its sleep. He keeps that for which he has ordained death, and sends the other to its appointed term. In this are signs for the thoughtful person. (Surah 39:42)

The Mysterious Templars

In the West, however, the BSD had a much harder time surviving. Being outlawed by the official church, it had to rely on secrecy for its teachings to continue to be passed down from generation to generation. Certain idiosyncrasies of the legendary Christian order of the Knights

Templar (1118–1314 A.D.) suggest they were intimately involved in that mission. The seal of the Templars, for example, depicted two knights riding together on a single horse. Like the enigmatic Templars themselves, this odd symbol has remained a mystery for hundreds of years, and dozens of different theories about its meaning have been advanced. The orthodox explanation was that it symbolized the Templars' poverty, but their order was one of the richest and most influential institutions in Europe. The binary soul doctrine seems to suggest a more reasonable explanation. The Templars, of course, were Christians and would have looked to their religion's rich heritage for inspiration in designing all their symbols and logos. Their unique seal seems powerfully reminiscent of a key passage in one of Christianity's earliest gospels: "Jesus said, 'It is impossible for a man to mount two horses or to stretch two bows. And it is impossible for a servant to serve two masters'" (Gospel of Thomas 47).

The Templar's seal almost seems to have been designed as a specific response to this passage in the Gospel of Thomas. If the BSD's problem can be symbolized by one man's inability to ride two horses, its solution can be symbolized by two men's ability to ride one horse. The Templar seal is yet another elegant symbol of the soul and spirit uniting within a person. When the two halves of one's being are at odds, straining in different directions like two separate horses, the person trying to ride them is unable to get anywhere. But if both halves of one's being are united, one becomes incredibly powerful and successful, no longer wasting energy fighting oneself. The Templars were known for just that—becoming extraordinarily powerful and successful in a very short period of time.

But did they know of the Gospel of Thomas? History certainly suggests that the Templars discovered *something* extraordinary while fighting the Crusades in Jerusalem, something which led them to adopt unorthodox religious practices and teachings that eventually attracted charges of heresy. It would not have been outside the realm of possibility for the Templars to have come across a copy of the Gospel of Thomas during their 70-year occupation of ancient Judea. The Roman authorities outlawed the Gospel of Thomas in the fourth century, and they controlled the Holy

Land, but with the rise of Islam two centuries later, that control vanished. By the time the Crusaders retook Jerusalem, those censorship policies had long remained unenforced in Palestine, and bootleg copies of Thomas' forbidden gospel may well have been available.

The Templars' mysterious battle flag, known as the *Beauséant,* also seems related to the binary soul doctrine. Consisting of two equal but opposite vertical blocks, a black one atop a white one, this flag suggests that the Templars' secret teachings revolved around the integration or unification of two equal but opposite elements. It seems odd, however, for a Christian order to adopt a flag that raises black above white. Black is usually equated with evil and white with good, and an upper position represents preference or dominance while the lower suggests inferiority and subservience. If that weren't strange enough, these black and white fields are of equal shape and volume, suggesting that the flag designer viewed them as equal opposites. This all seems inconsistent with the views of official Christianity, which holds good to be superior to evil. But if these black and white fields represent the two halves of the human psyche, the Templars' flag makes perfect sense. According to the binary soul doctrine, whereas the two halves of our being are equal opposites, the unconscious or "black" half must be "raised up" within each of us for our spiritual salvation to begin.

The Templars were also famous for their veneration of the Virgin Mary, but curiously depicted her with black images, rather than the more traditional white. Hundreds of these Templar-era Black Madonnas still exist in Europe, mostly in France. While the majority are found in churches and sanctuaries, a few Black Virgins have been moved to museums. Most were sculpted out of wood; a few are paintings and several others are frescoes. These black images cannot help but remind the BSD student of similar religious images of the Egyptian *ka,* which were also often rendered in black, almost as if they were negatives or reverse images.

Why would the Templars redesign in black religious imagery that had previously been consistently portrayed in white? Probably for the same reason they raised black above white in their battle flag. Two chief symbols of the unconscious soul are femininity and the color black. Taken together, the symbolism of their seal, their flag, and their penchant for Black Madonnas suggest a strong connection to the BSD. Like the Gnostics, the Templars seem to have also understood that achieving the Christian salvation required worshiping (that is, recognizing and embracing) the dark or "invisible" contents of the feminine unconscious.

While both our halves must be united and balanced, the way to accomplish this is to place the black *above* the white. Since humanity's whole spiritual problem has always been one of repressing, denying, and rejecting the unconscious, balance can only be restored by compensating for our present imbalance. Just as the ancient Egyptians believed that Osiris, as great as he was held to be, could only be saved by his female counterpart, Isis, so too did these Templars apparently believe that the female side of our beings possessed the power to restore our equilibrium and wholeness, healing our inner divisions and "making the two one."

As if to confirm this, the Templars' chosen name for their flag, the French term *Beauséant,* translates directly into English as "beautiful bottom" or "beautiful buttocks." While this translation has been odd enough to keep most would-be interpreters busy searching for alternate translations, it makes perfect sense to the student of the binary soul doctrine, which insists that the path to spiritual success begins via deep soul-searching, exploring one's own backside, searching the darkest, bottommost levels of our own psyches. And just like the ancient Gnostics, the Templars seem to have believed that what awaits us in that dark hemisphere possesses surpassing beauty.

The Freemasons, another mysterious group rumored to have descended from the Templars, tellingly use the compass and square for their own logo. Since a compass draws circles, a female symbol, and a square draws squares, a male symbol, this choice of emblem again seems to reflect a symbolic union of equal but opposite masculine and feminine forces, suggesting that it too descends from the ancient world's binary soul doctrine.

Masonic symbolism also places a similarly dualistic emphasis on the two large cast-bronze pillars that once stood on either side of the entrance to the temple in Jerusalem, obscurely teaching that when these two pillars are conjoined, they will create a desirable state of stability and endurance. They are mysteriously said to be the two pillars of the universe, which, when united together, support and sustain it. Tradition reports that in

Solomon's original temple, one of these pillars was black and the other was white; and together they somehow explained all the mysteries of the universe. Even though they were identical in every other respect, they were not only given different coloring, but were actually given separate names as well, obviously to distinguish between them and emphasize their "separate but equal" status.

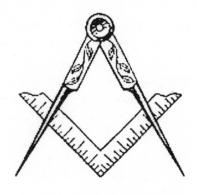

The Sacred Marriage

Unfortunately, this mission to pass on the binary soul doctrine secretly in the West created its own problems. Any cultural attempt to perpetuate a religious tradition through secrecy would encounter a recurring cultural dilemma, people who somehow stumbled across slivers of the secret doctrine and jumped to the wrong conclusions about that tradition. They would either rail against its imagined errors or, far more destructively, embrace their mistaken assessment of the secret faith and start teaching that error to others as an exciting new religious truth.

For instance, many different cultural expressions of the binary soul doctrine chose to symbolize humanity's ultimate spiritual goal with the same metaphor: the union of "man" and "women," that is, two equal but opposite masculine and feminine elements. Unfortunately, many have mistakenly concluded from such symbolic glimpses that their salvation could be achieved through physical sex, when in fact the *true* Sacred Marriage has always been an inner psychological achievement, occurring between one's inner feminine and masculine elements. What the apostle Paul taught seems consistent with the BSD on this point: It would be best for a person to remain celibate if possible, for the most direct path to personal wholeness would seem to be a solitary inner path, and the urge for physical sex is just a reflection of a far more fundamental psychological urge for personal wholeness via the reunion of the inner soul and spirit.

This Sacred Marriage, or *hieros gamos,* was a fundamental tenet of the Valentinian school of Christian Gnosticism. Valentinus, the second-century Gnostic who almost became pope, taught that salvation required both halves of one's spiritual being to join permanently. Unfortunately, many interpreted the symbolic teaching of the union of the inner masculine and feminine components as a religious excuse to indulge in promiscuous sex. Such "sacred sex" traditions were reportedly practiced by the Templars.[9] Such misinterpretations may have done more harm to binary soul traditions than any other single factor.

Valentinus' powerful teachings about the Sacred Marriage between the soul and spirit were transformed into today's legend of Saint Valentine, the patron saint of romantic love. Fortunately, even in error one can sometimes find helpful truths. Marriages and other committed relationships can be very useful tools in preparing oneself for the inner spiritual transformation called Sacred Marriage. In order to achieve a successful marriage, one must learn to relate to one's spouse, and this invariably requires one to first "get in touch" with one's inner "other half." A man generally has to rediscover his "inner female" in order to relate to his wife, and a woman has to do the equivalent to understand her husband.

Yet another aspect to the ancient religious tradition of Sacred Marriage that the binary soul doctrine would seem to inform is one which has received considerable popular attention in the last 20 years: the legend that Jesus Himself married, and fathered a bloodline that eventually produced the royal families of Europe. Both the best-sellers *Holy Blood, Holy Grail* and *The Da Vinci Code* have advanced this hypothesis, and while the BSD does not address the many intricate details of those arguments, it does suggest a new factor that may tend to support the same general conclusions. These "holy blood" theories have been condemned by traditional Christianity, largely because they suggest that Jesus did not die on the cross, but instead went on to live a long life and sire a family.[10] The binary soul doctrine, strangely enough, seems to suggest that *both* scenarios may have occurred at the same time. Jesus may have been both the Yom Kippur atonement goat that was sacrificed, and also the Yom Kippur goat allowed to escape.

The Symbolism of Yom Kippur: A Tale of Two Goats

When we betray our ideals and integrity and our two halves divide at death, the BSD suggests, both halves are saddled with the guilt of that betrayal, but each suffers in a different way. Their division is not punishment so much as the *instrument* of punishment. Because of our guilt, one half is sacrificed and lost while the other simply wanders innocently away, unknowingly carrying the continuing stain of its guilt. While the unconscious soul dies, becoming imprisoned in the wretched realm of the dead, the conscious spirit merely loses its memory, which causes it to wander aimlessly into strange new experiences and new incarnations, where it eventually confronts the karma created by its sins. This conscious spirit is forced to experience the consequences of its previous actions in its subsequent incarnations without ever realizing why those turns of fate take place because it loses all memory of the original causes that led to those inevitable effects. Meanwhile, the other half of the self, the unconscious soul, suffers punishment from its guilt as well, by becoming imprisoned in a static, unchanging existence in a nightmare-like netherworld.

This whole scenario seems eerily reflected in the annual ritual once held on the ancient Jewish holiday of Yom Kippur, the Day of Atonement, the most important day in the Jewish calendar. In order to remove the sins of the people, Mosaic Law had introduced a ceremony to transfer all the people's guilt to a pair of substitutes, two simple beasts that would be punished in their stead.

The nature of this Jewish atonement ritual has a lot in common with the binary soul doctrine and, as it turns out, with the biblical account of Jesus' atonement for humanity's sins. The sacrifice on the Day of Atonement required two perfect male goats that had to be mirror images of one another. Both these goats were forced to bear the guilt of the people of Israel, but in very different ways. The High Priest would cast lots for the two goats and, according to how the lots fell, one goat would be designated the "Lord's Goat" while the other became the "scapegoat." After the sins of the people were symbolically transferred to both goats, the Lord's Goat was killed while the scapegoat was allowed to escape. Taking two pieces of scarlet cloth that represented the sins of the people, the High Priest tied one piece around the neck of the Lord's Goat, and the other around the scapegoat's horns, thus transferring the same blood-red guilt to both. After casting lots and assigning their fates, the High Priest would slaughter the Lord's Goat, immediately sprinkling its blood in the temple while verbally confessing the sins of the people. After this grisly chore, he would come out to the scapegoat and, symbolically laying his bloodied hands on the head of the second beast, he would confess the sins of his people all over again. After thus receiving the stain of guilt, the scapegoat was allowed simply to wander into the wilderness, symbolically taking the sins of the people away with it as it ambled off, unknowingly carrying the stain of its brother's blood on its head.

According to Mosaic Law, then, the sacrifice of the first goat wasn't enough by itself to achieve the objective of saving the people from their sins; for some reason, this second goat was once thought to have been needed as well. Both halves of the equation had to be dutifully performed before the sins of the people would be credited as fully forgiven. Traditional Judeo-Christian theology cannot explain the curious existence of the second goat in this ritual, but it makes perfect sense to the student of the binary soul doctrine. Obviously, this ritual originally symbolized the fate of the two halves of a guilty person's soul after his or her death; one half would die, and the other half would be left free to wander aimlessly from incarnation to incarnation. Yet both halves still bore the same guilt, and both suffered from it equally. While the unconscious half would die and go off to suffer in the land of the dead, its conscious partner would remain perpetually alive (by reincarnating) but would still suffer the consequences of its sin by encountering its own guilty karma in those subsequent lifetimes, proving that it carried the stain of its past sins. Thus, just as both halves of the soul suffer the consequences of our sin in very different ways, so too did both goats suffer the guilt of the people on the Day of Atonement, one bearing it in death, the other in life.

A Tale of Two Jesuses

An eminent man known as "Jesus Bar Abbas" was being held at the time, so when the people were gathered together, Pilate asked them, Which prisoner do you want me to set free? Do you want this Jesus Bar Abbas, or do you want the Jesus who is called the Messiah? (Matt. 27:15–17)

Christianity has long associated Jesus' death with the Jewish atonement ritual of Yom Kippur, declaring that He bore the entire burden of humanity's sin in our place. Even the apostle Paul made this connection. According to Old Testament theology, however, a crucial piece to the puzzle was missing: If Jesus was the sacrificial atonement offering, then where was the scapegoat who had to bear the same burden of guilt, but was still allowed to walk away alive from the sacrifice ritual?

There *was* another figure in this drama. Two men were brought before Pontius Pilate, and they had the same name, the same title, the same history, and the same status. As we shall see, they may even have been biological twins. And like the Yom Kippur ceremony, one of them was randomly chosen to live and the other forced to die, even though both were saddled with a similar burden of guilt.

Today, after 2,000 years of literary conditioning, we blithely distinguish between these two men, calling one by the name Jesus and the other by the name Barabbas. But according to a number of early Bible manuscripts, the Gospel of Matthew originally identified *both* of them as holy men named "Jesus." Although most Christians live their whole lives without ever hearing of it, the man we have come to know as Barabbas was originally identified in Matthew as "Jesus Bar Abbas." Today this Hebrew phrase translates as "Jesus, the Son of the Father," but to the Jews of Jesus' day, it would have been understood as "Jesus, the Son of God."[11] Scholars today widely believe that, in a clear violation of the original integrity of the New Testament, church authorities edited out the name Jesus from Jesus Barabbas.

The parallels between Pilate's two sacrificial offerings, however, go far beyond a simple name. To many people, the most astounding revelation in the entire Bible may be the fact that, just like the two identical goats in Judaism's Yom Kippur ceremony, the two men brought before Pontius Pilate were identical in a great many respects. Pilate identified one as "Jesus, the Son of God" and the other as "Jesus who is said to be the Messiah," both of whom were religious figures in custody for inciting a political insurrection. Two men with the same name and the same claim were in custody in the same place at the same time for the same crime! This simply cannot be a coincidence.

The Bible accuses Barabbas of inciting a political insurrection in Jerusalem at the very same time that Jesus did the same thing when He rode triumphantly into Jerusalem as the newly announced King of the Jews, gave speeches to vast crowds of supporters, and instigated a riot at the temple. Both men were obviously religious leaders as well as political figures; the Bible itself refers to Barabbas as the "Son of God," and Jesus made virtually the same claim for Himself. Indeed, Jesus had referred to God as His own Father in His public speeches so many times that the popular gossip might well have come to refer to Him by those very terms— Jesus Bar Abbas—"that Jesus who calls himself the son of the Father." And both were famous public figures in Jerusalem at the same time. Matthew describes Barabbas with the Greek word *episemos,* which translates as "notable" or even "eminent."[12] Jesus, of course, was equally famous, having been swarmed by adoring throngs of people in Jerusalem just days before His arrest.

And so, in a precise duplication of the annual Atonement Day ceremony that no Jew of the era could possibly have failed to recognize, Pilate had two virtually identical males marked for death, and proposed randomly to set one free and kill the other. And after the sacrifice, Pilate ritually washed his hands and declared himself innocent of guilt, which is also the last thing the High Priest traditionally did during the atonement ritual of Yom Kippur. The Jews of Jesus' era would no more mistake all this Atonement Day holiday symbolism than modern Americans would mistake the meaning of a fat guy in a red suit passing out gifts. The Christians of 70 years later certainly didn't:

> Note what he commanded: "Take two fine goats that look alike and offer them up. Let the priest take one of them as a whole burnt offering for sins." What should they do with the other? "The other one," he said, "is accursed." Note how the type of Jesus is revealed: "And all of you spit upon it and pierce it, and then tie scarlet wool around its head and send it out that way into the wilderness." . . . What does this mean? Pay attention: "The first goat is for the altar, and the other is accursed." Notice that the accursed one is crowned, because then they will see him on that day wearing a scarlet robe that goes down to his feet, and they shall say, "Isn't this the one we rejected and pierced and spat upon? Truly this is the same one who claimed then to be the Son of God. How alike he is to Him!" This is why the goats had to be fine goats that look similar to each other, so that when they see him coming then, they'll be amazed by the goat's likeness. Recognize in this the type of Jesus who was to suffer. (The Epistle of Barnabas 7:6–11)

Traditionally ascribed to the companion of Saint Paul, the Epistle of Barnabas was written sometime between 70 A.D. and 135 A.D. The early church had high regard for Barnabas's claims that all the commandments, rituals, and practices of the Old Testament should be interpreted allegorically. The work was even deemed canonical in some circles, being accepted as divinely inspired scripture by Jerome, Clement of Alexandria, and Origen. It was even included among the books of the New Testament in the Codex Sinaiticus and Codex Hierosolymitanus.

In the passage cited here, this early Christian work directly associates Jesus with the two goats of the Yom Kippur ceremony and then suggests something very interesting indeed. It declares that one of the two goats of the Yom Kippur ceremony is traditionally tortured (spit upon and "goaded," or "pierced with reeds") before it is set free, while the other goat is not tortured but instead put to death "whole." Declaring this ancient Jewish ritual to reflect Christ's own crucifixion and death strongly suggests that, just as so many ancient heresies insisted, one Jesus was beaten and tortured but quite another Jesus was hung upon the cross.

The Basilidians, a second-century Christian sect, believed that Jesus' image was transferred to another who was crucified in His place. This idea apparently still held currency four centuries later, for it wound up being incorporated into Mohammed's teachings as well. Islamic culture still maintains today that another man took Jesus' place on the cross, someone with the same physical appearance: "They did not slay him, neither crucified him, only a likeness of that was shown to them" (Koran 4:157).

Who Was the Scapegoat?

If there indeed were two Jesuses onstage alongside Pilate and both ended up being saddled with the same guilt, but one was murdered while the other was set free, what happened to the one who got away? Is there any way for us to figure out who this might have been? Who was the scapegoat who presumably also received humanity's sins, but had to carry them in life instead of death?

In the ancient Yom Kippur ritual, the scapegoat was allowed just to disappear into the wilderness. Similarly, some would say, Barabbas also disappeared from the pages of history. But did he really? If Barabbas was a scapegoat who was set free while still carrying the crushing burden of guilt placed on him, could he have realistically escaped into historical obscurity? Matthew identified him as a well-known public figure even before Jesus' crucifixion; could he have possibly disappeared from public life after having played such a major role in the foundational event of the Christian church?

What do we know about this mysterious Jesus Barabbas, who, if all the Yom Kippur parallels are not pure coincidences, apparently could have effectively substituted for Christ on the cross? We probably don't even know his real name, since the name "Jesus" (which means "God Saves") was frequently adopted by would-be Jewish messiahs in the first century. We do, however, know that Barabbas was presented as a perfect twin to Jesus, since he was seen fit at least to fill the predetermined role of the Yom Kippur scapegoat.

These parallels with the traditional Yom Kippur ceremony raise a most interesting question: Did Jesus know in advance that He was the one who was going to be picked? If the scene before Pilate was indeed intended to replicate the Yom Kippur ceremony, the identity of the sacrificial victim would not have been decided until the day of the ceremony. Is it possible that Jesus did not know whether He would end up on the cross or not? Such a thing may be hinted at in the heartbreaking scene where Jesus begs God, "Father, if it is possible, let this cup be taken from me" (Matt. 26:39). That plea takes on a poignant new significance if He expected to be standing onstage alongside Jesus Barabbas the next morning, but didn't know which of the two would be chosen for the cross. If these Yom Kippur parallels point true, then *both* men standing onstage alongside Pilate may have voluntarily chosen to be there, both of them equally prepared to accept the honor of the crucifixion, but neither knowing which of them it would ultimately prove to be.

And if these Yom Kippur parallels point true, then when he left the scene, the man once known as Jesus Barabbas would have been carrying a huge symbolic burden of guilt on his shoulders.

Jesus Had a Twin Brother?

Does any figure of the early church fulfill that guilty description? Yes—Judas, the legendary betrayer of Jesus, the only person besides Jesus who was originally portrayed as holding any guilt after the events of Christ's passion were completed. Even though Jesus had theoretically assumed all the sins of humanity on His shoulders with His crucifixion, Judas seems to be a glaring exception to that rule, portrayed as doomed from the earliest days of the church.[13] If anyone in Christian history ever shouldered a greater burden of guilt than Jesus took on, it was Judas. Like the scapegoat of Yom Kippur, he walked away from that event carrying far more guilt than before it started.

But was Judas an identical twin of Jesus? If he was the same Judas as the author of the Gospel of Thomas and the Book of Thomas, he might have been. As noted previously, the author of those works, whose name actually was Judas, was specifically identified as "Didymos Judas Thomas," or in other words, "Twin Judas Twin." In his Book of Thomas, he was described not only as Jesus' "brother,"[14] but indeed as His "twin and true companion."[15] And in the Acts of Thomas, Judas Thomas is depicted as not merely being Jesus' twin brother, but indeed His *identical* twin, looking so like Him that the two could easily be mistaken for one another:

> And he saw the Lord Jesus in the likeness of the apostle Judas Thomas, who shortly before had blessed them and departed from them, conversing with the bride, and he said to him, "Didn't you go out before them all? How can you be here now?" But the Lord said to him, "I am not Judas who is also Thomas, I am his brother." (The Acts of Thomas)

If this is the same Judas who wrote the biblical Book of Jude, he may well have been Jesus' biological brother, since Jude 1 identifies Judas as the brother of James the Just, and James was Jesus' brother.[16] Indeed, both the Gospels of Matthew and Mark explicitly declare that Jesus had four brothers—Joseph, Simon, James, and Jude.

The scapegoat of the Yom Kippur ceremony traditionally wandered far away from the site of the ceremony and, in much the same way, Judas Thomas also wandered far away from Jerusalem after Jesus' crucifixion, eventually winding up, according to legend, in India. Curiously, early Christian legends from eastern Syria identify this figure as the twin brother of Jesus, celebrating him as one of the foremost of the Twelve Disciples. If Judas Thomas indeed was both the infamous Barabbas and the even more infamous betrayer Judas, this would explain why he felt he had to flee his native land after Jesus' crucifixion. But most important, it would also explain why the Gospel of Thomas contains such unique insights found in no other Christian scripture. As Jesus' perfect twin and alter ego who could have just as easily assumed the mantle of Crucified Savior, Judas Thomas would have possessed insights into Christianity's mysteries unequaled by any other apostle. If any of Christ's followers were to grasp fully His teachings, no one would be a more likely candidate than His own twin brother. If Jesus and Thomas were perfect equals, then even though Jesus Himself never left any written teachings while He was alive, the Gospel of Thomas would present the same teachings as if He had, containing the same perspective, insights, and depth of understanding. It would truly be unique among all Christian scriptures, as indeed it appears to be. It would be scripture authentically written by the very Jesus who stood before Pilate. Well, one of them, anyway.

If Judas was Jesus' twin brother, and they bilaterally agreed to take on the burden of humanity's guilt, this would also explain Judas' apparent betrayal of Jesus in the Garden of Gethsemane. If they were twins, only one conclusion can be reached: They must have been partners, and the whole arrest scene was mutually planned out in advance. After all, as endless biblical students have noted down through the millennia, Jesus *needed* someone to betray Him in order for His planned sacrificial crucifixion to take place as scheduled. Without Judas' willing collusion, Jesus' entire plan to save the human race would have hinged not only precariously, but also rather distastefully, on the sinfulness of one man. Paradoxically, if that uninformed Judas had been too *good,* Jesus could never have saved anyone. Such a plan, of course, casts Jesus as one willing to benefit from the misfortune of others. If He intentionally took advantage of the failings of Judas, that would not only diminish the glory of any salvation He might have thus wrought, but might itself negate it, as it would be a sin (counting on the worst in people) on Jesus' soul, thus disqualifying Him from being a pure sacrifice. On the other hand, if Judas was a willing participant in the scheme and voluntarily agreed to become the most hated man in history in order to help Jesus save humanity, his willingness to sacrifice himself also for the greater good would make Jesus' success just that much more glorious.

Were Jesus and Judas secretly working together to redeem humanity? In Gethsemane, Jesus called Judas his *hetairos.*[17] Usually translated "friend," this word can also indicate a state of partnership or comradeship. And Jesus needed a very special friend indeed to help Him with this mission. At the Last Supper, Jesus appears to collude with Judas; not only does He not attempt to dissuade Judas from the action they both know he is about to perform, but Jesus actually urges him to go ahead with it.[18] Even though the Gospels of Matthew and John both insist that Jesus openly identified Judas as His betrayer in front of all the other disciples at the Last Supper, no one there raised a finger to stop him.[19] Instead, as Judas leaves to hand over his Master to the authorities, Jesus implies to the rest of His followers that Judas was about to perform a special, necessary, and even Godly service, so that the "Son of Man may be glorified and God glorified in him."

If there had been no Judas to identify Jesus in the dark of night, the authorities would have been forced to arrest Him in public, which might well have sparked mass riots. Instead of a single notable sacrifice that history would remember for millennia, our children would grow up reading about mass casualties occurring that day. Or more likely, since Jesus' followers would have been the ones most likely to die in those riots, history would never have recorded the birth of Christianity at all. Thus, despite all the abuse heaped up against Judas over the millennia, the simple fact is that Jesus never would have been able to accomplish what He needed to do without having a brave partner who was also willing to take on an impossibly heavy burden of derision and guilt. Judas was, indeed, humanity's scapegoat. For 2,000 years, the figure we have come to know as Judas has been an object of unique human condemnation. To accept such an onerous burden knowingly, his willingness to take on guilt had to equal Jesus' own willingness to do so. Just like the two doomed goats of the Atonement Day sacrifice, both had to be equally willing to accept a burden of unimaginable guilt for their plan to succeed.

Judas Priest

Judaic tradition has long entertained the hypothesis that there would be two separate but equal facets to the Messiah, one priestly and one kingly. For millennia, however, Jews have disagreed over whether these two facets would both exist in the same man, or if there would actually be two separate Messiahs, a priestly one and a kingly one. The Dead Sea Scrolls prove that at least one major element of Jewish society fully expected two such Messiahs to emerge side by side. Contemporaries of Jesus and Judas, the society of devout Jews known as Essenes were convinced that the coming of those two Messiahs was imminent, virtually right on their doorstep. Christianity's spin on this ancient hypothesis, of course, was that when Christ appeared on Earth the first time, it was as the priestly Messiah, and when He returns in His Second Coming, it will be as the kingly Messiah.

Perhaps the mystical Essenes who wrote the Dead Sea Scrolls were right, after all, and both Messiahs *did* arrive on schedule in first-century Palestine. If Judas and Jesus were operating together in a secret partnership, perhaps they split these Messianic roles between them. It does seem that Judas was a priest, since, when he went to the temple to argue Jesus' innocence before the priests, the Bible testifies that he entered the *"naos,"* the Holy Place of the sanctuary of the temple, to speak to them.[20] Only priests were allowed to enter that inner portion of the temple. If Judas was allowed to enter the inner temple, he must have been a priest.

But was he the priestly *Messiah*? Or just a sinner? Like Barabbas, Judas' role in Jesus' crucifixion is also portrayed very unfavorably in the Bible. He is said to have betrayed Jesus for a paltry payment of 30 pieces of silver, which probably amounted to no more than a few hundred U.S. dollars. Such a small payout was obviously not the motive for his actions. And the stated reason why the authorities needed Judas in the first place doesn't really hold water either. The Jewish religious leaders, it is said, figured they had to arrest Jesus at night, away from all the massive crowds who followed Him everywhere during the day. All those followers, it was feared, would riot if they saw Jesus getting arrested, so they had to catch Him at night and needed someone to lead them to Him. But if Jesus really had all these crowds of faithful followers, then where were they when Pilate asked the crowds to decide between Jesus and Barabbas? These two stories just don't match up; either Jesus had those crowds in His hip pocket or He didn't. Either the Judas story is bogus, or the Barabbas story is.

Perhaps *both* are. We already know that the official church changed the original text of the Barabbas story. The question is, was the original report of Judas' role in this drama *also* rewritten? If church authorities saw fit to adulterate the original report they received about Jesus Bar Abbas, there is no telling what else they might have done, and where their treacherous revisions of the Holy Bible ultimately ended. Obviously, in order to erase intentionally such an intriguing and mysterious element as Barabbas' first name, these biblical editors must have felt that their own agendas were more important than the integrity of the revealed scriptures they were entrusted to protect and preserve.[21]

There is, in fact, compelling evidence that the biblical reports concerning Judas *were* changed after the fact, just as those of Barabbas were, since in its present form the Bible describes two mutually exclusive versions of Judas' death. In Matthew 27:5, we read that Judas "went away and hanged himself," but in Acts 1:18 we read instead that "Judas bought a field; there he fell headlong, his body burst open and all his intestines spilled out."[22] In Matthew, the priests buy the "Field of Blood" after Judas' death, but in Acts, Judas buys it himself before he dies, and somehow they both buy it with the same blood money Judas reportedly received from betraying Jesus. Obvious editorial inconsistencies such as this have done incalculable harm to claims of biblical inerrancy over the millennia. Just as they rewrote the original report about Barabbas, so too they apparently also altered the original data about Judas. Why? Why would they resort to fabricating reports of Judas' death? The question answers itself—because, very early in the nascent church's existence, when all the original apostles were still alive, someone in authority wanted the public to believe that Judas was dead. Why so? Perhaps because that was the only way this particular scapegoat could hope to walk away.

Could Judas, Thomas, and Barabbas have all been one and the same person? Such an identification could have been hidden by the early church's widespread use of nicknames. Both Thomas and Barabbas, after all, were nicknames, not true names. In fact, *all* the major figures in the early church, including Peter, James, John, Thomas, Lazarus, Barabbas, and Judas had nicknames. Simon was christened "Peter," which in today's vernacular would be like calling him "Rocky." James and John were "sons of thunder." Judas was "the twin." Jesus Barabbas was "son of the father." Lazarus was "the Osiris," "the one raised from the dead." And finally, we have the mysterious, little-mentioned twelfth apostle whose name variously appears in the Bible as Jude, Judas, Thaddaeus, or even Lebbaeus.[23] The simple fact that the canon can't even agree on this disciple's name raises nagging questions about his true identity. Even so, the Bible comes very close in Acts to identifying Judas as Barabbas. When a doctrinal crisis occurred and the original apostles had to send a delegation from Jerusalem to Antioch to clarify church teachings, a prominent church leader named "Judas Barsabbas" was chosen:

> Then the apostles and elders, with the whole church, decided to choose some of their own men and send them to Antioch. . . . They chose Judas (called Barsabbas) and Silas, two men who were leaders among the brethren. (Acts 15:22)

This peculiar nickname, *Bar Sabbas*, doesn't seem to mean anything in Aramaic. "Bar" means "son of," but "Sabbas" is no known Aramaic personal name or family name. Barsabbas is, however, so close to Barabbas that the simplest stroke of a pen could have transformed the one into the other. If so, this passage might have originally read "They chose Judas, the one said to be Barabbas." Choosing Jesus' brother for this mission would have made sense. The first doctrinal dispute in the original church had just arisen and had to be decisively addressed. The original apostles were still living in Jerusalem at that time and would have wanted to man their delegation to Antioch with figures of such undisputed position and authority that the Antiocheans would have had no ground to challenge their teachings. They not only would have wanted to send one of the original Twelve, but indeed the most prominent apostle they had available. If Jesus had a twin brother who had stood beside Him on that stage with Pilate, no other figure could have possibly held greater clout in the early church. Of course, if the original church had viewed Judas as a traitor, he would not have been honored. But at least one second-century sect, the Cainites, taught that Judas was not evil at all, but a great hero who deserved honor instead of condemnation.

The figure of Jude Thaddaeus is only mentioned five times in the gospels. But if, as the story in Acts suggests, the early church held Jude in such great esteem, then why does he have such a minor role in the rest of the Bible? In addition to Acts, Christian tradition also grants Jude unique status, saying that after the resurrection, *he* was the one who retrieved Christ's burial cloth, which many believe to be the Shroud of Turin. Of course, if Jude had been Jesus' twin, it would make sense for him to claim possession of his brother's shroud.

Two Halves Made One

Thousands of years ago, cultures all around the globe once taught the same catechism: that the whole universe reflected an original primordial duality, a divine whole comprised of two equal but opposite elements dancing together in perfect unison. Such a Divine Dyad is even reflected in one of the most frequently used names for "God" in the Old Testament: *Elohim* is a composite of the feminine plural of god *(Eloh)* and the masculine plural of god *(Im)*. Everything in our universe, BSD cultures once believed, reflected the United Dyad from which they arose, everything being comprised of two equal but opposite elements that reflected the qualities of the Dyad's divine halves. Certainly the human mind follows that same rule, being comprised of one half that is dominant and out in the open, and another half that is recessive and hidden.

If the ancient world's doctrine of such a divine duality is correct, the nature of the Messiah would have to follow that same binary pattern. Just as the human mind has two halves, even though we tend to be aware of only one of them, so too there would have been two Messiahs, even though we were aware of only one of them at the time. And just as we tend to reject, deny, ignore, and all too often even demonize the contents of our unconscious minds, we probably would have done the same thing to that other Messiah, the one who, just like our unconscious minds, was hidden and demonized: Judas Thomas, the *other* Jesus. The other half of the Son of God.

Could there have truly been two Christs? Amazingly, this seems to have genuinely been an open question in the minds of a great many people in the earliest years of the faith, and the idea even seems to be supported by certain passages in the Old Testament. The Hebrew Prophet Zechariah, for instance, specifically prophesied the coming of two Messiahs:

> I see, and behold, a lampstand all of gold, with a bowl on the top of it, and seven lamps on it, with seven lips on each of the lamps which are on the top of it. And there are two olive trees by it, one on the right of the bowl and the other on its left. (Zech. 4:2–3)

In his vision, Zechariah saw the Jewish menorah with an olive branch on either side of the candlestick. When he asked what the two olive branches were supposed to mean, he was told, "These are the two Messiahs who stand beside the Lord of the whole earth" (Zechariah 4:14). Those two olive branches, then, represented *two* Christs. This depiction of Zechariah's two Messiahs is even found on the state seal of Israel!

It is well known that many Gnostics originally believed there had been two Christs, one of whom was a being of pure spirit, while the other had a normal body of flesh. Of course, after the crucifixion, that would indeed have been the case if one of them had been crucified and the other allowed to escape. One would have been in spirit, while the other would have still been alive. And despite the official church's campaign to exterminate Gnosticism, this idea about two Messiahs does not seem to have quickly faded over time, but instead tenuously persisted even in the face of violent opposition. In fact, almost 500 years after Jesus' crucifixion, Constantinople Patriarch Macedonius II felt the need to inform Emperor Anastasius that he rejected the teaching that there had been two Sons or two Christs. Even that, however, didn't fully resolve the controversy, since the church found it necessary to refute the same idea all over again a few years later at the Second Council of Constantinople. What could have triggered such a refutation? To the student of the BSD, it can mean only one thing: Powerful cultural voices were still questioning, even at that late date, whether there may have originally been *more* than one Messiah. Although the voices of the Gnostics had been driven underground, they were apparently still being heard.

Similarly, many early heresies insisted that Jesus had not truly died on the cross, but that a substitute had died there in His place. Even Islam subscribes to this belief. If there had actually been two identical Messiahs, however, and one died while the other lived, such beliefs would be instantly explained. At least one early Christian sect not only believed that there had been two Messiahs, but that Judas Thomas himself had been the second Messiah:

> In a fragment from another apocryphal work, Jesus, approaching Simon Peter and Judas Thomas, addresses them "in the Hebrew language." There seems to have been some obfuscation, perhaps deliberate, in the translation of the original Coptic text, but what Jesus appears to say is: "Greetings, my venerable guardian Peter. Greetings, Thomas [Twin], my second Messiah."[24]

If Judas Thomas indeed was a second Christ, a scapegoat who "got away," what happened after that? Did Thomas leave any other legacy that might further flesh out the lost history of Original Christianity? If Thomas was Christ's twin brother, Jude, that would explain history's persistent rumors about Christ leaving behind a direct bloodline of descendants. According to the fourth-century church historian Eusebius, the apostle Jude sired a line of descendants called the Desposyni.[25] If Jude and Jesus were identical twin brothers and equal Messiahs, Jude's descendants might have been credited as Jesus' own offspring. Judas Thomas did not merely produce a family, however; he actually produced a whole church of his own. If the Roman Church was founded by Constantine, then the Indian Church was founded by Thomas. Church records hinting that Thomas traveled to the land of the Hindus are fleshed out by Indian traditions, which insist that Thomas emigrated from Palestine to India by boat, taking passage on a trading vessel that sailed down the Red Sea and across the Persian Gulf to arrive at the port of Cranganore on India's southwest coast in 52 A.D. Today, some six million Indians call themselves Mar Thoma (Saint Thomas) Christians, proudly claiming to be direct blood descendants of converts baptized by the apostle.

The Indian church of Saint Thomas turned out to be a unique sociological experiment, left alone to evolve in almost perfect isolation from the rest of Christiandom. If their local legends are correct, the seed Thomas planted in the rich spiritual climate of India was left undisturbed for over 1,500 years, which seems to have allowed it to preserve many customs, beliefs, and traditions that were edited out of the official church. For centuries, the Christians of Saint Thomas had women deacons, kept the Jewish Sabbath, and followed a liturgy that included fixed days of fasting and abstinence. In fact, they still used two of the oldest Christian liturgies in existence—the Mass of Addai and Mari, and the Liturgy of Saint James—which date all the way back to the original church in Jerusalem before its destruction in 70 A.D. They even sang in Aramaic, the original language of Christianity.

The Mar Thoma Christians, however, did not merely follow a more primitive form of Christianity; they subscribed to a fundamentally different set of teachings from the Roman church. The Christians of Saint Thomas believed wholeheartedly in reincarnation, and they also believed that Saint Thomas had been a Messiah or Christ in his own right:

> This cult amounted to a kind of St. Thomas religion, and this is attested to by Bishop Jordan, the French Dominican friar who was sent to Quilon by Pope John XXII, in 1330, to convert the Syrians to the Roman creed. Friar Jordan soon had to abandon his Indian flock as incorrigible, and in *Marvels Described,* writes, "In this India there is a scattered people, one here, another there, who call themselves Christian, but are not so, nor have they baptism, nor do they know anything about the faith: nay, they believe St. Thomas the Great to be Christ."[26]

All that changed in the seventeenth century, when a Portuguese archbishop named Menezes forced the Saint Thomas Christians to abandon their ancient traditions and adopt the teachings and practices of Catholicism instead. All their sacred texts and writings were confiscated and destroyed, and they were forced to embrace alien beliefs and practices, such as Mary being the mother of God, and the use of images and icons. They were even forced to dress in "Catholic" attire and forbidden to use Hindu musicians in their services. According to local tradition, thousands who refused to compromise their original faith were labeled "Judaizers" and burned at the stake, while others fled for their lives to other areas of India.

Prior to this outside interference, however, the Saint Thomas Christians had been such a remarkably stable church and one that took such pride in its origins that it still preserved the original songs, liturgies, and language of its founder. But once the official church stepped in, India's church became infected with the same disease afflicting all the rest of the world's churches and immediately started fracturing into smaller and smaller sects. What had successfully remained a single, unified church for more than 1,500 years shattered apart into the Latin Catholic Church, the Syro-Malabar Catholic Church, the Jacobite Syrian Church, the Nestorian Church, the Anglican Church, the Marthoma Syrian Church, and the Syro-Malankara Catholic Church.

Fortunately, even though the historical records of the Saint Thomas Christians were all put to the flame, their cultural legends survived, preserved in the memories of India's six million Christians. Hundreds of traditional songs about Saint Thomas, as well as two ancient full-length ballads that seem to date from the earliest years of Christianity, are still sung in India today.[27]

All this devotion raises a perplexing question: If the Saint Thomas Christians were so conscientious about preserving the legacy they received from the apostle Thomas, then why did they believe in reincarnation, which was the case when the Catholics showed up in 1599? Was the belief there from the beginning? Did Thomas teach a Christianity to the Indians that incorporated both reincarnation and resurrection? Did he, in other words, teach the binary soul doctrine? It certainly seems that he may have. The Christians of Saint Thomas were almost fanatically obsessive about preserving the original contents of their faith when Rome finally caught up with them, but even so, they still believed in a Christianity that included reincarnation. Either that belief originated with Thomas or, despite their apparent devotion to authenticity, it somehow managed to slip in later.

The official church, of course, maintains that Thomas did *not* teach a reincarnationist Christianity to the Indians, but that they instead allowed their own country's widespread belief in reincarnation to slip in eventually and corrupt Thomas' original teachings. This argument does not hold up, however. If Saint Thomas Christianity had *not* originally included reincarnation, it would have been virtually impossible for it to have found any acceptance in India's strongly pro-reincarnationist culture. A cultural debate over reincarnation would have immediately arisen, especially since Christianity's original message revolved around the concept of providing a way to survive death. This debate would have completely dominated public opinion about and interest in this strange new religion. Since India's primary faiths—Hinduism, Buddhism, and Jainism—were all strongly pro-reincarnationist, Christianity would have been unique, labeled from the first as "that non-reincarnationist religion." Christianity would have stood out like a sore thumb. If, as the official church maintains, it then chose to reverse itself on that issue at some later point, the religion would have lost whatever respect it might have otherwise accrued in the eyes of the people. It could never have survived a reversal on the one issue it originally became known for in their country. Yet when the official church took over the Indian church in the seventeenth century, it found Saint Thomas Christians not only to be devoted reincarnationists, but also highly respected in Indian society. The only explanation for this would be if Thomas had preached reincarnation right from the beginning.

If Thomas taught a version of Christianity that included reincarnation, it almost certainly would have been the binary soul doctrine, for no other theology is able to reconcile the multiple conflicts between reincarnation and resurrection. As it turns out, a number of elements in the Book of Jude would seem to support this hypothesis. In Jude 10, for instance, he complains that many in the early church were ignorantly condemning teachings they didn't understand; this is the very argument Gnostics were leveling against the orthodox in those earliest days. In Jude 6, he mysteriously mentions angels who fled their homes and betrayed their responsibilities, an apt metaphor for conscious spirits who abandon their unconscious souls at the end of each life. Jude reports that those angels were condemned to remain bound in darkness until Judgment Day, which again is metaphorically consistent with the BSD's teaching that the conscious spirit's penalty for that act of betrayal was to remain bound in the darkness of memory loss until Judgment Day. And in Jude 4, 8, 11, and 12, he repeatedly criticizes these same individuals for practices that misinterpreted key tenets of theology. Most probably, given the text, they had been using the Gnostic tradition of Sacred Marriage as an excuse for licentious sex. Jude didn't criticize them for subscribing to that Gnostic theology itself, but merely for adapting it to their own immoral purposes. It is particularly interesting that Jude in the text condemns these faithless Christians as "twice dead," which would seem to be a clear reference to the second death that figures so prominently in the binary soul doctrine. Declaring them to be both fruitless and uprooted, his terminology reminds the student of the BSD that sinners have no roots (recollection of their own pasts), nor can they hope to see their own fruit (subsequent incarnations).

Unfortunately, since Rome consigned the Indian church's ancient scriptures to a fiery holocaust, all physical evidence that might have demonstrated the presence of the BSD in the early Indian church has been lost. Thomas *himself* may be that evidence, however. By recognizing the connection between the BSD and Israel's traditional Atonement Day ritual, we noticed that Jesus Christ and Jesus Barabbas seemed purposefully to recreate that same ritual, taking the places of the sacrificial goats. By then recognizing the logical connection between Barabbas—who had to be Jesus' perfect twin in order to be a proper scapegoat in that ritual—and Judas Thomas—who indeed was said to be Jesus' twin brother—we were left asking if the apostle Thomas had been a *second* Messiah, perhaps even the second savior predicted by the Old Testament and expected by the Essenes. Was Thomas truly the Atonement Day scapegoat who got away, a second Messiah, a second Son of God? And if so, how would we know?

The Old Testament is silent on the eventual fate of the scapegoat, reporting only that it was always allowed to wander far away, just as Thomas did. Nonetheless, one cannot help but wonder, if there had indeed been *two* Messiahs standing on that stage beside Pilate, *two* Jesuses equally ready and willing to take the cross, would they then have *both* possessed the power to raise from the dead? The Acts of Thomas, yet another ancient Christian scripture, seems to feed this suspicion, ending on a very curious and intriguing note, with yet another empty tomb. Just like his more famous twin brother, Thomas met his death with a lance in the side. And when Judas Thomas was finally laid to rest in his own sepulcher in India, it was also later discovered to be empty.[28] The text of the Acts of Thomas goes on to explain the empty tomb by suggesting that the body was probably robbed by those wishing to use it for magical purposes, but one cannot read this rationalization without being reminded that the very same theory was used by those arguing against Jesus' own resurrection four decades earlier:

> Now it came to pass after a long time that one of the children of Misdaeus the king was smitten by a devil, and no man could cure him, for the devil was exceeding fierce. And Misdaeus the king took thought and said: I will go and open the sepulchre, and take a bone of the apostle of God and hang it upon my son and he shall be healed. . . . And he went and opened the sepulchre, but found not the apostle there. (The Acts of Judas Thomas)

And here, perhaps, we finally find the origin of the ancient report about "Doubting Thomas" who insisted on physical proof that Jesus had risen from the grave, demanding to touch Jesus' wounds with his own fingers. That one incident condemned Thomas to be forever labeled the "apostle of little faith," even though he paradoxically exhibited the *greatest faith* of all the apostles in the Lazarus incident, when he was ready to die immediately:

> [Jesus] told them plainly, "Lazarus is dead, and for your sake I am glad I was not there, so that you may believe. But let us go to him." Then Thomas (called Didymus) said to the rest of the disciples, "Let us also go, that we may die with him." (The Gospel of John 11:14–16)

During the Lazarus incident, Thomas seems to have had complete faith in the power of resurrection, even *before* he personally witnessed Lazarus' decayed body rising from the dead. But when Jesus subsequently died and rose from the dead Himself, Thomas displayed far more personal interest in Jesus' Resurrection body than any of the other apostles did. Was this because he had suddenly and inexplicably lost his previous faith in resurrection, or was this interest a far more private matter, knowing that the day would eventually come when he himself would experience the same miraculous phenomenon his twin brother had just gone through?

The BSD repeatedly appears alongside this notion of dual Christs.

Basilides, a Christian Gnostic who had a following in first-century Alexandria, taught a dualistic form of Christianity that included a belief in both reincarnation and resurrection, and he insisted that someone else substituted for Christ on the cross. And both the Mandaeans (who claim to have been the original followers of John the Baptist) and the Manichaeans believed in dual souls that divide at death, and they also maintained that someone took Christ's place at Calvary. Like many contemporary Muslims, modern Mandaeans specifically identify Thomas as that substitute:

> All Mandaeans believe that not only was Judas Thomas Jesus' twin, but that it was this Judas who was crucified in Jesus' place. They believe that Jesus afterwards took on the identity of his brother, calling himself Thomas, and that he was the true author of The Gospel of Thomas, as well as supposedly The Gospel of John.[29]

This unorthodox suggestion of a second Christ also appears in Leonardo da Vinci's *The Last Supper,* where the second figure from the left seems a perfect twin of the Christ sitting at the center of the table, even wearing the same clothes. And, as many have become aware through such books as *Holy Blood, Holy Grail* and *The Da Vinci Code,* the mysterious Church of Mary Magdalene at Rennes-le-Château, France (which was once the heartland of the BSD-believing Cathars), also depicts twin Messiahs. Mysterious renovations of the church in the late nineteenth century placed statues of Mary and Joseph on either side of the altar, each holding an identical Christ child.[30] From Zechariah's "olive tree" prophecy of the coming of twin Messiahs, to the Essenes who felt the arrival of those two Messiahs was imminent, to early Christian groups who insisted that two Messiahs had indeed arrived, to Manichaean, Mandaean, and Islamic teachings that a look-alike substituted for Jesus on the cross, to Mar Thoma Christians' tradition that Judas Thomas had been a Messiah in his own right, to Leonardo da Vinci's depiction of two Christs in his Inquisition-era work, to a nineteenth-century display of twin baby Jesuses in a Catholic church in France, this hypothesis has simply refused to die a quiet death.

Zechariah's two olive trees make just one other appearance in the Bible, in the Book of Revelation, and there again they are said to symbolize God's two special servants. In Zechariah, the two olive trees are openly identified as divinely anointed Messiahs. In Revelation, they are similarly identified as God's specially empowered prophets. Revelation uses the exact same phrase in Zechariah, "the two olive trees that stand before the Lord of the earth," making it clear that these are the very same figures Zechariah prophesied about centuries earlier:

> And I will give power to my two witnesses, and they will prophesy. . . . These are the two olive trees and the two lampstands that stand before the Lord of the earth. . . . Now when they have finished their testimony, the beast [will] kill them. . . . After three and a half days a breath of life from God entered them, and they stood on their feet. . . . Then they heard a loud voice from heaven saying to them, "Come up here." And they went up to heaven in a cloud. (Rev. 11:3–12)

It is interesting to note that Revelation depicts both of these servants preaching God's word for a time, and then they are murdered, and then they both rise from the dead and ascend into heaven. It is even more interesting to note that the tense of the verbs changes halfway through these passages. The passage literally declares that these two Messiahs *already* died, *already* rose from the dead, and *already* ascended into heaven. Was the author of Revelation describing a future event, or was he trying to secretly preserve forbidden knowledge of Christianity's past by inserting it into scripture disguised as a future event? Does Revelation record the dual Messiahship, dual murders, and dual resurrections of Jesus and Thomas?

Official Christianity has long criticized Judaism for failing to recognize its long-awaited Messiah when He finally showed up, but the truth of the matter may be more complex than that. If the Jews could miss one Messiah in their midst, they could probably miss two. And if a people who had been breathlessly anticipating the imminent arrival of their Messiah for centuries could miss Him when He appeared, the majority of Christians could probably overlook one as well. We may never know for sure if Thomas was really a second Christ, or if the Gospel of Thomas was truly written by one of Israel's long-awaited Messiahs. But there would be something deliciously appropriate in discovering that the Christian salvation that was designed to heal humanity's divided hearts, finally allowing both halves of our beings to work perfectly together as one again, was orchestrated by two Messiahs who worked perfectly together as one Themselves.

Conclusion

A Christian Manifesto

The light shines in the darkness, but the darkness has not understood it.
—The Gospel of John 1:5

By the fifth century, it had become a capital crime to possess any literature critical of official Christianity. The Romans were killing Christians again, but unlike the first persecutions, believers no longer had the option of escaping the sword by paying lip service to Caesar. This time, a loved one could be cut down simply for possessing something that seemed to be contraband literature. People had no choice but to make sure that everything even potentially questionable was removed from their homes and destroyed.

The death penalty is a powerful deterrent, which is why humanity's understanding of Christian origins is now so one-sided. Today, apologists for the official church confidently trot out texts and lists from the second and third centuries that genuinely seem to support their argument that the Gnostic scriptures were rejected by the majority of believers right from the beginning. But since any texts that might have shown otherwise are certain to have been destroyed, such arguments rest on nothing but compromised evidence.

Thanks to the rampant paranoia of those centuries, the church found itself unwilling to preserve the works of *any* of its first historians; the writings of Papias, Julius Africanus, Hegesippus, and many other authors were all washed away by the tide of Roman censorship. Papias, who was said to have personally met the apostle John, wrote his histories in vain, for they have all vanished. Julius Africanus, the first Christian historian to produce a universal chronology, studied extensively in the Gnostic hotbed of Alexandria, which is perhaps why his work is also missing. And Hegesippus, who was said to have used both a Gospel of the Hebrews and a Syriac Gospel (probably the Gospel of Thomas), is poignantly called the father of church history even though his works were all allowed to disappear.

After this purge of the works of Christianity's first historians was complete, the church was left with virtually nothing earlier than the histories of Eusebius of Caesarea, an orthodox writer from the fourth century who is now generally credited as the "first" major Christian historian. This is indefensible. For hundreds of years, the church was the most powerful institution on earth. If it had wanted these eyewitness reports on the earliest developmental stages of Christianity to be preserved, they would be but a click away on the Internet. Instead, they are phantoms, empty forms filled with nothing but the content of our own imaginations.

In the practice of law, compromised evidence is deemed inadmissible for good reason. If you walked into a courtroom seeking justice only to discover that your opponent had been allowed to destroy preemptively all evidence that might have supported your position, you could pretty much guess which way the remaining evidence would lean. The official church, by its own admission, destroyed all evidence that might have supported the Gnostic scriptures. Knowing this, it is intellectually dishonest for orthodox apologists to point to extant second-century lists of approved scriptures as evidence of anything but their own organization's conspiracy. Since such lists are all that remained after their editing and censorship, they reflect nothing beyond that editing and censorship itself.

The church was not content with simply censoring undesirable texts; it also felt the need to modify the texts it chose to keep. In Bart Ehrman's masterful 1993 work *The Orthodox Corruption of Scripture,* he painstakingly demonstrates that the early church widely engaged in corruptive textual modification practices.[1] A specialist in the study of partial and whole New Testament manuscripts, Ehrman presents compelling evidence that orthodox scribes freely added and subtracted from the canonical texts to emphasize their own theological agendas.

This all leads to one revolutionary question: Could Christ's original teachings have truly been lost? Such things do happen; founding a major world religion is no guarantee that one's teachings will survive. Born in 216 A.D., the Iranian prophet Mani founded what was once a vastly popular religion. Manichaeism spread across Europe, the Middle East, India, and China, and survived well into the fourteenth century. Mani personally wrote seven canonical scriptures, but widespread political censorship eventually erased all those texts from the face of the earth. Although he founded a world religion that lasted for more than a thousand years, *none* of Mani's written works survived history intact. The same thing, it seems now, happened to Original Christianity, and if we had not discovered the texts buried at Nag Hammadi, the world would never have known that this "bait and switch" took place. When the BSD was edited out of Original Christianity all those years ago, the faith lost two major tenets: the doctrine of reincarnation and the importance of integrity.

Hello Again, Old Friends

The ancient church listed five complaints against belief in reincarnation, all of which are completely satisfied by the binary soul doctrine:

1. People seem to have no memory of previous lives.
2. Reincarnation seems to conflict with resurrection.
3. Reincarnation seems to minimize the Christian salvation.
4. Reincarnation requires a distinction between body and soul.
5. Scriptural support for reincarnation seems subjective and speculative.

Of course, the BSD's concept of an after-death soul division immediately explains why memory loss occurs between lives, and it reconciles reincarnation and resurrection by providing a separate element for each: The spirit reincarnates while the soul is only restored via resurrection. And instead of minimizing the Christian salvation, the BSD shows it to be tremendously more glorious than the official church ever imagined, providing each of us with not merely one life saved, but a vast personal legacy of past-life selves that would all be saved and reunited. The final two complaints are not criticisms of a doctrine, but misreadings of the Bible itself, for the canon clearly distinguishes between body, soul, and spirit in numerous passages, as well as openly declaring that Elijah came back as John the Baptist, possessing the very same spirit that had previously incarnated as Elijah. Thus the BSD satisfies *all* the church's ancient challenges to reincarnation.

While editing reincarnation out of Original Christianity was a great loss, losing the faith's original appreciation of the importance of whole-ness, purity, and integrity was a far more destructive sacrifice. As soon as the nascent church started to distinguish itself from Judaism, a fundamen-tal issue arose, which continued to torment the faithful for centuries to come: What was more important for salvation, a person's purity and integrity or a person's faith? This issue arose in the very first years of the church, when the disciples who had walked with Jesus during His ministry all held that a person's purity was of absolute importance, whereas Paul insisted that all the old rules governing purity were now irrelevant, and the only thing that mattered after Christ's Resurrection was a person's faith.

Centered in Jerusalem, the Jewish Christian movement, originally called "the Way," included the Twelve Apostles along with many of Jesus' other followers. This group initially required its members to continue fol-lowing Jewish dietary laws, arrange for ritual animal sacrifices in the tem-ple, and have their male children circumcised. But Paul challenged these teachings, arguing that Jesus had rendered the whole purity issue irrele-vant; instead of relying on one's purity to get to heaven, one now had to rely exclusively on one's faith in Jesus' promise of salvation.[2] (Tellingly, however, even Paul seemed to have originally been a little confused about this whole issue, since he is on record as observing the purity obligations on at least two separate occasions after his conversion.[3])

This issue reemerged with a vengeance in 251 A.D., when the congre-gation of the faithful again found itself torn between those who believed purity to be more important than faith, and those who viewed faith as more important than purity. At that time, two different popes arose, Novatian and Cornelius, each championing one of these two positions. The issue remained a sore point in the church for centuries to come, as did the schism between the Novatianists and the official church.

The scriptures found at Nag Hammadi make it clear that the most well-known conflict in the early church revolved around this same issue. However, that ancient dispute between the Gnostic and official churches, the BSD suggests, was based on a misunderstanding. One side thought that Christ's original message was one of faith, while the other thought it was one of purity, but they both misunderstood. It was not a question of either/or, but both/neither. Christ taught neither purity *nor* faith alone, but purity *and* faith. Once the two branches of the church started choos-ing one or the other, the true faith was already lost.

In the end, the official church won the political war against the

Gnostic Church, but that victory came at the price of purity and integrity.[4] Born in a bloodbath, the official church became the ultimate symbol of man's inhumanity to man. From the torture chambers of the Inquisition to the mindless barbarities of the Crusades, from the attempted genocide of the Cathars and Huguenots in France to those of the Jews and Moors in Spain, the church became the epitome of unspeakable corruption.

Like Father, Like Son

> You belong to your father, the devil, and you want to carry out your father's desire. He was a murderer from the beginning, not holding to the truth, for there is no truth in him. When he lies, he speaks his native language, for he is a liar and the father of lies. (John 8:44)

The church's students learned the lessons it taught. Western civilization was built on the foundation of the official church's corruption and reflects it as a son reflects his father. Today, much of the world sees the United States as a den of thieves and murderers, convinced that the U.S. invasion of Iraq was nothing but a blatant land-grab. While many Americans aggressively dispute that perspective, others might wonder if we are deluding ourselves. Even a casual look at the news suggests that our civilization is infested through and through with thievery, from the dishonest executives at the top of the food chain to the blatantly dishonest folk at the bottom who insist it is their god-given right to steal anything they can find online from the music and motion picture industries. With executives at huge companies like Enron, Martha Stewart Living Omnimedia, Edward Jones, ImClone Systems, WorldCom, Tyco, Rite Aid, Qwest, Arthur Anderson, Halliburton, Merrill Lynch, Citigroup, Adelphia Communications, and Xerox all getting caught cheating in recent years, America's current business motto seems to be that "crime not only pays but pays big enough to cover the potential costs of getting caught." Meanwhile, what Americans can't steal up front, we often steal after the fact; defaulting on our debts via bankruptcy has become so widespread it is almost our new national pastime. And as this is being written, the Bush administration is taking the same route, embracing a weak dollar as a means of getting out of the problem of its $500 billion per year trade deficit.

Does *anyone* in American culture still respect integrity? Still encourage it? Still think it is the most advantageous path a person can walk in life? Even a brief look at popular culture gives the impression that much of

America feels that personal integrity is nothing but a liability. And until that changes, the United States will just keep growing more and more corrupt, and ensnaring itself in more and more conflicts of its own making.

The ancient BSD insisted that the average human being has no integrity, that the two halves of our mental being are not successfully communicating with one another. However, there's a far more familiar word for this: lying. One half of our being has been lying to itself about the other half of our being, and we've been doing this for so long we now do it almost completely unconsciously, without even being aware of it. If an alien species ever shows up willing to give us a truly unbiased opinion of our species, they will surely say that "lying to ourselves" is what we do best.

The conscious mind has been refusing to accept input being generated by the unconscious. The unconscious, meanwhile, has continued to generate more and more input, which has built up, and built up, and built up. Each time we lie to ourselves about ourselves, we reinforce the division within us a little more, adding yet more psychic debris to a growing pile that we actively struggle against, actively repressing it.

A Baptism into Self-Honesty

> Why is my language not clear to you? Because you are unable to hear what I say. (John 8:43)

This wall of repressed material in the unconscious is our whole problem. So long as this material remains, we will never have integrity as individuals, or communities, or nations, or religions. How do we fix this problem? One thing is certain—we don't fix it by simply *pretending* that we have integrity. Integrity is not reacquired through superficial posturing or behavior modification. The way to acquire true integrity is to correct the communication failure, and that requires getting rid of the blockage preventing communication between our conscious and unconscious. And the only way to do *that* is to allow all that repressed psychological material to reach its destination—our conscious minds.

But we cannot do this on our own, because our whole system has been compromised, and are now so completely corrupted and malfunctioning that we can no longer fix ourselves. A corrupted system cannot repair or regulate itself. After our many lifetimes of self-deception, we are so full of all sorts of deceptive unconscious psychological garbage that we can no longer know at any moment if we are really being truthful to ourselves or if we are just being unwittingly manipulated by yet another automatic unconscious knee-jerk reaction to stimuli. Until Jesus arrived, we were trapped in a circular dilemma: Until we cleaned out our neglected mental closets, we would have no integrity, but because of our lack of integrity, we couldn't clean out our mental closets.

To break this stalemate, we had to find an outside element still possessing the purity and integrity we lacked, so that it could guide us out of the dilemma we had created for ourselves. Original Christianity, of course, maintained that Christ Himself was that guide, but also insisted that the solution He offered was conditional. We needed to: (A) believe that He did indeed exist and could be contacted, (B) open a line of communication with Him in our hearts and minds, and (C) ask Him to guide us out of our unhealthy cycle of behavior by pointing out all the ways we betrayed our ideals in the past.

In 12-Step programs, this process is called "taking a moral inventory." In contemporary culture, it is called "soul-searching." In Toltec thought, it was called "recapitulation." This same fundamental step was also required of all believers in Original Christianity: "a baptism of repentance for the forgiveness of sins." In the beginning, baptism had nothing to do with the ritualistic confession of faith it has become today, but was instead an excruciating emotional purge. Original Christianity called it "an immersion," submerging seekers in their sinful memories, baptizing them in their unacknowledged self-disgust and heartbreak over having betrayed their highest ideals. It was a profoundly transformative experience of heightened self-consciousness and self-honesty.

The path of integrity is an internal path, ultimately independent of any cultural institution or organized religion. It is the way by which all true religions guide their followers to eternal life, and without which, none will. Such a cleansing was the first step in a great many different spiritual disciplines, but it has been forgotten by most New Age approaches, while official Christianity reduced it to an empty ritual performed on newborn infants. Nonetheless the original form of baptism still exists and still has the same power to restore our purity, wholeness, and integrity today.

This, Original Christianity believed, is the path Jesus guides us down inside our own minds, whether or not we even realize He is involved with our process at all. He doesn't mind. He doesn't care if we know His real name (we don't) or His true history (we don't). We don't even know ourselves, so how can we dare to pretend we know Jesus? Fortunately, it doesn't matter if we do or not, if we know His name or not, if we call ourselves

Christian or not. All He cares about is our reacquisition of our integrity. As long as we are trying to go in that direction, He is there helping us along the path and guaranteeing we will eventually reach our destination safely.

Blasphemy: Hatred in the Name of God

Many cultural versions of the binary soul doctrine maintained that duality is the signature of the universe itself and that everything in existence comes ready-made with two equal but opposite elements engaged in an endless dance. A corollary of this idea being that things tend to be defined by their opposites, wise men once cautioned their students to "be very careful in choosing your enemies, for you will become just like them."

On 9/11, when enemies were perceived as attacking us from religious motives, it became virtually impossible to avoid a religious response. President Bush confirmed this early on, by almost immediately appearing in the pulpits of American churches. Since then, one of America's top generals told church audiences that the war on terrorism is a battle with Satan, while Malaysian Prime Minister Mahathir Mohamad told a summit of Muslim leaders that Jews unfairly rule the world, calling upon the world's 1.3 billion Muslims to join together to achieve a "final victory" over the world's Jews.

With such stories in the news, can anyone think the age of religious warfare is over? Fortunately, the rediscovery of the binary soul doctrine provides the world a rare opportunity to reevaluate its religious beliefs objectively, a chance to embrace the common foundation underlying Islam, Judaism, and Christianity and thus heal the ancient divisions among them. With the revelation that all three traditions' beliefs about the afterlife have their origin in the same mechanics of the human psyche, these religions have a chance to return to their roots, shedding the corruptions, misunderstandings, and wrong turns that transformed them into the horrors we've inherited today.

But until the West again embraces Christianity's original worship of personal integrity and reintroduces the healing practice of true soul-searching baptism, our culture will remain too corrupt and mentally unbalanced to see its enemies clearly enough to have any chance of truly ending war. These enemies are popularly portrayed as hate-filled religious fanatics, but that's what they say about us as well. Even though both Christianity and Islam preach love rather than hate, people in each camp enthusiastically hate, condemn, and kill their opposites in the name of God. The reason we can embrace these contradictions is because our minds are still sick. As slaves of our inner spiritual corruption, we often fail to recognize consciously those elements of ourselves that are most abhorrent to us. Instead of admitting we possess these unattractive traits, we ignore and deny their presence within us.

Unfortunately, self-deception is not the end of the story. This refusal to admit the truth to ourselves about the way we are and what we have done does not disappear simply because we choose to ignore it. On an unconscious level, we still know the truth about ourselves. Our unconscious still knows we possess this abhorrent quality and continues to attack it, trying to purge this undesired trait. This unconscious self-repulsion causes us to feel a tremendously compelling urge to reject and condemn this trait, but since we are not admitting to ourselves that we possess this trait, we are unable to do so. Nonetheless the unconscious will not stop pestering us about it until we admit our error and repent.

That leaves us in a bind. We cannot repair the fault, nor can we escape our continuing inner urge to repair it. So we look for other places where it might be found, so we can condemn it there instead. We project onto others those traits of our own that we hate, but cannot admit we possess. We feel such a strong inner need to condemn these traits that we unconsciously seek them out in others, and once we have convinced ourselves that we have found these hated traits in others, we feel very comfortable condemning them in that context.

No matter how many others we are driven to persecute and condemn, however, our inner drive is never truly satisfied until we turn our searchlight back on ourselves, finally rooting out and expelling our own inner faults. Only then will we find the peace we seek. Once we have rooted out our own inner faults, we find, seemingly miraculously, that we no longer seem to observe these hated faults everywhere we look. The bottom line is, the more we rail against some hated trait in our enemies, the more we unconsciously identify with that very trait and the more we unconsciously condemn ourselves for the very thing we openly condemn in others.

How to Win a Holy War

> *Jesus said, "You see the mote in your brother's eye, but you don't see the board in your own eye. When you take the board out of your own eye, then you will see well enough to remove the mote from your brother's eye." (The Gospel of Thomas 26)*

Yes, we are in a religious war, but ultimately it has nothing to do with a fight between Islam and Christianity. The conflict before us today is much more fundamental, having to do with humankind's betrayal of its own sacred ideals. As soon as humans decided that instead of loving their neighbors, they could control and manipulate them, war became inevitable. America's political opponent in this war is completely irrelevant, because that opponent is just a mirror that God graciously provided to help us become conscious of our self-betrayals. If the enemy in this conflict hadn't turned out to be Islamic militants, it would have been some other equally challenging group; one way or another, the mirrorlike role of our equal opposite would have been filled, and the drama played out.

All peoples and nations on earth, according to the Bible, live and breathe and have their being *inside* God (Acts 17:28). It follows, then, that everything in our lives can only be truly understood in that context. If so, then there is really only one relationship that has ever existed or ever will: our relationship with God, the relationship of the part to the Whole. Every other relationship we seem to have in this world is just a reflection and representation of that primary relationship. If we seem to have a problem with one another, it is because we are really having a problem in our relationship with God. And if we correct that primary relationship, then all our earthly relationships will reflect the same health that our relationship with God enjoys. If we want peace with our fellow humans, we must first find peace with God.

This is not news. Humanity has always known this. Nonetheless the war that the United States is in won't go away until the war accomplishes what it came for—to force us to confront fully our self-deceptions and self-betrayals. Islam is not our enemy in this battle, but our dearest friend, for it is taking on the thankless task of forcing the Christian West to confront its sins, nudging us back toward our original ideals, so we can finally fulfill Christianity's exalted potential. There is no way around this obligation, for we owe it to both ourselves and our Creator. One way or another, our culture is doomed to suffer a painful process of self-confrontation, and this war won't truly end until we do. The outer battle may change, assuming different shapes, designs, and appearances, but it won't disappear from our path until the inner reason for its existence has been satisfied.

The only way to win this outer war is first to address the secret conflict raging in each of our hearts. This war calls the United States to a *true* baptism of repentance. While authentic baptism is always painful, it is well worth it, for once we are healed, all our worldly relationships can then finally be healed as well. As long as we remain sick, all our relationships will be sick as well, for our inner spiritual disease will corrupt all we do. We must, both individually and as a people, confront, acknowledge, condemn, and repent our sins in this world. This repentance must occur both on the individual and collective levels of our being.

We in the West must publicly confess and wholeheartedly condemn the many deceptive, immoral, and illegal practices of our FBI, CIA, NSA, and similar organizations. Our country must admit trying to manipulate secretly the internal affairs of foreign nations and democracies, and must make amends where we can. We must start measuring the Israelis and Palestinians with the same moral yardstick and admit failing to do so in the past. We must ensure open and transparent elections, not allowing our powerful to manipulate our weak secretly. We must prevent our rich from secretly manipulating our markets, our well-connected from secretly escaping our justice, and our jailers from secretly torturing our prisoners. On every level, from the highest governmental agency to the innermost crannies of every human heart, we must utterly reject the practice of worshiping darkness—that is to say, we must stop putting our faith in the power of lies and secrecy.

Evil can only thrive in darkness, so light must be shined into every dark corner. This is the only cure for the moral crisis threatening our civilization. We can no longer tolerate living in denial—neither the denial of our self-deception nor the denial of governmental deception. Until we find the faith, courage, and integrity to confront and expose our lies, they will just keep knocking on our doors, blindsiding us and derailing our lives. No substitute or stopgap measure can even temporarily save our children from the grief of this confrontation. Once the United States stands up once again, however, as a people of true honor and uncompromised integrity, a country driven by its ideals of truth, justice, and brotherly love rather than its fears and anxieties, we will again be a nation the world community will respect and wish to emulate.

Jesus insisted that we always have to clean up our own internal problems before trying to fix anyone else's, but once we *do* bite the bullet and attend to our sins and clean out our eyes, we will see clearly enough to help our fellow nations see clearly as well. Once we are all seeing clearly together, we will be able to address and peacefully resolve problems between us.

To proceed on that assumption alone, of course, would be an act of pure faith, a daring leap into the unknown. The question before us is this: Once we have suffered through the grief of purging ourselves of our sins, will we then really see new solutions to our problems miraculously appear before our minds' eyes, or not? We cannot hope to see those solutions *before* we clean out our eyes and can only take it on faith that those solutions will become apparent to us once we do. It is a leap of faith, pure and simple. All we have to go on are the promises of those who have walked the path before us. Jesus promised that once we heal our self-inflicted wounds and become whole again, we could then be the pure light unto the world that America's forefathers envisioned:

[Jesus said,] "There is light within a person of light, and it shines on the whole world. [But] if it does not shine, it is dark." (The Gospel of Thomas 24)

Appendix A

The Second Council of Constantinople

Until the Second Council of Constantinople in 553 A.D.,[1] no specific condemnation of the doctrine of reincarnation had occurred within the church, even though it was well known that many different sects had been teaching forms of Christianity that included reincarnation. Although the Council of Nicaea had implicitly outlawed all unapproved teachings 200 years earlier, it had not specifically addressed reincarnation. Apparently, great numbers of Christians still subscribed to this belief in the sixth century, because the church felt it necessary at that time to single out reincarnation and condemn it *explicitly*. At the Second Council of Constantinople, the belief in reincarnation was bundled together with other ideas under the catchall phrase "preexistence of the soul," and condemned as a crime punishable by death.

As had been the case in Nicaea, a lot of politics were involved. This council was summoned by the Emperor Justinian, *not* Pope Vigilius, the official head of the Christian church. In fact, the pope refused to attend the council because he felt Justinian was playing politics with the church, unjustly manipulating the council to arrive at a predetermined conclusion. At first, the pope refused to support the decisions of the council, but was eventually coerced into reversing his opinion.[2] The Western church, which had also refused to accept the council's decisions, then excommunicated Pope Vigilius for his reversal and split away from the church of Rome. The schism lasted for more than a hundred years.

As if that weren't disturbing enough, another facet to the story of the Second Council of Constantinople puts the validity of its condemnation of reincarnation into even greater doubt. There seems to be some question whether Origen was actually discussed at the council at all, or if the emperor deceptively added the condemnation of Origen into the official written record after the fact. The council was under the full control of Emperor Justinian, who was even more insistent than Constantine had been on enforcing religious conformity. He closed non-Christian schools, baptized nonbelievers by force, and all but wiped out some Christian "heretic" groups with fierce persecutions. The emperor had an anxious agenda involving Origen; before the council had even formally opened, Justinian ordered the bishops assembled there to address the dispute over Origen's teachings.

Inconsistencies in subsequent documents, however, leave historians uncertain if Origen was ever formally condemned at the council. Some learned writers believe he was, while an equal number deny this. In any event, it does not seem that Pope Vigilius' reversal specifically included a condemnation of Origen, nor do the later popes Pelagius I (556–561), Pelagius II (570–590), or Gregory the Great (590–604) seem to have known of Origen's condemnation at this council. Nonetheless, even though this church council has been widely viewed as invalid by later historians, its recorded judgments were entered into the law books, effectively outlawing all discussion of reincarnation within the boundaries of the empire. From the point of view of public teaching, the doctrine of rebirth completely disappeared from European thought after 553 A.D.

It was just driven underground, however; it actually took another 1,000 years of bloodshed to eradicate the concept from Western religion.

Appendix B

The War between America's Soul and Spirit

Every kingdom divided against itself will be ruined . . .

—Jesus Christ

Numerous cultures that subscribed to the binary soul doctrine believed that the whole universe reflects the duality we observe in the human soul. Many nations around the world taught their children variations of the very same creation myth: that God created the universe by dividing Himself in two and then mating one half of His infinite Self with the other half. This universe we live in, they believed, was the magical offspring of that divine marriage, with every facet of that universe, including the human soul, still reflecting that original duality. This is why, they explained, we find ourselves in a reality where everything has a two-part, divided, or binary form. They believed this was why the root structure beneath trees looks just like the branch structure above them, and why the shape of virtually all living things is symmetrical, having equal but opposite right and left sides. They thought this was why we have two equal but opposite sexes, why electricity and magnetism have positive and negative poles, and why every action produces an equal but opposite reaction.

Recently, the world has witnessed this same dynamic in American politics. For some time now, the population of the United States has been divided into two equal but opposite political parties, which are, as it turns out, perfect reflections of the two halves of the human psyche.

The Democratic Party: Voice of the Human Soul

Just as the right hemisphere of the brain controls the left side of the body, the Democratic Party is also popularly referred to as "the Left" side of America's political body. And just as the right half of the brain is more dominant in women, the majority of women tend to vote Democratic. Like the right-brain unconscious, Democrats embrace holistic concepts like the "interconnection of all things" and the "brotherhood of man," prioritizing these values over left-brain ideals such as independent individualism and personal responsibility. Unfortunately, this emphasis on the needs of the group over the rights of the individual often translates into higher taxes. Like the unconscious soul, the Left feels more confident when dealing with subjective internal matters (i.e., domestic affairs) than objective external affairs (foreign relations) and, also like the repressed unconscious, Democrats tend to identify with society's weaker and more downtrodden elements. Like the nurturing unconscious, the Left has assumed the feminine role of caregiver in society. Like the right half of the brain, the Democratic Party focuses its attention on what people have in common, and this focus on connections and relationships makes diplomacy one of its primary strengths. This focus on connections, however, also gives Democrats a tendency to be more inclusive and tolerant than exclusive and intolerant, which frequently translates into larger government.

Like the unconscious soul, Democrats tend to think in broad inclusive patterns that allow for flexibility, nuance, and uncertainty, and seem uncomfortable with the rigid black-and-white distinctions so dear to the left-brain conscious mind. Indeed, like the mystical unconscious, the Democratic Party seems remarkably comfortable with uncertainty. Despite the Republican Party's claim to be more religious, Democrats often seem to demonstrate greater faith in the face of uncertainty. In the recent presidential election, for example, the states most likely to suffer future terrorist attacks voted *against* the candidate running on a "War Against Terror" platform, while those states *least* likely to suffer a terrorist attack voted *for* him. Obviously, the Democratic populace of the East and West coasts is not nearly as worried about safety and certainty as the Republican populace of the rural states.

The Republican Party: Voice of the Human Spirit

The Republican Party emphasizes left-brain ideals like personal freedom and individualism, strength and self-reliance, and justice and order, while tending to distrust subjective right-brain values like emotion, nuance, and empathy for the downtrodden. Just as the left-brain mind controls the right side of the body, the Republican half of American politics is often simply called "the Right," and just as the rational conscious mind is more dominant in men, the majority of men vote Republican. The conscious mind exercises its dominance over the weaker unconscious and, in much the same way, the Republican Party favors the interests of the wealthy and powerful over the less fortunate elements of society. Like the objective left-brain conscious mind, the Republican Party tends to be more adept with external matters (i.e., foreign affairs), but less skillful dealing with the messy subjectiveness of domestic culture. Just as the dispassionate conscious mind distrusts the subjective feelings of the unconscious, so too do Republicans often dismiss feelings of empathy as worthless, referring to them as "bleeding-heart liberalism."

The left-brain conscious mind tends to notice details and differences more than patterns and connections. This tells us that it primarily views itself as a whole unto itself, rather than as a part of a larger whole. Always noticing the differences between itself and everything else, it feels separate from, and independent of, the world around it. The Republican Party is a group of people who seem to look at life with this same detached, objective perspective, elevating the rights and privileges of the individual over the needs of the group. Like the left half of the brain, Republicans tend to be more exclusive than inclusive, focusing more on the distinctions and differences between people than on the connections and relationships between them.

Like the conscious spirit, the Right prefers clearly defined distinctions, being uncomfortable with flexibility, subtlety, and uncertainty. Instead of exhibiting faith in unknown matters beyond its control, the Republican Party's sense of security, like the dominant conscious mind, seems to rest more on its own strength, control, and dominance.

Republicans often prefer definitive left-brain demonstrations of strength and authority to gentler right-brain expressions of brotherhood, empathy, diplomacy, or faith.

Already Deeply Integrated?

Both parties are equally valid reflections of the highest ideals of the American people. It is not these ideals that are causing us trouble, but the working relationship between them. BSD cultures around the world taught that the only solution to humankind's problems was to integrate the two halves of our being so they would work in perfect harmony. In much the same way, it is growing clear to more and more Americans that the only way to prevent our country from ripping itself apart is to do the same with our two political parties.

The red and blue states on the map we saw during the 2004 presidential election suggested our country was geographically divided into distinct Republican and Democratic territories, but the map was deceptive. Within those states, their separate counties were haphazardly shuffled into Democratic and Republican checkerboard patterns, and within each county, the difference between Democratic and Republican votes was often no more than a few percent one way or the other. Our country, states, and counties are not nearly as divided as they have been made out to be.

Our Inner Partisans

Indeed, none of us is as purely partisan as we might believe. Just as each of us possesses both a conscious and an unconscious, it would not be wrong to say that we each also have both a Republican and a Democrat living inside us. And while we may lean one way or the other on election day, in our daily lives these two halves of our being share the stage within each of us.

Thanks to research by Dr. Fredric Schiffer, professor of psychiatry at Harvard University, it is now possible to introduce ourselves to these two inner partisans. Simply by covering one eye or the other, we can manually control which side of the brain is dominant at any given moment.[1] If we cover our right eye and look out through the left only, this provides extra stimulation to the right side of the brain, awakening our inner Democrat.

Similarly, covering the left eye stimulates our inner Republican. If we take an hour or so, and honestly ask ourselves the same set of political questions twice, once with the left eye covered, and then repeating the same set again with the right covered, we often come up with strikingly different answers depending on which side of the brain is being stimulated at the time. Using two simple pairs of safety glasses, one with the left eyepiece taped over, the other with the right, Dr. Schiffer discovered that we each have these two distinct points of view within us all the time, and can access them independently of each other:

> Sitting with patients who have rather dramatic changes in their outlook on life and the world within seconds of putting on taped safety glasses is an amazing experience. Seeing the patient's entire demeanor change . . . over a relatively short period of time—is a compelling experience.[2]

Once we realize that both these partisans live and breathe within each of us, it no longer makes sense to adore one political party and demonize the other, because to condemn either is to reject, deny, and ignore part of our own being. Unfortunately, as long as the majority of Americans keep trying to embrace one half of this social equation and destroy the other, our prospects of restoring the peace, stability, and prosperity we once knew seem all but impossible. Just like each half of the human psyche, each side of this social equation can, on its own, only offer a crippled and incomplete solution to America's challenges. American history teaches us that whenever either party has had control of both the presidency and the Congress, the result has been excessive spending and an unbalanced budget. But when the presidency and Congress are spread across both parties, they tend to arrive at a healthy balance, helping spending to remain under control and the nation to remain stable.

Any extreme imbalance between Republican and Democratic forces in our society, just like an imbalance between conscious spirit and unconscious soul, is likely to bring pain, disease, and death. The future of our society depends on bridging this gap, reintegrating the two halves of America's being. Just as the ancient Christians taught so long ago, we must indeed "make the two one." This change cannot be legislated from the top down, however, but must transform society from the bottom up. The current divide between the Democratic and Republican Parties cannot be reconciled until we first resolve the spiritual battle raging in each of our hearts. Politics is really a spiritual issue and simply reflects the underlying spiritual realities of the populace. Since the political landscape is a reflection of the population's underlying spiritual condition, any attempt at changing the reflection instead of its source is doomed to fail. If America is divided, that division must be addressed at its root: the inner spiritual conflict raging in every human heart. As soon as we start being true to ourselves and embrace both these vital aspects of our inner being, the alienation between the Democratic and Republican parties will begin to diminish, and a productive and fruitful cultural exchange between them can resume.

Democrats and Republicans are the soul and spirit of American politics. We need both, and we need them working together in harmonious unison. If the system lost either of these voices, the country would disintegrate. If we no longer had anyone representing and defending the needs of the collective, the nation would collapse, but the same is also true of the rights of the individual. Both sides of the equation are equally essential. We need them just as much as we need both men and women, both night and day, both summer and winter. But we will only reconcile them with one another after we first reconcile our own souls and spirits.

For a nation to be whole, its people must be as well.

Endnotes

Chapter 1

1. Arthur Ponsonby, *Falsehood in Wartime,* Newport Beach, Calif.: LSF Publishing, 1928, 1991.

2. In a *Today Show* interview broadcast August 30, 2004, President Bush said the United States could never win the war against terrorism.

3. Matthew 10:38–39, Matthew 16:24–25, Luke 14:26–27, John 12:26. Certainly the martyrs of Christianity's first three centuries understood this.

4. Associated Press, Washington, October 16, 2003.

5. Jonathan Petre, "Williams worried by leaders' religious rhetoric," *Telegraph News Limited,* February 22, 2003.

6. After having been hunted, persecuted, and killed for centuries by the Romans, the authorities of the official church embraced the same strategies against its own enemies as soon as they had the power to do so. Shortly after Christianity became the official religion of the empire, being a Manichaean, or Gnostic, carried the death penalty.

7. A few of these ancient works, such as the Gospel of Thomas and the Gospel of Truth, were finally recovered at Nag Hammadi, after being lost to history for more than 1,500 years.

8. Among scholars of Thomas, the view that Thomas preserves the earliest sayings of Jesus is almost universally accepted. Other New Testament scholars, however, have been slower to accept this conclusion, as the discussions that went on for decades among Thomas scholars are only just now beginning to filter out to the rest of the fragmented and parochial world of biblical scholarship.

9. "The original stage of Peter may well be the earliest passion story in the gospel tradition." See Robert J. Miller (ed.), *The Complete Gospels,* San Francisco: HarperSanFrancisco, 1994, p. 400.

10. Historians disagree over whether Constantine really ever converted to Christianity at all. He worshiped the Roman sun god at the same time he professed to be a Christian. After his "conversion," he built a triumphal arch in Rome that featured the sun god, and a statue of the sun god for Constantinople. All his coins featured the sun. He made Sunday (the day of the sun god) into a day of rest when work was forbidden. Christianity incorporated worship of the Roman sun god into its rites during Constantine's reign, praying toward the rising sun, worshiping on Sunday, and celebrating Jesus' birth on December 25 (the birthday of the sun god). Constantine's character never reflected Jesus' teachings, even after his so-called conversion. He remained vain, superstitious, and violent, with little respect for human life. He reveled in slaughtering

the enemy during military campaigns, forced prisoners to fight wild beasts, and even had a number of his family members executed. Constantine supposedly waited until just before he was dying before asking to be baptized, and, in fact, historians disagree as to whether he was actually baptized at that time.

11. The Jewish historian Josephus reported that reincarnation was widely taught in Judea in the first century, and was even taught by the Pharisees. See his *Jewish War* 3.8.5 and *Antiquities of the Jews* 18.1.3. This historical report is given even greater credence by the fact that Judaism went on to incorporate officially the doctrine of reincarnation as *"gilgul"* in the Zohar, a classic of Jewish mysticism purportedly written in the second century.

12. The *ka*-name of Amonemhat I was "He who repeats births," the *ka*-name of Senusert I meant "He whose births live," and the *ka*-name of Setekhy I was "Repeater of births." Pharaohs sometimes claimed to have more than one *ka* (soul), claiming, in effect, to possess multiple selves, identities, personalities, and so on; this suggests that these ancient Pharaohs claimed, just as "holy men" of the East do today, that they remembered their past lives and identities.

13. A great many biblical passages seem to refer to reincarnation. See my books *The Division of Consciousness* and *The Lost Secret of Death* for more.

14. See: Morton Smith, *Clement of Alexandria and a Secret Gospel of Mark*, Cambridge, Mass.: Harvard University Press, 1973.

15. Clement was venerated as a saint down to the seventeenth century.

16. Clement's *Hypotyposeis* is no longer extant, but numerous fragments have been preserved in a handful of Greek works. Photius argued in his work *Bibliotheca* that Clement taught reincarnation in *Hypotyposeis*. While he soft-peddled reincarnation, Clement may have been more open with other elements of the esoteric tradition he inherited from his teachers. In Clement's day, the distinction between orthodox and Gnostic was not nearly as defined as it would become later. Even though Clement was a towering leader of the church in his day, he referred to the most advanced and purest Christians as "Gnostics." There was a huge difference, Clement insisted, between the faith of the ordinary Christian and the knowledge of the perfect Christian. The perfect Christian, he maintained, receives profound insights into the mysteries of the religion, which ordinary Christians must accept on faith alone. Emphasizing the moral worth of religious knowledge, Clement extolled Christian perfection, referring to the perfect Christian as "the true Gnostic." Despite all this, however, Clement had no notable or lasting influence on the subsequent history of Christian theology, except for his influence on the young Origen. Most of his works, including *On First Principles, On Prophecy, On Angels, On the Devil, On the Origin of the Universe, On the Unity and Excellence of the Church, On the Soul, On Resurrection, On Marriage*, and others, have been lost to history. We can only imagine what other early Christian insights Clement might have tried to share with us in those works.

17. See Origen's *Commentary on John 6:7* and *Commentary on Matthew 10:20*.

18. From his *De Principiis*.

19. Even so, the current of reincarnational thought in Christianity was so strong that the church was eventually forced to condemn reincarnation more *explicitly* a few hundred years later, at the Second Council of Constantinople. See appendix A.

20. No one really knows how many people were put to death during the Inquisition because, of course, the Roman Catholic Church was the only entity that had any chance to keep records. Estimates range from a low of 7,000 victims to a high of 67 million.

21. David Barrett, et al. (eds.), *World Christian Encyclopedia: A Comparative Survey of*

Churches and Religions in the Modern World, New York: Oxford University Press, 2001. More conservative surveys still list more than 660 distinct Christian denominations.

Chapter 2

1. The Gospel of Thomas 39 and 102.

2. Ezekiel 37:11–14, Isaiah 26:19–21, and Daniel 12:1–3.

3. Cultural next-door neighbors Israel and Egypt used this same term. Since the "second death" was the separation of the soul and the spirit from each other, the "first death" would seem to have been the separation of the soul and spirit from the physical body.

4. For more on this, see my earlier books *The Division of Consciousness* and *The Lost Secret of Death,* which catalogue the many ancient religions that once subscribed to the binary soul doctrine and explore the likely psychological consequences of such a division. These are the first fruits of my 18 years of study of the binary soul doctrine.

5. For a more extensive discussion of Egypt's version of the binary soul doctrine, see chapter 1 of my book *The Lost Secret of Death.*

6. Curiously, such cultures could not agree on which was the more important. Israel identified more with the soul, India more with the spirit.

7. *Librum de vera religione,* chapter 10.

8. The common beliefs of these different nations are explored at length in chapter 8 of my book *The Division of Consciousness,* and chapters 1 and 13 of *The Lost Secret of Death.*

9. Early Christians regularly distinguished between the soul and spirit, as can be seen in Thessalonians 5:23, Hebrews 4:12, Gospel of Mary 5:10, Gospel of Philip 67:4, Acts of John 82, Acts of Paul 3:24, Prayer of the Apostle Paul 2, Secret Book of James 4:20, Apocalypse of Peter 219, Epistle of the Apostles 22–25, Book of Baruch (Justin) Contra Celsus Chapter XVIII (Origen), Against Heresies 5:4:1 (Irenaeus), and Hymn against Bardaisan (Ephraim).

10. The Bible directly associates this division of soul and spirit with both the "second death" and also the "keys to death and the afterlife." In the Book of Revelation, the only place in the Bible where the phrase "the second death" appears, the phrase "double-edged sword" also appears. This phrase only appears in two places in the New Testament: in Hebrews 4:12, where it is associated with the division of the soul and spirit, and in Revelation 1:16–18, where it is associated with the keys to death and the afterlife.

11. See the seminal 1998 work by Fredric Schiffer, professor of psychiatry at Harvard University, *Of Two Minds: The Revolutionary Science of Dual-Brain Psychology* (New York: Free Press). In his book, Schiffer reports that many in his field now associate left-brain consciousness with the classic Freudian conscious mind, and right-brain consciousness with the Freudian unconscious.

12. I explore these postmortem psychological processes in depth in *The Lost Secret of Death.*

13. While a discussion of these connections is beyond the scope of this book, I explore them at length in *The Lost Secret of Death.*

14. Henry R. Percival (ed.), *The Seven Ecumenical Councils of the Undivided Church,* Vol. XIV in series edited by Philip Schaff and Henry Wace, *Nicene and Post Nicene Fathers,* Grand Rapids, Mich.: Wm. B. Eerdmans, 1988.

15. Eleventh Canon, Fourth Ecumenical Council.

16. Hebrews 11:5 declares that Enoch did not experience death but was taken by God.

17. Long before the Council of Nicaea, one of the first great schisms in the church occurred over this very issue. One half of Christianity felt that the purity, perfection, and sinlessness of the church must not be compromised, while the other half insisted that faith was more important than sinlessness. In 251 A.D., two different men, Novatian and Cornelius, were independently consecrated as pope, each representing one of these two views. Novatian's supporters, who called themselves *katharoi*, or Puritans, believed the church must be devoted first and foremost to purity, and this emphasis found great support from the church at large. Although Novatianism eventually fell under imperial persecution, the Novatian Church was an identifiable entity until the seventh century, and its ideals and name were taken up again by Europe's Cathars in the tenth to twelfth centuries. To combat those later Cathars, of course, the Roman church instituted the infamous Inquisition, which continued until the nineteenth century. Thus we can see that the Roman Church's abandonment of the path of purity in the early years of the faith continued to have repercussions for the next 1,600 years.

18. John 1:25.

19. As I explore in detail in *The Lost Secret of Death*.

20. Arthur Janov, *The New Primal Scream*, Wilmington, Del.: Enterprise Publishing, [nd], p. 6.

21. And so it does—not the safety and security of our physical person but of our self-image and self-esteem.

Chapter 3

1. I suspect they not only occurred simultaneously, but in fact are both effects of the same cause, a cause which, à la Julian Jaynes (author of *The Origin of Consciousness in the Breakdown of the Bicameral Mind*, Boston: Houghton Mifflin, 1976), fundamentally changed the way the human mind functioned, making us more adept at reading and writing, but less adept at retaining our memories from one life to the next.

2. Such as Egypt, China, and Mesoamerica. See chapter 13 of *The Lost Secret of Death*.

3. *Epic of Gilgamesh*, tablet 1.

4. Ibid., tablet 2.

5. The Judaic prophecies of the Old Testament *do* make similar claims of spiritual cannibalism occurring during the Universal Resurrection of Judgment Day, but the wording of the texts leaves them somewhat more open to interpretation. See chapter 4 for more on this, along with chapter 9 of *The Division of Consciousness* and chapter 15 of *The Lost Secret of Death*.

6. See the analysis of the "dark tunnel" experience in chapter 3 of *The Lost Secret of Death*.

7. Or did the story originally describe Utnapishtim as being "one-eyed," which could have been a symbol for an integrated consciousness?

8. See chapter 11 of *The Lost Secret of Death*.

9. See: Giorgio De Santillana and Hertha Von Dechend, *Hamlet's Mill*, Jaffrey, N.H.: David R. Godine, 1977.

10. See chapter 4 of *The Division of Consciousness* for an expanded discussion of this.

11. Willis Barnstone and Marvin Meyer (eds.), *The Gnostic Bible*, Boston: Shambhala, 2003, p. 119.

12. Also see chapter 4 of *The Division of Consciousness* for more on this Primordial Division.

Chapter 4

1. If the recollection and reacquisition of all our past-life memories, thoughts, and emotions did not proceed according to some organizing principle, the integrity of the data would be compromised. It would be like taking all the books in a library, ripping out their pages, throwing all those pages randomly together in a heap on the floor, and then trying to make some sense of it all. It would be a recipe for madness, which reminds us that, way back in the Old Testament, madness was indeed listed as one of the consequences of being unfaithful to God (Deut. 28:15–28, Jer. 25:16, Zech. 12:14).

Chapter 5

1. From Lance S. Owens, "The Gospel of Thomas and the Hermeneutics of Vision," www.gnosis.org/naghamm/gth_hermen.htm, 2004.

2. Hippolytus and Origen both refer to a Gospel of Thomas, while Paul and Clement seem to have even quoted from it.

3. Their obscurity, however, does have a parallel in the canon. A great many passages in the Old Testament books of the prophets, especially Isaiah, Jeremiah, and Daniel, contain equal if not even greater levels of obscurity. *The Division of Consciousness* demonstrates how the binary soul doctrine unlocks many of the most puzzling of these Old Testament passages.

4. John Dominic Crossan, *The Birth of Christianity*, San Francisco: HarperSanFrancisco, 1998, p. 410.

5. The siglum *Q* comes from the German *Quelle*, meaning "Source."

6. Helmut Koester, *Ancient Christian Gospels*, Philadelphia: Trinity Press International, 1990, p. 86.

7. Another lost text from early Christianity, the Didache, or Teaching of the Twelve Apostles, was discovered in a monastery in Constantinople and published by P. Bryennios in 1883, and may date as early as 50–70 A.D.

8. Crossan, p. 408.

9. Matthew 5:48, 19:21.

10. Matthew 9:2–6, 12:31, 26:28.

11. 1 Corinthians 2:6–7, 1 Corinthians 3:1–3.

12. See: Matthew 13:11, Mark 4:11, Luke 8:10, 1 Corinthians 2:7, and 1 Corinthians 4:1.

13. This is either a coincidence, or an intended (and therefore meaningful) parallel of the binary soul doctrine's habit of recognizing pairs of separate and distinct yet equal elements.

14. In the upper reaches of the Euphrates valley in Eastern Syria, Saint Thomas was believed to have been Jesus' biological twin brother. This Syrian tradition was later adopted by the Saint Thomas Christians in India. See Bart D. Ehrman's *The New Testament: A Historical Introduction to the Early Christian Writings*, New York: Oxford University Press, 1997, p. 178.

15. In the Book of Thomas, he is named Judas Thomas, and specifically stated to be Jesus' twin brother.

16. Or some later editor edited it out of the Gospel of John.

17. Matthew 13:55, Luke 6:16, Acts 1:13, Jude 1:1.

18. It seems unlikely that this emphasis of Thomas' twinhood was an irrelevant detail that just happened to get mentioned in passing. The gospels don't include irrelevant details about any of the other apostles. It doesn't mention, for example, that one of them was clubfooted or short or tall or bald or had a scar or lisp. It must have had some meaningful relevance to the story of Christianity's origins.

19. Ancient Semitic scribes often employed a literary style that relied heavily on repetition. God creates humankind no less than three times in Genesis 1:27–29, and we are informed who the tenants of the ark were six separate times in Genesis chapters 6 through 8. In chapters 1 and 2 of the Book of Amos, the expression "For three transgressions and four, I will . . ." is repeated no less than eight times. In Amos chapter 4, the phrase "yet you have not returned to Me" occurs five times, ending each time with "prepare to meet your God." The prose of Leviticus, Numbers, Deuteronomy, and Ecclesiastes is similarly repetitive. Exodus and Deuteronomy each contain a copy of the Decalogue, and much of chapter 38 of Isaiah is a repetition of 37.

20. See chapter 12 of *The Lost Secret of Death*.

21. For more on John's baptism, see *The Lost Secret of Death*.

22. Modern science is only just now starting to illuminate the edges of this truth, with its discovery of the way the very consciousness of the observers affects the outcome of some experiments in quantum physics. But Thomas suggests that the connection goes much deeper.

23. This seemingly modern psychological insight was kept alive for many years in the early church. Consider this elaboration on the same theme found in the Gospel of Philip: "As for ourselves, let each one of us dig down after the root of evil which is within one, and let one pluck it out of one's heart from the root. It will be plucked out if we recognize it. But if we are ignorant of it, it takes root in us and produces its fruit in our heart. It masters us. We are its slaves. It takes us captive, to make us do what we do not want; and what we do want, we do not do. It is powerful because we have not recognized it. While it exists it is active. Ignorance is the mother of all evil. Ignorance will result in death, because those who come from ignorance neither were nor are nor shall be."

24. I explore this dynamic more thoroughly in *The Division of Consciousness*.

25. The original name of the Egyptian city where the Greek version of the Gospel of Thomas was unearthed was Oxyrhynchus, from the name of a sacred fish, the modern binni. In biblical times, this city, named after a fish, was known as a great Christian center.

26. Again, note the occurrence of a "doubled double" in this passage. Instead of one crop, we now find two, the second of which is twice as big as the first.

27. Luke 12:49.

28. This saying also reminds the reader of Saying 82 of the Gospel of Thomas: "He who is near me is near the fire, and he who is far from me is far from the kingdom."

29. In Sayings 58, 70, 82, and others.

30. Matthew 8:22.

31. *The Lost Secret of Death* explores a wealth of scriptural evidence that early Christians struggled to rediscover and reassimilate their past-life souls.

32. See: Robert Eisenman, *James, the Brother of Jesus*, New York: Penguin, 1997.

33. Matthew 16:23, Philippians 3:10–13.

34. Reminding us of Saying 6.

35. Eusebius reported that James the Just, the brother of Jesus and the leader of the church from 33 A.D. to 62 A.D., was a vegetarian (Ecclesiastical History 2.23.5–6) and suggested that the Twelve Apostles had been strict vegetarians as well (Proof of the Gospels 3.3). In 1 Corinthians 8:13, the apostle Paul took an oath to become a lifelong vegetarian, and several early Christian groups, including the Nazarenes, Ebionites, and Kathari, were all said to be vegetarians.

36. Genesis' story of the primordial division of the soul and spirit, otherwise known as the "Great Fall," is explored in *The Division of Consciousness*.

37. The canonical Bible does not seem to declare overtly that all people preexisted their current lives, but it does report that at least one man besides Jesus did: Job. See Job 38:4–12, and for more, see *The Division of Consciousness.*

38. Acts 3:21.

39. In *Seek to See Him* (New York: E. J. Brill, 1996), April de Conick pointed out that in Philo's *Noah's Work as a Planter,* five sorts of trees were named in the garden: trees of life, of immortality, Knowledge, comprehension, and knowledge of good and evil.

40. In fact, this passage in Thomas suggests that it will be *impossible* to resist these invaders and prevent them from taking over; an alternate translation of this passage reads, "They are naked in their presence so as to give it back to them," indicating that they are not only naked before them, but also completely powerless before them.

41. See also passages 61 and 108.

42. Ephesians 2:14.

43. This notion that it is possible to arrive at a place of such complete harmony with the physical universe that it automatically provides all one's needs and responds to all of one's requests is a major theme in the Gospel of Thomas, appearing in Sayings 13, 14, 19, 106, and 113.

44. Which is the same message later Gnostic works also reported. See again those passages listed in the discussion of Saying 11.

45. This same phrase is used to refer to the Universal Resurrection in Matthew 12:41.

46. See also Saying 47, "an old patch is not sewn on a new garment," for more on this theme.

47. Luke 12:31.

48. This theme of emptiness is echoed again in Saying 97 and is carried still further in later Gnostic works like the Gospel of Philip and the Gospel of Truth.

49. Luke 11:17.

50. Several fragments of a Greek version of the Gospel of Thomas were found among the Oxyrhynchys Papyri in the late nineteenth century. These fragments consist of the preamble and Sayings 1–6, 26–28, 30–32, 36–38, and 39, as well as a saying not found in the Coptic version, which follows 32.

51. By the time things have gotten so out of control that these hordes of past-life selves are already invading, nothing can be done to stop them from moving in and taking over, and resisting them at that stage will do no good. If one wished to fight against this invasion, one would need to integrate them manually *before* Judgment Day started to unfold. However, their invasion, thanks to Jesus, will be brief. I explore this dramatic episode in the Judgment Day scenario in detail in *The Division of Consciousness.*

52. See *The Lost Secret of Death* for more on this.

53. This passage can also be translated as "Come into being as you pass away," which at first glance seems to fit the theme of the Gospel of Thomas—"how to survive death"—as well as "Be passersby" does. "Come into being as you pass away" suggests, however, that a person's needed spiritual transformation occurs at or just after the moment of death, whereas the Gospel of Thomas repeatedly emphasizes that one must enter the kingdom of heaven before one dies, not that one will enter it at the moment of one's death.

54. See *The Division of Consciousness* for more on that Primordial Division.

55. The Jews entered a divided sea, another metaphor suggesting they were entering the realm of division. In fact, the two most meaningful Old Testament events, the creation of Genesis and the escape of Exodus, revolved around the same theme: finding life amid divided waters. See Genesis 1:6 and Exodus 14:17–21.

56. Discovered in the last years of the nineteenth century and translated for the first time in the 1964 work by Edgar Hennecke *New Testament Apocrypha* (Philadelphia: Westminster Press), p. 156, this epistle is credited to Paul's disciple Titus.

57. Writers seem undecided about the usefulness of such dialogues. In some scriptures, the Gnostics recommend using prepared dialogues to address various "authorities" they expect to meet in the afterlife. But in other scriptures, they state that the only way to avoid being enslaved by those authorities in the afterlife is to have achieved full enlightenment and salvation, in which case such prepared dialogues would be unnecessary. Such dialogues, then, may have been nothing more than last-ditch efforts to avoid the inevitable, much as Egypt's mummification processes seem to have been.

58. Eli Siegel, *Self and World: An Explanation of Aesthetic Realism*, New York: Definition Press, 1981.

59. Joel 2:32.

60. John Dominic Crossan, *The Birth of Christianity*, San Francisco: HarperSanFrancisco, 1998, pp. 578–579.

61. Matthew 21:42, Mark 12:10, Luke 20:17, Acts 4:11, and 1 Peter 2:7.

62. Symbolized by Adam.

63. Symbolized by Eve.

64. According to Jewish tradition, the first letter, first word, first sentence, first chapter, and so on of the Bible all have something in common, and that common element, whatever it may be, is absolutely essential to comprehending fully God's revealed message to humanity. The first line in the Bible is usually translated "In the beginning God created the heavens and the earth." The Hebrew word that the author of Genesis chose to use, however, for "create" was *bara*, which actually means "to divide," to separate, cut, or cleave. Thus we find, just as Jewish tradition maintained, the first letter and first word of the Bible indeed both revolve around a single concept: division into two parts. See *The Lost Secret of Death* for more.

65. Passages 21, 40, 57, 65, and 73.

66. Jesus said to her, "I am the resurrection and the life. He who believes in me will live, even though he dies; and whoever lives and believes in me will never die" (John 11:25–26).

67. See *The Division of Consciousness* and *The Lost Secret of Death* for more on this.

68. "You shall have no other gods before me. You shall not make for yourself an idol in the form of anything in heaven above or on the earth beneath or in the waters below. You shall not bow down to them or worship them; for I, the LORD your God, am a jealous God" (Exodus 20:3–5).

69. For more on this, see chapter 1 of *The Lost Secret of Death*.

70. Adam and Eve had children only after disobeying God in Eden; Abraham and Sarah, and Jacob and Rachel only conceived after the two husbands slept with other women. And Isaac and Rebekah remained barren until Isaac finally broke down and prayed to God, presumably to repent an undisclosed sin (possibly repenting a lifetime of bitterness over having been marked for sacrifice by God as a child?). For more on this, see chapter 11 of *The Lost Secret of Death*.

71. W. Schneemelcher and K. Schaferdiek, "Second and Third Century Acts of Apostles," in Wilhelm Schneemelcher (ed.), *New Testament Apocrypha*, Philadelphia: Westminster Press, 1965, p. 172.

72. See *The Division of Consciousness* and *The Lost Secret of Death* for more on this.

73. "Blessed is the man whom God corrects; so do not despise the discipline of the Almighty" (Job 5:17).

74. See also in the Nag Hammadi text titled Treatise on the Resurrection: "The

thought of those that are saved shall not perish. . . . Does not that which is yours exist with you? Yet, while you are in this world, what is it that you lack? This is what you have been making every effort to learn. . . . Nothing, then, redeems us from this world. But the all which we are—we are saved. We have received salvation from end to end. Let us think in this way! Let us comprehend in this way!"

75. See *The Division of Consciousness* for more on this.

76. A variation on Luke 15:3–7 and Matthew 18:12–14.

77. See *The Division of Consciousness* for more on this.

78. See *The Division of Consciousness* for a discussion of this process.

79. The Exegesis on the Soul 133:4–9.

Chapter 6

1. Compare this Hindu passage from *The Law of Manu:* "Man is not a simple, but a complex being: that substance which gives a power of motion to the body, the wise men call the 'knower of the field' or the vital spirit. . . . Another internal spirit called . . . the great soul attends the birth of all creatures embodied, and thence in all mortal forms is conveyed a perception either pleasing or painful [the soul makes good/bad value judgments]. These two, the vital spirit and reasonable soul, are closely united . . ."

2. Yuri Stoyanov, *The Other God,* New Haven, Conn.: Yale University Press, 2000, p. 87.

3. Exodus 20:5.

Chapter 7

1. For a fuller account of this BSD in ancient Judaism, see *The Lost Secret of Death.*

2. In the passage normally translated "God created the heavens and the earth," the Hebrew word normally translated as "created" is *bara,* a verb that actually means to divide, separate, cut, or cleave.

3. From the Haggadah, a Jewish legend from the Misrash.

4. Genesis 15:1–18.

5. Hebrews 11:37, Martyrdom of Isaiah 5:2.

6. As quoted in Willis Barnstone, *The Other Bible,* San Francisco: Harper & Row, 1984, p. 6.

7. Willis Barnstone, *The Gnostic Bible,* Boston: Shambhala, 2003, p. 533.

8. *The Other God,* p. 104. Mani's father belonged to a puritan Judeo-Christian movement called the *katharioi,* which may have been related to the *katharoi* that supported Novatian in 251 A.D., as well as the Cathars of France a thousand years later.

9. Lynn Picknett and Clive Prince, *The Templar Revelation,* New York: Bantam, 1997.

10. Even if Jesus did father a child as many are speculating today, the meaning of the survival of that bloodline may have implications far beyond the nature of Europe's royal bloodlines. If Jesus sired a son by the year 50 A.D., and each of that son's descendants also had at least two offspring, who themselves also had two offspring, and so on, it would be mathematically possible for every living person on the planet today to be His direct blood descendant. If so, then the idea of humanity being saved by Jesus' blood raises a whole new set of possibilities.

11. Several early manuscripts of Matthew, including manuscripts in the Caesarean group of texts, the Sinaitic Palimpsest, the Palestinian Syriac lectionaries, and some manuscripts used by Origen in the third century, support the fact that Barabbas' name was originally Jesus Barabbas, and some modern New Testament translations reflect this, such as *The New English Bible, The Scholar's Version, The Message,* and *The Contemporary*

English Version. According to a note by Origen, the long-lost Gospel of The Hebrews translated or interpreted this word "Barabbas" as "Son of their Master" (teacher).

12. Although modern translations often use negative words like "notorious," the Greek word *episemos* has no inherently negative connotations and is even related to a word honored in biblical tradition: epistle.

13. Even though he repented before he died.

14. The Book of Thomas 138:19.

15. Ibid., 138:7.

16. Why did the names Simon, James, and Judas each appear *twice* in the list of Christ's Twelve Apostles? Was there a shortage of first names in Palestine during the time of Christ? Or were these records clumsily edited to cover up something?

17. Matthew 26:50.

18. John 13:18–35.

19. Matthew 25:26, John 13:21–28.

20. Matthew 27:3–5.

21. The second-century writings of Celsus provide a unique portrait of Roman attitudes toward the early Christians. He openly accused the church of compromising the original integrity of the Holy Gospels, editing the text on the fly during debates. He doesn't seem to be making these accusations out of whole cloth, either, because many textual variants have been found in ancient New Testament manuscripts. For example, there are more than 70 variations of the Lord's Prayer in different manuscripts of the Gospel of Luke.

22. The early second-century historian Papias, who Eusebius called "a man learned in all things, and well acquainted with the scriptures," gives yet another version of Judas' death, describing him succumbing to something like elephantiasis. This tells us that no less than three different versions of Judas' death were circulating at the dawn of the second century.

23. In Matthew 10:2–4 and Mark 3:16–19, the name Jude does not appear in the list of the apostles, but rather the name Thaddaeus. "Judas" is the Greek form for the English "Jude."

24. From Michael Baigent, et al., *The Messianic Legacy,* New York: Holt, 1986, pp. 96–97, quoting a translated passage from a fragment of the Gospel of Bartholomew.

25. Eusebius, *History,* 3:19.

26. Ishwar Sharan, *The Myth of Saint Thomas and the Mylapore Shiva Temple,* New Delhi: Voice of India, 1991.

27. In addition to this living oral tradition, the theory that Thomas traveled to India also finds support in the third-century Acts of Thomas. And like both the Gospel of Thomas and the Book of Thomas, this scripture also insists that Thomas was Jesus' twin and that his true name was Judas.

28. According to Indian tradition, Saint Thomas died in 72 A.D.

29. Paul William Roberts, *In Search of the Birth of Jesus,* New York: Riverhead, 1995, p. 118.

30. The classic BSD theme of equal but opposite duality saturates the interior of this building. The floor is designed with black and white squares, and the statues in the church are arranged in groups of two, either facing one another or side by side. These statue pairs seem to be mirror opposites of each other, either visually, or metaphorically, or both. Most statues are placed between two stations of the cross, and in the same way that the statues face each other, so do most of the stations of the cross. The two statues of Joseph and Mary are almost perfect mirror images of each other, and the two infant Jesuses in their arms are exact mirror opposites. This theme of duality is further rein-

forced by the repeated occurrence of the number 22 within the church. The 22-letter inscription "Terribilis Est Locus Iste" ("This place is terrible") greets everyone entering the church, and the same number occurs time and time again throughout the building. This number, a doubled "two," is reminiscent of the name Didymus Thomas, or "twin the twin." Legend has it that the church's mysterious renovator, Bérenger Saunière, the priest at Rennes-le-Château from 1885 until his death in 1917, discovered something in or near the church that simultaneously made him incredibly wealthy and contemptuous of his Roman Catholic hierarchic superiors, and inspired him to encode a mysterious religious secret into his renovations of the church.

Conclusion

1. Bart D. Ehrman, *The Orthodox Corruption of Scripture*, New York: Oxford University Press, 1993.

2. Galatians 2:11–14.

3. Acts 16:1–5; 21:17–26.

4. The official church won because it aligned itself with the conscious spirit, and so was able to capitalize on the strengths of the left-brain mind, such as linear, hierarchical organization. The Gnostic Church, aligned with the subjective unconscious, was much more poorly suited to engage in an objective power struggle.

Appendix A

1. Which was then as far removed from Christ's ministry as we are today from Columbus's voyage to the New World.

2. His initial refusal to support the decisions of the council forced the pope into hiding until he finally reversed his opinion, probably under duress. Curiously, after (supposedly) accepting the council's decision, but before he could complete his journey back home, the pope died. This coincidental timing has caused many to suspect foul play, questioning whether the reports of his reversal were fabricated after his death, and whether, indeed, his death was accidental at all.

Appendix B

1. Fredric Schiffer, *Of Two Minds: The Revolutionary Science of Dual-Brain Psychology*, New York: Free Press, 1998, p. 47.

2. Ibid., p. 50.

Bibliography

Baigent, Michael, Richard Leigh, and Henry Lincoln. 1982. *Holy Blood, Holy Grail.* New York: Delacorte.

———. 1986. *The Messianic Legacy.* New York: Holt.

Barnstone, Willis (ed). 1984. *The Other Bible.* San Francisco: Harper & Row.

Barnstone, Willis, and Marvin Meyer (eds.). 2003. *The Gnostic Bible.* Boston: Shambhala.

Bhattacharyya, Sibajiban. 1987. "Indian Philosophies." In Mircea Eliade (ed.), *Encyclopedia of Religion.* New York: MacMillan.

Bible. English. New International Version. 1978. New York: New York International Bible Society.

Boldman, Robert. 1999. *Sacred Life, Holy Death: Seven Stages of Crossing the Divide.* Santa Fe, N.M.: Heartsfire Books.

Branden, Nathaniel. 1997. *The Art of Living Consciously: The Power of Awareness to Transform Everyday Life.* New York: Simon & Schuster.

Brandon, S. G. F. 1969. *The Judgment of the Dead.* New York: Scribner.

Bremmer, Jan. 1987. "Soul: Greek and Hellenistic Concepts." In Mircea Eliade (ed.), *Encyclopedia of Religion.* New York: MacMillan.

Brown, Dan. 2003. *The Da Vinci Code.* New York: Doubleday.

Buckley, Jorunn Jacobsen. 1987. "Mandaean Religion." In Mircea Eliade (ed.), *Encyclopedia of Religion.* New York: MacMillan.

Budge, E. Wallis. 1967. *The Egyptian Book of the Dead: The Papyrus of Ani in the British Museum.* New York: Dover.

———.1973. *Osiris and the Egyptian Resurrection, Vol. II.* New York: Dover.

Burkett, Elinor, and Frank Bruni. 1993. *A Gospel of Shame.* New York: Viking Penguin.

Chopra, Deepak. 2000. *How to Know God: The Soul's Journey into the Mystery of Mysteries.* New York: Crown.

Crehan, Joseph. 1976. "Near Eastern Societies." In A. Toynbee, A. Koestler, et al. (eds.), *Life after Death.* New York: McGraw-Hill.

Crossan, John Dominic. 1998. *The Birth of Christianity.* San Francisco: HarperSanFrancisco.

Davies, Steven. 1987. "Soul: Ancient Near Eastern Concepts." In Mircea Eliade (ed.), *Encyclopedia of Religion.* New York: MacMillan.

De Conick, April D. 1996. *Seek to See Him: Ascent and Vision Mysticism in the Gospel of Thomas.* New York: E. J. Brill.

De Santillana, Giorgio, and Hertha Von Dechend. 1977. *Hamlet's Mill.* Jaffrey, N.H.: David R. Godine.

Ehrman, Bart D. 1993. *The Orthodox Corruption of Scripture.* New York: Oxford University Press.

———. 1997. *The New Testament: A Historical Introduction to the Early Christian Writings.* New York: Oxford University Press.

Eisenman, Robert. 1997. *James, the Brother of Jesus.* New York: Penguin.

El Mahdy, Christine. 1989. *Mummies, Myth, and Magic.* New York: Thames and Hudson.

Freud, Sigmund. 1965. *New Introductory Lectures in Psychoanalysis.* New York: Norton.

Fromm, Erich. 1950. *Psychoanalysis and Religion.* New Haven, Conn.: Yale University Press.

Gallup, George, Jr., and William Proctor. 1982. *Adventures in Immortality.* New York: McGraw-Hill.

Gnoli, Gherardo. 1987. "Iranian Religions." In Mircea Eliade (ed.), *Encyclopedia of Religion.* New York: MacMillan.

Goleman, Daniel. 1997. *Emotional Intelligence: Why It Is More Important than IQ.* New York: Bantam.

Grant, Michael. 1993. *Constantine the Great.* New York: Scribner.

Janov, Arthur. [nd]. *The New Primal Scream.* Wilmington, Del.: Enterprise Publishing.

Jaynes, Julian. 1976. *The Origin of Consciousness in the Breakdown of the Bicameral Mind.* Boston: Houghton Mifflin.

Jung, C. G. 1969. *The Collected Works of C. G. Jung,* Vols. 7 and 8. Princeton, N.J.: Princeton University Press.

Knight, Christopher, and Robert Lomas. 1996. *The Hiram Key.* New York: Barnes & Noble.

Koester, Helmut. 1990. *Ancient Christian Gospels.* Philadelphia: Trinity Press International.

Laing, R. D. 1960. *The Divided Self.* New York: Pantheon.

Layton, Bentley. 1987. *The Gnostic Scriptures.* Garden City, N.Y.: Doubleday.

Long, J. Bruce. 1987. "Underworld." In Mircea Eliade (ed.), *Encyclopedia of Religion.* New York: MacMillan.

Long, Max Freedom. 1965. *The Huna Code in Religions.* Marina del Rey, Calif.: DeVorss.

May, Gerald G. 2004. *The Dark Night of the Soul.* San Francisco: HarperSanFrancisco.

Milavec, Aaron. 2004. *The Didache: Text, Translation, Analysis, and Commentary.* Collegeville, Minn.: Liturgical Press.

Miller, Robert J. (ed). 1994. *The Complete Gospels.* San Francisco: HarperSanFrancisco.

Novak, Peter. 1997. *The Division of Consciousness.* Charlottesville, Va.: Hampton Roads.

———. 2003. *The Lost Secret of Death.* Charlottesville, Va.: Hampton Roads.

Ornstein, Robert. 1997. *The Right Mind: Making Sense of the Hemispheres.* New York: Harcourt Brace.

Owens, Lance. 2004. "The Gospel of Thomas and the Hermeneutics of Vision." Gnostic Society: www.gnosis.org/naghamm/gth_hermen.htm.

Percival, Henry R. (ed.). 1988. *The Seven Ecumenical Councils of the Undivided Church.* Grand Rapids, Mich.: Wm. B. Eerdmans.

Picknett, Lynn, and Clive Prince. 1997. *The Templar Revelation.* New York: Bantam.

Ponsonby, Arthur. 1928, 1991. *Falsehood in Wartime.* Newport Beach, Calif.: LSF Publishing.

Ries, Julian. 1987. "Immortality." In Mircea Eliade (ed.), *Encyclopedia of Religion.* New York: MacMillan.

Rig Veda. 1994. Edited by Barend A. van Nooten and Gary B. Holland. Cambridge, Mass.: Harvard University Press.

Rinpoche, Sogyal. 1993. *The Tibetan Book of Living and Dying.* San Francisco: HarperSanFrancisco.

Riviere, Claude. 1987. "Soul: Concepts in Primitive Religions." In Mircea Eliade (ed.), *Encyclopedia of Religion.* New York: MacMillan.

Roberts, Paul William. 1995. *In Search of the Birth of Jesus.* New York: Riverhead.

Robinson, James M. (ed.). 1977. *The Nag Hammadi Library in English.* San Francisco: Harper & Row.

Ruskan, John. 2000. *Emotional Clearing: A Groundbreaking East/West Guide to Releasing Negative Feelings and Awakening Unconditional Happiness.* New York: Broadway.

Sanchez, Victor. 2001. *The Toltec Path of Recapitulation.* Rochester, Vt.: Bear & Co.

Schiffer, Fredric. 1998. *Of Two Minds: The Revolutionary Science of Dual-Brain Psychology.* New York: Free Press.

Schneemelcher, Wilhelm (ed.). 1965. *New Testament Apocrypha*. Philadelphia: West-minster Press.

Segal, Alan F. 2004. *Life after Death: A History of the Afterlife in the Religions of the West*. New York: Doubleday.

Seidel, Anna. 1987. "Afterlife: Chinese Concepts." In Mircea Eliade (ed.), *Encyclopedia of Religion*. New York: MacMillan.

Sharan, Ishwar. 1991. *The Myth of Saint Thomas and the Mylapore Shiva Temple*. New Delhi: Voice of India.

Siegel, Eli. 1981. *Self and World: An Explanation of Aesthetic Realism*. New York: Definition Press.

Smith, Morton. 1973. *Clement of Alexandria and a Secret Gospel of Mark*. Cambridge, Mass.: Harvard University Press.

Springer, Sally P., and Georg Deutsch. 1985. *Left Brain, Right Brain*. New York: W. H. Freeman.

Stout, Martha. 2001. *The Myth of Sanity*. New York: Viking.

Stoyanov, Yuri. 2000. *The Other God*. New Haven, Conn.: Yale University Press.

Strong, James. 1984. "Dictionary of the Hebrew Bible." *The New Strong's Exhaustive Concordance of the Bible*. Nashville, Tenn.: T. Nelson.

Tober, Linda M., and F. Stanley Lusby. 1987. "Jewish Afterlife." In Mircea Eliade (ed.), *Encyclopedia of Religion*. New York: MacMillan.

The Upanishads, Breath of the Eternal. 1948. Translated by Swami Prabhavananda and Frederick Manchester. Hollywood, Calif.: Vedanta Press.

Van Baaren, Th. P. 1987. "Afterlife: Geography of Death." In Mircea Eliade (ed.), *Encyclopedia of Religion*. New York: MacMillan.

Watterson, Barbara. 1984. *The Gods of Ancient Egypt*. New York: Facts on File.

Way of Life: A New Translation of the Tao Te Ching. 1983. Translated by R. B. Blakney. New York: New American Library.

Wheeler, Ramona Louise. 1999. *Walk Like an Egyptian*. Mount Shasta, Calif.: Allisone Press.

Zandee, Jan. 1977. *Death as an Enemy According to Ancient Egyptian Conceptions*. New York: Arno Press.

Index

About the Author

    Peter Novak is the acclaimed author of two books. A former librarian, Novak has spent the past 18 years researching our cultural legends and their connection to modern psychological findings. He lives in La Porte, Indiana.

Hampton Roads Publishing Company

. . . for the evolving human spirit

HAMPTON ROADS PUBLISHING COMPANY publishes books on a variety of subjects, including metaphysics, spirituality, health, visionary fiction, and other related topics.

For a copy of our latest trade catalog, call toll-free, 800-766-8009, or send your name and address to:

HAMPTON ROADS PUBLISHING COMPANY, INC.
1125 STONEY RIDGE ROAD • CHARLOTTESVILLE, VA 22902
e-mail: hrpc@hrpub.com • www.hrpub.com

ML

4/06